THE
TRIADS

THE
TRIADS

The Growing Global Threat
from the Chinese Criminal
Societies

Martin Booth

St. Martin's Press
New York

Library of Congress Cataloging-in-Publication Data

Booth, Martin.
The triads : the growing global threat from the Chinese criminal societies / Martin Booth.
p.   cm.
ISBN 0-312-05524-2
1. Triads (Gangs)   I. Title.
HV6441.B59   1991
364.1′06′089951—dc20   90-49183   CIP

First published in Great Britain by Grafton Books.

First U.S. Edition: March 1991
10 9 8 7 6 5 4 3 2 1

CONTENTS

Note on Chinese Proper Nouns   vi
Preface   vii
Introduction   ix

1   In the Kingdom of the Sons of Heaven   1
2   Monks and Emperors   17
3   The City of Willows   33
4   A Century and a Half of Crime   40
5   A Pair of Mr Bigs   72
6   The Men of Pak Fa'an Gai   88
7   Triads International   107
8   Fighting the Triads   133
9   The Red Turbans Revisited   152

APPENDIX 1:
'Overthrow the Ch'ing and Restore the Ming'   159

APPENDIX 2:
From *The Hung Society* by J. S. M. Ward and
W. G. Stirling (1925)   160

APPENDIX 3:
From *Triad Societies in Hong Kong* by
W. P. Morgan (1960)   170

APPENDIX 4:
Commissioners' Report on the Penang Riots, 1868   197

Select Bibliography   205
Photo Acknowledgements   206
Index   207

NOTE ON CHINESE PROPER NOUNS

In recent years, the Government of China has sought to standardize the writing and spelling of Chinese personal and place-names. Quite often, this new orthography has resulted in the newly appointed name looking totally different from the original when spelt in English. For example, the city formerly known as *Canton* is now called *Guangzhou, Peking* is now *Beijing* and the province of *Fukien* is now *Fujian*.

As most readers will be more familiar with the former nomenclature, and because most of the events outlined took place when the former names were in use, it is the earlier versions which are used throughout the text.

PREFACE

In spite of the current media coverage their activities are attracting, the Triads remain an obsessively secretive and closed criminal fraternity. Little is commonly known about them since they are far less readily penetrated than, for example, the Mafia, with whom they are often inaccurately compared. Yet they occupy a position centre stage on the international crime scene today.

Their grip on local Chinese communities throughout the world is fearful enough for those concerned, be they in Hong Kong, Sydney, Toronto, San Francisco, London, or Glasgow. But their activities at street level – extortion, vice, gambling – pale into insignificance beside what is now their major sphere of activity: drugs. The stark fact now facing law enforcement agencies is that the Triads control 90 per cent of the world's heroin trade. Taken together with their other activities, including their increasing involvement in financial and computer crime, this makes them potentially the single most dangerous organized crime threat now facing the international community.

One important fact to grasp at the outset is that these criminals – ruthless to those who betray them, merciless to those who oppose them – are by no means a modern phenomenon. Their origins can be traced back to before the time of Christ, though the edges of Triad history are blurred by legend, mythology, and folklore. The rituals still in use by Triad lodges are, in essence, centuries old; their traditions have their roots in ancient warrior codes of honour and patriotism, not – as now – the dishonour and cowardice of the street thug. We can never hope to understand the Triad mentality, or effectively counter the Triad threat, until this ancient and complex historical context is understood. That, in part, is the purpose of this book, which should ideally have been written by a Chinese author. I hope that in due course one will emerge who will be able to offer a definitive historical account of the Triad phenomenon. In the meantime, very much as a stopgap, I offer this book.

But I have also had another, equally important, purpose in mind: to awaken public awareness – in particular the awareness of government and government agencies – to the threat the Triads now pose. Quite simply, it is a threat that cannot, and must not, be ignored.

During the writing of *The Triads* I have been indebted to the senior officers of the Royal Hong Kong Police Force. Without them the book could not have been written. In particular I should like to thank Chief Superintendent John Dunn and Chief Superintendent David Hodson. I also owe a considerable debt to John Powell, without whose librarianship skills much of my research reading would have been impossible.

Martin Booth

INTRODUCTION

I was sitting on a bench in a small park in Tsim Sha Tsui East in Kowloon in November 1988. It was a fine and balmy autumnal morning with clear blue skies, hot sunlight but comparatively low humidity. Some Chinese children were romping in a nearby play area with their amahs, and an old man, his trouser legs rolled up to the knee, was perched upon a low wall, reading one of the many Hong Kong Chinese-language daily newspapers through spectacles with pebbled lenses. Seated unobtrusively on another wall under the shade of some trees was a young Chinese man in his early twenties.

Dressed in a pair of new sneakers, designer-cut jeans, a shirt, and an Yves St Laurent pullover, he too was reading a newspaper, but the English-language *South China Morning Post*. Every few minutes, he was approached by one of another three younger men who spoke to him for a few moments then left, having handed him some money. He issued no receipts but made a note of the transaction on a small cheap child's notepad.

I followed one of the delivery boys and saw him enter one of the many stereo/camera shops which exist in the nearby streets of the tourist shopping wonderland of that area of Kowloon. He was not in the shop for long and, upon leaving it, he headed back in the direction of the park.

Two months previously, I had been in the fourth-floor premises of a tailor, in a twelve-storey building about five minutes' walk from the tiny park. The building is fairly old by Hong Kong standards and the two lifts serve alternate floors only: if one enters the lift serving the even-numbered floors, there is no way of reaching an odd-numbered floor without returning to ground level and starting again. The tailor was having my suit altered in a back room and I was standing by the cash desk chatting to him when the lift door opened.

From the lift stepped a Chinese youth of about 18: he was dressed shabbily and had long, unkempt and dirty hair, which is unusual – young Hong Kong Chinese men are characteristically well dressed and clean, no matter how poor they are, and they generally keep their hair short. The youth was carrying a wooden tray with food on it which had been prepared at a cooked-food stall in an alley just down the street.

He dropped the tray on the cashier's desk and demanded payment. The tailor informed him that he had not ordered any lunch. The youth insisted he had, glancing at me all the while in an uneasy manner. The tailor stated quite emphatic-ally but courteously that he had not ordered the food and that he took his lunch every day in a restaurant in nearby Cameron Road. The youth asserted forcefully that there was an order for the food from the tailor in that particular building. He produced a scrap of paper with the order written upon it. At this point, the tailor informed him quite politely that there was another tailor's business on the floor above and that the youth had taken the wrong lift. At this, the youth scowled, swore, and pressed the lift button, muttering to himself until it arrived.

The tailor was visibly upset by this confrontation: he regretted causing the youth a loss of face for, in doing so, he might have encouraged a small reprisal – a polythene cup of cooking fat over a bolt of cloth being delivered, perhaps.

Both of these instances are small examples of the Chinese Triad societies at work today in Hong Kong. Such activities are commonplace in the streets of the colony and are accepted – if reluctantly – as a part of the cut and thrust of everyday business life by the hundreds of thousands of shopkeepers, factory owners, taxi drivers, coolies, office workers, and restaurateurs whose lives are affected. 'Squeeze' hits everyone.

The Triad societies are Free China's criminal underground. They are proscribed in mainland China, where membership is likely to result in a death sentence. In Hong Kong it can lead to a prison sentence; but Hong Kong is at present, and has been since 1841, the Triad societies' world headquarters. Wherever there is a Chinese community, throughout the world, there is at least one Triad society making a criminal living from it, surviving parasitically by 'squeeze' – a metaphorical expression of long standing in the East covering protection rackets, the control of service industries (even as small as the delivery of noodles from a cooked-food stall), the operation of labour markets, the running of gambling and vice establishments, and generally taking advantage of every opportunity for profit within the Chinese community.

This situation has existed for well over a century and a half but has largely been specific to Chinese communities. Few foreigners have come into contact with Triad society operations, and unless they have been either police officers in oriental British colonial police forces, the taipans of the big trading companies dealing with China or tin miners in Malaya in the nineteenth century, they have had no cause for concern. But the situation is now changing.

In Britain, America, Australia, and Canada, the Chinese communities are expanding fast. With the imminent handover by the British Government of Hong Kong to the sovereignty of the People's Republic of China in 1997, large numbers of Hong Kong Chinese are emigrating. The vast majority of these are law-abiding, hard-working, and educated Chinese whose entrepreneurial skills and business acumen is much sought after. A minority are equally skilled criminals equipped with ruthless efficiency and dedication.

They are not leaving Hong Kong to set up business afresh in their newly adopted land. Most of them are leaving to join society brothers already resident overseas and making, in some instances, vast incomes from crime, most of it still restricted to the expatriate Chinese communities.

Canada is often the first choice of country for emigrating Triads. The west coast around Vancouver and Victoria has a large Chinese population, amongst which are a number of Chinese ex-Hong Kong police officers who escaped from the anti-corruption drive of the 1970s and who now live in Canada, often under assumed names. Most of these were and are Triad members.

The next favourite destination is Australia, where there is also a large resident Chinese population, an economic environment ready for exploitation, and a huge non-Chinese population ripe for expanding the Triads' most lucrative trade: narcotics.

A third choice of destination is the USA. But here the Federal Bureau of Investigation (FBI), the CIA, the FDA (Federal Drugs Administration), the US Customs and Coast-guard, the immigration authorities, and various local police forces make life somewhat tougher for the Triads; further-more, the 'ethnic' criminal is not such a problem as he might be in Australia or Britain. Laws exist in the USA to combat organized and syndicated crime (the RICO Statutes) and the fight against narcotics dealing is in full gear. Nevertheless, heroin from South-east Asia, largely smuggled and sold by the Triad societies and their link brotherhoods in the USA, is still available and heroin abuse is still a major problem. Since the FBI successfully broke the traditional American mobster syndicates – the Mafia – the Triads have moved in to the vacuum: every single gramme of heroin now sold in New York is Chinese-supplied, often by way of Hong Kong.

In Britain, the Triad societies have existed since at least the early nineteenth century. Today, they control much of the Chinese community. The 14K Society, the Shui Fong, the Wo Shing Wo and its related group the Wo On Lok, the Sun Yee On – all of them Hong Kong-based societies – have officers and lodges in Britain. They even receive senior office-bearers flown in to Britain from Hong Kong to sort out inter-society disputes. They also temporarily import their own hit-men and assassins.

In Hong Kong, the police are experienced and ever-vigilant in their fight against the Triad societies. The law is being restructured to accommodate the problem, and a tribunal has been set up to offer immunity from prosecution to members of Triad societies who renounce their membership. Spectacular successes in arrests in recent years have boosted both police morale and public confidence. Yet the problem remains on the streets – protection rackets, loan sharking, prostitution, gambling, and narcotics.

The problem lies in the fact that the Triad society system is not merely a criminal fraternity. It is a part of Chinese history, mythology, and legend. Its roots lie over two thousand years deep in the soil of Chinese culture. It is these roots that we must first uncover.

THE
TRIADS

1

IN THE KINGDOM OF THE
SONS OF HEAVEN

'POLICE PRAISE FOR WITNESS AS TRIAD GANG IS
JAILED'
'TRIADS' SECRET MEETING STARTS HEROIN ALERT'
'TRIAD GANG THREATENED TO SEVER MAN'S LEG'
'TRIAD CHIEF JAILED'
'POLICE PREPARE FOR INFLUX OF TRIAD
CRIMINALS FROM HONG KONG'

Just a selection of sensational headlines from recent press reports concerning the growth of Triad activity in the UK and elsewhere. The ruthless commitment of the Triads to crime and violence is unquestionable; but it was not always so, and remnants of a different past are still embedded in Triad ritual and symbolism. Fighting the Triads on a practical level is one thing. Understanding them – getting under their skin and into the complexities of their cultural and historical heritage – is another; but it is no less vital if the growing Triad threat is to be countered effectively.

In order to do this – to begin to understand the motivation and mechanisms of the Chinese secret societies known as the Triads, though often inaccurately nicknamed the 'Chinese Mafia' – it is essential to have some appreciation, however superficial, of their long and complex history, much of it based in legend and half-truth. Of course today the Triads and the Mafia have common 'business' interests, and both are formidable and efficient criminal organizations. But the organization of the Sicilian Mafia is structured round a small group of families who are often involved in long-drawn-out vendettas against each other; and both in Italy and the USA the Mafia have had some serious setbacks and have experienced a definite loss of power and influence in certain key areas of their operations. The Triads, on the other hand, must be seen against a larger canvas. They arose from and within the largest nation on earth, their genesis and, indeed, their fundamental psychology being located not in oscillating family or clan union and disunion but in reactions to the invasion and conquest of their land by outside forces. And, unlike the Mafia, their power as an international crime organization is now increasing – dangerously so.

The Triads are related historically to secret societies whose primary aim was originally patriotic: the re-establishment of the Chinese as rulers of China. The Chinese Imperial system came into being in 255 BC with the foundation of the Ch'in dynasty. It lasted only 49 years but was responsible for constructing the foundations of a unified state. In 202 BC, after an interregnum of several years, it gave way to the Western (or Early) Han dynasty (206 BC–AD 220) under which centralization took place and China began to develop a national identity. The emperor was regarded as divine, the Son of Heaven, an absolute monarch; a ruler not only by position and power but by personal example. Under the moral doctrines and codes of conduct laid down by Confucius the emperor was obliged to gain the respect and loyalty of his subjects by his righteousness, probity, mercy, and benevolence. If he failed to attain, or maintain, such standards of behaviour, then he was said to have forfeited the Mandate of Heaven and the people were justified – indeed it was their duty – to rise up and depose him. Natural disasters were taken as signs that the emperor was not living up to his responsibilities; a flood, an earthquake, a famine – frequent catastrophes throughout Chinese history – or portents such as an eclipse of the sun or a passing comet were interpreted as sufficient cause for an uprising. From the birth of the Chinese nation, therefore, rebellion was part of the very fabric of life and became inbred, as it were, in the national psyche.

Such a climate encouraged the foundation of groups who saw their role as preparing for the overthrow of Imperial authority, not so much out of mere political disaffection, but as part of what was thought of as the natural order of things. The first reference to a secret society which might be seen as a precursor of the Triads is to the 'Red Eyebrows', who rouged their eyes and originated in what is today the province of Shantung. In AD 9 the Western Han dynasty was overthrown by a usurper called Wang Mang. In the popular risings that followed, the Red Eyebrows played a major role, and Wang Mang's turbulent reign came to a violent end with his assassination and the foundation of the Eastern (or Later) Han dynasty in AD 25. But the Red Eyebrows, no longer fighting for a patriotic cause, continued to exist, struggling for survival as bandits and outlaws. They became an embarrassment and liability to the Imperial administration and an army was sent to suppress them. This the Imperial forces did by the simple expedient of rouging their eyebrows, which caused so much confusion amongst the genuine Red Eyebrows that they were routed and massacred. A historical precedent had been set. Here was a secret society that had responded to the call of Imperial authority at a time of national danger but who had subsequently been persecuted by the regime they had helped back to power.

The sheer size of China made absolute Imperial rule impossible, and so under the Early Han dynasty a civil service bureaucracy was established which, although directly responsible to the Imperial throne, seldom communicated with it. These autonomous and autocratic local administrations were ripe for corruption, making the whole machinery virtually impossible to dismantle. This system of government remained more or less intact for two thousand years, only being finally abandoned with the foundation of the Republic of China in the early twentieth century. A position in the civil service was thus both highly respectable and potentially very lucrative, and competition was extremely keen. Recruitment to the service was by written examination only and hundreds of thousands of men (women were excluded) sat the examinations annually. Inevitably a great many candidates failed, resulting in large numbers of literate, educated, but unemployed and unemployable men. The system bred disaffection, a situation opponents of the Imperial government were quick to exploit.

Life for the masses was based on rural communities, and people's lives revolved around their immediate locality. As a result, private associations sprang up to protect local interests: rice- or wheat-growers joined together to maintain their markets; metalworkers, weavers, stonemasons, and livestock farmers formed the equivalent of trade guilds. It was a small step for such groupings to become centres of subversion during times of political unrest – either against the local administration or against the Imperial throne itself. Often discontent was nurtured by those who had failed to gain admittance to the civil service: an educated élite with a grudge to bear is always a dangerous thing.

The nature of Chinese society provided a fertile soil in which secret societies could thrive. For these political associations secrecy was crucial, since the price of discovery by the authorities was torture and death. Their survival therefore depended on the loyalty of their members and strict measures evolved to ensure that such loyalty was enforced. Ritual initiation was the primary means of binding members together since it imposed religious as well as moral obligations upon the membership. Secret society rituals drew on three religious sources: Taoism, Buddhism, and what is best described as Confucianism, all of which provided the societies with a vast lexicon of symbols, images, ceremonies, and magical vocabulary.

Taoism, founded by Lao-tzu in the sixth century BC, combined shamanism, alchemy, and ancestor worship and was in many ways tailor-made for secret societies in the emphasis it placed on the continuity of the family or clan unit and on loyalty to the past – be it blood ancestors or society founders and their ideals. Buddhism, introduced into China in the Later Han dynasty, was, like Taoism, periodically proscribed by the authorities. Forced underground, both religions became ripe for use by the secret brotherhoods, even on occasion becoming secret sects in their own right.

The turbulent reigns of the Later Han emperors saw a number of rebellious groups rising to threaten their authority. Amongst them were two in particular: the Copper Horses and the Iron Shins. Around AD 170 a popular leader emerged in north-eastern China named Chang Chueh, who claimed to be directly descended from the hereditary founders of Taoism. With a reputation as a healer and a mystic he soon gathered a substantial following and by AD 180 his adherents had coalesced into a society called the Yellow Turbans. In less than a month, commanded by 36 generals, they had overrun most of northern China.

The activities of the Yellow Turbans were originally inspired by political disaffection with Imperial rule; but once in power they became not so much a regional government but more a religious movement with semi-criminal undertones. Patriotism was not part of their motivation: they were far more interested in benefiting their members at the expense of those outside the society, and anyone who opposed them was eradicated. In the years following the Yellow Turban uprising, with the Imperial government in disarray, there was widespread anarchy, out of which arose three figures (possibly three of the 36 generals) who were to become both national and legendary heroes: Kwan Yu, Liu Pei (a member of the Chihli royal family, the Imperial Han clan), and Chang Fei. It was said that the trio swore a blood oath to each other in a peach garden, making them figures of archetypal significance to all later secret brotherhoods, including the Triads. Indeed Kwan Yu, murdered by Liu Pei's enemies, was deified in the late sixteenth century as Kwan Ti, the god of war, wealth, literature, and – significantly for Triad history – oath-taking brotherhoods.

The Han empire came to an end in AD 220. Two years later the Three Kingdoms were established, founded by Liu Pei: Shu in the south-west (of which Liu Pei became emperor);

Wu in the north-east; and Wei in the north. The Three
Kingdoms lasted until 280 and on their collapse the Western
Chin empire was founded, but in 304 northern China was
again divided, this time into the Sixteen Kingdoms, whilst
southern China became the Eastern Chin. The Sui dynasty
brought about a brief reunification before the emergence of
the first of the truly great dynasties, the T'ang.

Crucially for Triad history, Buddhism was proscribed
three times during the three hundred years of T'ang rule. It
went underground, and with it went large numbers of
adherents. During the first of the T'ang purges Buddhism
established its own secret organization from which the first of
China's truly organized secret societies sprang. Buddhist
symbolism and ritual has remained a core part of Chinese
secret societies, including the Triads, to the present day.

The fall of the T'ang dynasty in the early tenth century
produced another period of disunity before the Sung dynasty
came to power in 960. Towards the end of Sung rule China –
for the first time – began to come under threat from external
invaders, amongst them the Mongols under their leader
Kublai Khan, who deposed the Sungs and proclaimed himself
the first emperor of the Yuan dynasty. Resistance to Mongol
rule was widespread but disorganized and centred in the
south, where pro-Sung sentiments were strongest. But
gradually rebel groups began to amalgamate under three
leaderships: the pirate Fang Kuo-chen, the Buddhist monk
Chu Yuan-chang, and the White Lotus Society.

The White Lotus Society was one of the most powerful
secret organizations of its time. Like other similar societies it
changed its name from time to time to avoid discovery or
infiltration, becoming the White Lily Society, the White
Yang Society, or the Incense Smelling Society. It had
affiliations with a number of other religiously-based groups,
such as the Eight Diagrams Sect (also called the Celestial
Principles Sect), the Nine Mansions Society, the Heaven and
Earth Society, also known as the Hung League and the Triad
Society.

Legend states that the White Lotus Society had been

founded by the famous Buddhist teacher Eon (Hwui-yin). At Rozan, south of the Yangtse River, Eon established a community that worshipped the Amitabha Buddha – the Buddha of the 'Pure Land', a mystical state of existence to which devotees could obtain entry through prayer and meditation. The community, which also included laymen, was centred upon eighteen monks, known as the Eighteen Sages of Rozan, and had been left alone to pursue its own course until the advent of the T'ang dynasty, when rigorous persecution of Buddhists in general and members of the Amitabha sect in particular began. In 1344, after a long period of semi-dormancy, the White Lotus Society was revived and reconstructed by Han Shan-tung. In that year, in league with four other rebel leaders, Han Shan-tung rose up against the Mongols and succeeded in destabilizing the Yuan dynasty. The Society was now known as the Red Turban Rebels after the red headbands they wore in battle.

Eventually the Mongols were driven from China and one of the rebel leaders, a Buddhist monk called Chu Yuan-chang, assumed imperial power in 1368 as Hung Wu, the first of the Ming emperors. Though secret societies had wielded political influence in China before, it had never been on such a scale – a government overthrown, foreign usurpers driven out, and a new specifically Chinese dynasty founded. It was the White Lotus Society that gave the new dynasty its name: Ming Wang was the name borne by two prophets (one known as Big, the other as Little) sent by Buddha to establish peace and order from revolutionary chaos. Hung Wu was Chinese, and that is a key fact for the understanding of Triad history. (To the Chinese, a true Chinaman comes from southern China – the provinces roughly situated south of the Yangtse River. The nearer a man's ancestors hailed from to the coast of southern China, the more 'Chinese' he was considered. Well into the present century, southern Chinese referred to themselves as the 'men of China'.)

For most of the three centuries of Ming rule the White Lotus Society remained discreetly secret and politically detached, being neither officially recognized nor proscribed.

In 1621, however, it began to support a rebel called Su Hung-u. Quite why the White Lotus Society finally took against the full-blooded Chinese Ming dynasty, which it had so decisively helped establish, is not known for certain. But take against it they did, with the result that in 1644 China was conquered by the foreign Manchus, who established a dynasty, known as the Ch'ing dynasty, which lasted into the twentieth century.

The next documented record of the White Lotus Society is an Imperial edict of 1662 in which the second Ch'ing emperor, K'ang Hsi (1661–1722), rigorously proscribed secret societies, as well as taking drastic measures against Buddhism and Taoism. Other edicts followed which made other societies illegal: the White Lily Society, the Incense Burning Society, the Origin of Chaos Society, the Origin of the Dragon Society, and the Hung Society were specifically named. K'ang had established a firm hold on most of China, but in the south Ming sympathies were still strong, and were to remain so for the whole of the dynastic period. The secret societies were forced underground and began to coalesce into units of Ming-centred defiance, developing common rituals, as well as secret signs and phrases by which they might know each other.

From this time the White Lotus Society is mentioned less frequently in official documents and seems to have become amalgamated in some way with the Hung Society – certainly the 1662 edict assumed a close alliance between the two. In due course the Hung Society underwent further metamorphosis, to become known as the Triad Society, the name evolving perhaps from the Three United Society, yet another name for the Hung Society.

To the Triads the number 3 is of central significance, both mathematically and mystically: 3 multiplied by 3 (3 squared) equals 9; and any number that adds up to 9 is divisible by 9. For example: 1,804,563, which reduces to 9 by adding all the digits together (27) and then adding the result together (2+7=9). To the Chinese, 3 is the mystical number denoting the balance between Heaven, Earth, and Man. Three is the number of creation (compare the Christian Trinity) and there are also three Buddhist treasures, and man is said to have three souls – a concept that finds an important place in Triad ritual.

It is not known exactly when the Hung Society was founded, but it was certainly in existence by the middle of the seventeenth century and was well established by 1700. The centres of its activities were the provinces of Fukien and Kwantung, especially the city of Canton. It seems to have been fundamentally religious in nature at first, its governing deity being Kwan Ti, deified by the Ming emperor Wan Li at the end of the sixteenth century and adopted by several other secret societies as their tutelary god. To protect itself from infiltration by the Manchu authorities, the Hung Society had a variety of local names: for example, the Ghee Hin (or Justice and Prosperity) Society, outwardly just another of the many friendly societies or trade guilds.

The third Ch'ing emperor, K'ang Hsi's son Yung Ch'eng (reigned 1722–35), issued a number of edicts against secret societies, including the White Lily Society, the White Lotus Society, and the T'in Tei Hui – the Hung Society under yet another name: the Society of Heaven and Earth, whose aims were the moral reform of the people, the maintenance of religious belief and practice, and the encouragement of Chinese nationalism and patriotism. Its famous motto, which remains relevant today in relation to the Triads, was 'Overthrow the Ch'ing and restore the Ming' (see Appendix 1).

It was during the reign of Yung Ch'eng that we can identify the true historical beginnings of the Triads. The central event was the destruction of the Shao Lin (sometimes known as the Shiu Lam or Siu Lam) monastery. In Triad history, the monks of Shao Lin, who had assisted the emperor in his campaign against the Eleuths, a Mongol tribe in what was to become the province of Sinkiang, are seen as supremely accomplished warriors and strategists, deadly exponents of the martial arts, and bound together by rigid bonds of loyalty and discipline. It was these qualities that made them a threat to Imperial power – like the Red

Eyebrows over fifteen hundred years earlier – and brought about their annihilation. So runs the legend, for which there is little basis in historical fact.

One figure who undoubtedly did fight openly for the Ming cause was a pirate chief called Cheng Ch'eng-kung, known in English as Koxinga, who drove the Dutch settlers out of Formosa (Taiwan) and established a headquarters from which he exercised control all along the China coast from the mouth of the Yangtse to present-day Vietnam. His influence extended to the mainland province of Fukien, where there were many Ming supporters and where, according to legend, the Shao Lin monastery stood.

The greatest threat to the Ch'ing dynasty came in the early years of the nineteenth century, during what became known as the Taiping (meaning 'great social harmony' or 'universal peace') Rebellion, led by Hung Hsiu-ch'uan (1814–64), the son of a Hakka farmer who lived near Canton. Although not directly instigated by the Hung/Triad Societies, the Taiping Rebellion gave them ample opportunity to further their opposition to the Ch'ing dynasty. Hung, like many before him, had studied hard for the civil service examinations but had failed them. This was almost certainly because he was from the south, where Ming sympathies ran high, and from Canton in particular, a Triad stronghold, rather than because he was not intellectually competent. Hung's failure embittered him against the Manchus and he decided, as a result of a sketchy knowledge of Christianity, to instigate a holy war against the emperor, the local landowners, and the established religions. He formed the Society of God Worshippers and by 1848 had a powerful army under his command. The Society of God Worshippers and the Triads had close links and many rank-and-file Triad members joined the Taiping Rebellion, as well as Triad leaders such as Luo Dao-gang. The word *taiping* itself was of great importance to the Triads, who sometimes referred to themselves as 'men of Taiping'. It appears in Triad ritual, for instance, as Tai Ping Market, the Market of Universal Peace.

But the alliance between Hung's followers and the Triads

was not a permanent one. For one thing, the Triads had no wish to associate themselves with the eclectic and rather peculiar theology of the God Worshippers, who believed in the Eighteen Hells of Buddhism, made food offerings in the Taoist fashion to family cult altars, and read the Christian Bible during their ceremonies. It was also a puritan cult: gambling, prostitution, extortion, and opium smoking, amongst other things, were accounted grievous sins, and by this time such activities provided the Triads with their main sources of income.

Although possessing only rudimentary knowledge of Christianity, Hung and his followers became fanatical on its behalf, turning their zeal not only against the emperor but also against Buddhists and Taoists. Idols were destroyed, temples ransacked and burned, monks murdered. This severed the alliance with the Triads, who were, historically and ritualistically, Buddhist in their allegiance. Nevertheless, they did not overtly oppose Hung but rather allowed his rebellion against the Ch'ing rule to gain momentum. The rebellion moved from success to success. In 1851 Hung proclaimed a Taiping state, the Heavenly Kingdom of Great Peace. The following year, after taking several major cities, the rebels captured Nanking (which Hung renamed Tianjing, the Celestial Capital) and Hung proclaimed himself Emperor of China. In due course the Imperial forces regained the initiative and the rebellion finally collapsed in 1864, when Hung committed suicide. It had taken a decade to put down the rebellion, at a cost of some twenty million lives (at a conservative estimate) and the destruction of vast tracts of land.

While the Imperial army was occupied with the Taiping rebels, the Triads were busy massing an army in the south. They captured the port of Amoy and the important regional centre of Shanghai. They also laid siege to Canton and Kweilin; but surprisingly they did not consolidate these gains and in spite of their successes failed to pose a serious threat to the Ch'ing throne. Why the Triads did not take advantage of the situation and press home their gains remains a puzzle.

Perhaps they had lost the political will to do so, because by this time their criminal interests had become extensive, involving the cultivation and sale of opium outside the registered – and taxed – government network.

For some years after the death of Hung the Manchu emperors faced sporadic local outbursts of Taiping or Triad unrest. These were ruthlessly put down. Amongst them was the trouble caused by the Small Knife Society in Shanghai in 1853–5 and Amoy in 1853, and by the Red Turbans (affiliated to the Triads, but not related otherwise to the Red Turbans of the fourteenth century) who attempted to seize Canton in 1854. At other times local Triad groups attacked *yamen* houses, government rice stores and prisons. The Imperial throne also faced non-Buddhist and non-Triad rebellions: the Chinese Muslims rose up in 1863 and remained in revolt for a decade in the north-west, whilst in the 1870s ethnic unrest broke out in Chinese Turkestan, supported politically and financially by the British government.

At the same time, Europeans – known as *gweilos*, 'white ghosts' – were beginning to exploit the enormous commercial potential of China, adding to the general confusion and disruption as they did so. Not until the end of the nineteenth century did the Emperor Kuang Hsu begin even to consider stabilizing reforms, but these were abandoned when the Dowager Empress Tzu Hsi took over the throne and virtually imprisoned the emperor in the Forbidden City.

Tzu Hsi instigated a jingoistic anti-foreigners policy, in spite of the fact that, strictly speaking, she was one herself. So skilled a manipulator was she that she even succeeded in attracting some of the pro-Ming faction to her cause, thereby bringing about the Boxer Uprising of 1900.

The Boxers were not a true Triad Society, though they could claim descent from the White Lotus Society, the Eight Diagrams Sect, the Red Fists Society, and the Big Knives or Ta Tao Hui, all of which were secret societies under the Triad Society umbrella. Their correct name was I Ho Chuan, the Righteous Harmony Fists. The nickname of Boxers was given to them by a Christian missionary who was also a correspondent for the Shanghai-based newspaper, the *China Daily News*. The Boxers originated in the province of Shantung and were first recognized by the provincial governor, Li Ping-heng, in May 1898 when he noted in a report that secret societies were causing riots by exploiting the tensions that existed between local Chinese and Christian foreigners and converts. The latter were called 'secondary devils' and were regularly burned out of their homes, hideously tortured, and then murdered. It seems likely that the Boxers were infiltrated by Triads, but they remained a predominantly religiously-based movement with a strong magical element in their rituals (they believed, for instance, that their bodies were invulnerable against the bullets of foreigners). They played on age-old superstitions and exploited the ingrained Chinese distrust of foreigners, as in this extract from a Boxer broadsheet:

> The Catholic and Protestant religions being insolent to the gods, and extinguishing sanctity, rendering no obedience to Buddha, and enraging Heaven and Earth, the rain clouds no longer visit us; but eight million Spirit Soldiers will descend from Heaven and sweep the Empire clean of all foreigners. Then will the gentle showers once more water our lands . . . If you gain five adherents [to the Boxer cause] your whole family will be absolved from all evils, and if you gain ten adherents your whole village will be absolved from all calamities. Those who gain no adherents to the cause shall be decapitated, for until all foreigners have been exterminated the rain can never visit us . . .

In the spring of 1899 the province of Shantung received a new governor, Yu Hsien, whose approval of the Boxers led to a rapid increase in their activities. As a result of diplomatic pressure from the Germans he was dismissed from his post, but was transferred by the Dowager Empress to the governorship of Shansi, where he became infamous for murdering forty-five Christian missionaries and their families in the space of one day.

His successor as governor of Shantung province, Yuan Shih-k'ai, moved against the Boxers, and was sternly reprimanded by the Empress for his troubles. In January 1900 the Empress issued an edict which effectively gave official support to the Boxers in their fight against the foreigners. Once again, history was repeating itself. The Imperial throne was using the secret societies who were theoretically opposed to it for its own ends.

But the Boxer Rebellion was a failure. The Imperial army was beaten back and the Imperial city of Peking was occupied by European forces. The foreigners had triumphed.

And what of the Triads? As they had done after the Taiping Rebellion, they failed to exploit the situation effectively, a further indication of the disintegration of their political interests. But it was not long before a figure emerged who changed all that and enabled the Triads finally to take on the Manchus, and win.

That figure was Dr Sun Yat-sen, leader of the Republican Party, which had strong support in the south of China. He was born in the province of Kwantung in 1866, the youngest of three sons in a poor agricultural family. At the age of twelve he was sent to Hawaii where his brother, fifteen years his senior, was a prosperous cattle farmer. Five years later he was attending an Anglican diocesan school in Hong Kong; from there he passed to Queen's College in Hong Kong and, at the age of twenty, entered Po-chi Hospital School in Canton. By now his political aim had been defined: to overthrow the Ch'ing dynasty. In 1887 he took up a position at the Alice Memorial Hospital in Hong Kong, where he met several other like-minded patriots.

After an unsuccessful attempt by the Republicans to stage a *coup d'état* in southern China in 1895 Sun Yat-sen was obliged to flee China. He travelled extensively, particularly in Japan and the USA, where there were large expatriate Chinese communities, and also to Britain and Europe, where Chinese undergraduates were studying at universities in Belgium, France, and Germany. Amongst these he gained support for the Republican cause: to overthrow the Ch'ing dynasty and replace it, not with another Imperial dynasty, but with a democratically elected government. Political support also came from the USA, which was seeking to extend its sphere of influence in the Far East, as well as from the Chinese expatriates and *émigrés*. More significantly, Sun Yat-sen's cause was also the Triads'.

Sun Yat-sen had been a Triad member from an early age, and in time he became a senior office holder. It is not known exactly when he took his oath of brotherhood, but he was at various times an official in a number of Triad societies, including the Hong Kong-based Chung Wo Tong Society, founded in 1890 to raise funds for the Republicans and to co-ordinate its activities. He was also a '426 Fighter' member of the Kwok On Wui Society in Honolulu and Chicago.

Until the late eighteenth century the Triads operated only within China and limited areas of South East Asia, their objectives being to protect local Chinese trade interests, to further the religious aims traditionally associated with them, and to undermine the Manchu dynasty. But as Chinese immigration increased over the first half of the nineteenth century, so Triad influence began to spread. Wherever there was a Chinese community there would be Triads. Triad lodges could be found amongst the Chinese laundrymen of San Francisco; in many communities that sprang up along the Oregon Trail there lived small groups of Chinese and as these expanded lodges were set up. There were lodges in Laramie, Cheyenne, Kansas City, Seattle, and Vancouver, lodges in the Californian gold-fields and the Klondike, and eventually lodges in New York and Boston. Many of these overseas lodges came under the supervision of the Hung Mun Society in Canton, a branch of this, the Chi Kung Tong group, being their active administrator.

In some places, such as Hong Kong, patriotic Triad societies were made illegal as a political expedient because of their opposition to the Manchu dynasty and support of the Republicans. This included Sun Yat-sen's own society, the Chung Wo Tong, even though – unlike some groups – it was not involved in criminal activity. In 1911, with Triad support, the Republicans staged a revolt in Canton which spread rapidly throughout southern China. The days of the Manchu dynasty were now numbered.

On 1 January 1912, after the fall of Nanking, the Republic of China was born, with Sun Yat-sen as its provisional president. Under foreign pressure he soon resigned this post to Yuan Shih-k'ai. One of the last acts of his brief presidency was to go to the tombs of the Ming emperors and publicly declare that the Ch'ing dynasty had been overthrown.

For the Triads it was a supremely glorious moment and their influence became all-pervasive. In order to rise in the civil service or the armed forces it was essential to be a Triad brother. Merchants, bankers, and businessmen quickly discovered that Triad membership oiled the machinery of commerce in a remarkable way. To Westerners this was corruption on a grand scale; to the Chinese it was a well established fact of public life. *Plus ça change* . . .

But mutual back-scratching quickly became something more sinister, and the Triads soon degenerated from pragmatic patriots into out and out criminals. The next stage in their history was about to begin.

2

MONKS AND EMPERORS

To the Western mind there are few prima-facie links between history and legend. To the Chinese, the dividing line between fact and legendary fiction is less clear cut. Into the grey area where the two overlap falls traditional history, which in China is often taken for literal truth.

The traditional history of the Triads is a fantastic amalgamation of real events and people, magical parable and folklore. Like legends the world over, those of the Triads undoubtedly have some tenuous roots in fact; but these have long been lost or reconstructed out of all recognition. The traditional history remains, however, as important as the authentic historical chronology of the Triads, for in it lies much of what the Triads wish to regard as the truth about themselves.

The traditional history of the Triads shows how modern members see themselves in relation to their past. As with any secret organization, an identity with history is central to their ritual, and consequently to their cohesion. An oath is only effective if it can be enforced by reference to the example of past members. The more this relationship can be enforced, the more effective it becomes. Continuity is of paramount importance. To the Triad office-bearer, being part of a continually unfolding history is a vital motive for his actions. He is not an individual acting on his own behalf, but a cog in a highly developed machine.

That history brings together myth and legend, heroism and defeat, magical strength and human failings, and has inspired some of the best-known stories in Chinese literature. This helps give a certain popular credibility to the Triads as a

whole, who are seen as being enmeshed in the greatness of
China's past. There are religious aspects to the traditional
history as well: Taoist ancestor worship, primitive magical
beliefs, Buddhism, and Confucianism all mingle together and
are given symbolic and ritualistic permanence.

There are several accounts of the Triads' traditional
history, two of which are of particular interest. One, which I
shall quote here, is taken from W. P. Morgan's *Triad Societies
in Hong Kong*, published in 1960 but researched and written a
decade earlier. This is a modern account obtained from Triad
informants in Hong Kong and now virtually unobtainable.
The other is drawn directly from another scarce volume, a
three-volume study, *The Hung Society*, made by J. S. M.
Ward and W. G. Stirling and published in 1925. Though it
deals specifically with the Hung Society at the turn of the
nineteenth century it reflects beliefs and symbols that have
remained unchanged for hundreds of years and that are
closely related to Triad mythology and ritual. It is given as
Appendix 2 (p. 160).

If one compares the two versions one can see how, in the
space of fifty years, the traditional history has been rewritten
and reassessed to the Triads' advantage. Ward and Stirling
based their account on secondary sources drawn from
colonial officers' reports and information gleaned from
academics and academic journals. Direct contact with the
Triads was for the most part absent. On the other hand, the
version recorded by Morgan is far more up-to-date and was
taken from a primary source. It contains far greater detail, a
heightened heroic and epic narrative, and a more complex
political background. Furthermore, Morgan obtained his
information direct from Triad members in Hong Kong. It is
reasonable to suppose that this version of their traditional
history is still broadly accepted by Triads today. Many of the
places mentioned in the narrative are either imaginary or now
untraceable. To simplify reading, the spelling of proper
nouns has been standardized. According to Morgan, the
story is as follows:

Towards the end of the reign of the Ming Emperor Sung Ching, the Empire was threatened from within and without. The Emperor was wholly preoccupied with pleasures of the flesh, and Imperial appointments and favours were lavished upon those who pandered to his tastes. As increasing control of the country passed into the hands of these sycophants, internal administration collapsed due to their concentration on self-enrichment and disregard for the needs of the people. Their crops devastated by a prolonged drought, and burdened by unceasing demands of the rapacious officials, the people of the country were on the point of starvation and ripe for rebellion. Beyond the Great Wall, the Manchurian armies were encamped, waiting to fall upon the collapsing Empire.

Disgusted with the corruption at Court, and convinced the Emperor had forfeited his mandate by ignoring the rights and needs of the people, a group of honest officials, including Kam Shun, Sze Ho Fat, Ku Ting Lam, Hung Kai Shing, Wong Hei Chung, Fu Ching Yuen, Wong Shuen Shan and Wong Po Chau, formed a secret organization under cover of a money-lender's shop. The aim of the organization was to recruit patriotic citizens to clear the Court of corrupt officials and restore the Ming dynasty to the level of honesty and efficiency it had once known. The move was too late, however, for the peasant Li Chi Shing (alias Li Chong) had already raised the standard of revolt and his starving followers swept through the country, capturing Peking and causing the Emperor to commit suicide. The Ming General Ng Sam Kwai, holding the Great Wall against a possible Manchurian invasion, could not tolerate the thought of a peasant on the Dragon throne and, hoping to attain the throne himself, entered into compact with the Manchus to drive out Li Chi Shing. The peasant rebels could not hold out against the trained armies of Ng Sam Kwai and the Manchus and were quickly defeated. Ng Sam Kwai's army had, however, borne the brunt of the fighting and suffered the most casualties so that on entry into Peking the stronger Manchus seized the throne themselves and set up Shun Chi as the first Emperor of the Ch'ing dynasty.

The organization set up by the honest Ming officials intensified its recruiting campaign and Ku Ting Lam set out their aims in a book called *Ming Yee Toi Fong Luk* – Record of the Enemies of Ming – which preached nationalism and resistance to the Ch'ings. Believing that they must act before the Manchus could consolidate their hold on the country, the organization rose into rebellion but was heavily defeated in a battle near Yenchow. Many of the leading officials were killed and of the survivors, Kam Shun sought refuge in a monastery while Wong Shuen Shan fled to Formosa. In Formosa, Wong Shuen Shan wrote a book setting out plans of action for defeating the Ch'ing occupiers and called it the *Kam Toi Po Luk – Kam Toi* Precious Records – after the name of a mountain on that island. This book was later given to Cheng Shing Kung, another Ming official who had earlier escaped to Formosa from the Ch'ing regime. Cheng Shing Kung studied the book and, in pursuance of plans set out in it, led an unsuccessful attack on the city of Nanking. After failing in this mission he retreated back to Formosa and on his death passed the book to his grandson, Cheng Hak Song, who continued to resist the Ch'ings until they finally managed to conquer the island, whereupon Cheng Hak Song committed suicide after placing the book in an iron chest and throwing it into the sea.

Some time after the conquest of Formosa by the Ch'ing, a rebellion by Ming supporters broke out in Szechuan province. This was led by Man Wan Lung, a monk, who had taken holy orders and changed his name from Wu Tai Hei after having committed a murder. While in the Ching Chung Shan monastery in Szechuan, he recruited supporters for the Ming cause and soon had sufficient followers to begin an armed uprising. He marched on Chengtu, the capital of the province, but lost his way in the mountain passes and obtained as a guide a man named Fong Pan Leung, who was in reality a secret agent of the local Ch'ing garrison commander. Warned by his agent, the Ch'ing commander set an ambush and destroyed the rebel army in the mountains of Mo Shang. Man Wan Lung was killed during the battle and his commanders and officials scattered. Many of them took refuge in the Siu Lam monastery in the Kaolin mountains, Po Ting district, Fukien province, where they continued to plot and gather supporters for fresh attacks against the Ch'ing. One of his leading counsellors, Chan Kan Nam, fled to the Pak Hok Tung – White Stork Grotto – in Wukwong district near the borders of Hunan and Kwangtung, where he began to draw up plans for attacks against the Ch'ing and to recruit followers to his cause.

Thus our heroes conducted themselves until, in the reign of the second Ch'ing Emperor, Hong Hei, rebellious tribes from the state of the Silu threatened an invasion of the country. The defending Generals were sore pressed and appealed to the Emperor to send them reinforcements. The

Emperor and his officials realized that they had no men of sufficient ability to cope with the situation and they decided to start a recruiting campaign throughout the country. It was announced that all men who could gather and lead forces to defeat the Silu rebellion would be rewarded with high honours and positions within the Ch'ing administration.

News of this appeal reached the ears of Cheng Kwan Tat, a nephew of the former Ming partisan Cheng Shing Kung. He was, at that time, residing at the Siu Lam monastery with his wife Kwok Sau Ying and his sister Cheng Yuk Lin where all were receiving instruction in the art of Chinese boxing. Cheng Kwan Tat informed Chi Yuen, the abbot of Siu Lam, of this news and at a general meeting of all the monks it was decided that they should offer their services to the Emperor. This decision was influenced by many factors. First they wished to prevent any further infiltration of the Empire by barbarians. Secondly they wished to put into practice the methods of warfare developed by them in the monastery. Thirdly they wished to gain confidence in their own abilities and at the same time impress the population with their feats so that the people would more readily join them when the time came to revolt. Fourthly they wished to alleviate the suspicions of the Ch'ing officials regarding their activities by pretending eagerness to fight in defence of the Emperor.

The abbot instructed his chief disciple, Tak Wan, to lead a hundred and twenty-eight monks together with Cheng Kwan Tat, his wife and sister, and report to the Emperor. From the Emperor, the monks asked only for sufficient provisions and weapons for their campaign and requested that no additional troops be sent with them. They marched against the Silu rebels and by their superior military skill defeated them within three months. On returning to Peking they were joyously acclaimed by the Emperor who wished to grant them titles and high positions in his government as a reward. The monks, however, declined his offers saying that they had only done their duty as patriotic citizens and their sole desire was to return to their life of peace in the monastery. Cheng Kwan Tat, not being bound to monastic rules, accepted the appointment of a garrison commander of the Ch'ing forces in the Wuchow district so that he might be in a position to supply information regarding troop movements to the monks at Siu Lam.

After the monks had returned to Siu Lam, the Grand Secretary of the Ch'ing Council, named Wong Chun Mei, became filled with jealousy at the honour shown them by the

Emperor and by the glory and gifts that were heaped upon Cheng Kwan Tat. He instilled a sense of insecurity into the Emperor by pointing out that this small band of monks had succeeded where his own generals and troops had failed, and might not their military superiority work equally as well against the Ch'ing as against the Silu invaders? He suggested that the reason they had refused appointments offered them was that they wished to return in a body to the south and there raise forces in preparation for a revolt against the Ch'ing. So great was the fear that grew in the Emperor's mind that he gave instructions to Cheung Kin Chau, High Commissioner of Fukien province, and Chan Man Yiu, Magistrate of Po Ting district, to destroy Siu Lam monastery and all its inhabitants. He also ordered the execution of Cheng Kwan Tat.

Cheung Kin Chau and Chan Man Yiu discussed methods of carrying out their orders. The monastery was located on a tall hill which commanded an excellent view of the surrounding terrain, so that a surprise attack was out of the question. The hill was also said to be honeycombed with tunnels leading to the monastery and even if the place were stormed it was likely that many of the inhabitants would escape through these secret passages. It was decided that, if possible, the monks should be drugged and then killed but in case anything went wrong all exits from the monastery would have to be guarded and to do this the location of the secret passages would have to be found out. Chan Man Yiu volunteered to try and find out the location of the passages and, disguising himself as an ordinary citizen, he wandered through the villages near Siu Lam hoping to pick up useful information.

One day, he came across a coolie whose shaven head bore the burn marks of a Buddhist monk. Curious, he sought friendship with the coolie and eventually learned that he had been a former monk of Siu Lam monastery. This man, Ma Yee Fuk alias Ma Ning Yee, had, in fact, been a prominent member of the monastic fraternity and had been ranked seventh among the brotherhood in martial ability. He had, however, made offensive overtures to the wife and sister of Cheng Kwan Tat and had also broken the Man Nin Po Tang – the Ten Thousand Years Precious Lamp – which was a sacred object presented to the monastery by the Persian government. For these misdeeds his credentials had been revoked by the abbot and he had been turned out of the monastery. His scarred head marking him as a renegade monk, he had been unable to obtain respectable employment and was reduced to earning his living as a common labourer. He was exceedingly bitter in his feelings towards the abbot and other members of Siu Lam and, on learning of Chan Man Yiu's real identity, agreed to assist in the destruction of the monastery. Apart from obtaining revenge against those who had reduced him to his present state, he was promised a reward in the form of a high official position if he would reveal the whereabouts of all the secret paths and also swear that his expulsion from the monastery had been due to his refusal to join the monks' conspiracy to overthrow the Ch'ing.

With the aid of the traitor Ma Yee Fuk, the troops of Cheung Kin Chau were quietly placed in position at the secret exits of the monastery, others were held close by to block the main gates when the signal was given. All were plentifully supplied with inflammable material with which it was intended to burn down the building. Chan Man Yiu, leading a small number of coolies carrying drugged wine in jars, approached the monastery openly. He informed the abbot that the wine was a personal gift to the monastery from the Emperor and requested that all the monks drink to the Emperor's health. The abbot was suspicious and tested the wine by dipping a magic sword into one of the jars. The sword changed colour and the monks, incensed by such treachery, sought to slay Chan Man Yiu who, however, managed to escape. On seeing Chan Man Yiu fleeing from the monastery, the troops of Cheung Kin Chau closed in and set fire to the buildings. Those at secret entrances also set fire to material in the tunnels and the smoke and flames prevented the monks from escaping in any direction. One hundred and ten perished in the flames and the remaining eighteen sought refuge in the great hall wherein was the image of Buddha and prayed for deliverance. Their prayers were answered by a large yellow curtain hanging in the hall dropping down and covering them. The curtain protected them from the flames, but the monks, suffering from the effects of smoke and injuries, all fainted. The Ch'ing troops, seeing the collapse of the monastery walls and observing no signs of life in the ruins, withdrew from the immediate area.

When the eighteen survivors recovered they found themselves trapped in the ruins but one of them, Tsoi Tak Chun, managed to knock a hole in the wall and they got out through that breach. The entire hill was still on fire but they passed safely over the burning grass and the smoke concealed their movements from the Ch'ing soldiers. They pressed on until they reached Ting Shan near Sheung Yeung city, Hupei province, and there thirteen of them died from the effects of their wounds and lack of food. They were cremated and their ashes wrapped in several bundles which were then carried by the remaining five survivors. These five, Tsoi Tak Chung, Fong Tai Hung, Ma Chiu Hing, Wu Tak Tai and Lee Shik Hoi, became the First Five Ancestors of the Society.

The First Five Ancestors continued their flight but were greatly weakened from lack of food to eat or water to drink. At times they managed to quench their thirst by drinking the dew collected on the blossoms of lotus flowers but they were unable to find any food to sustain themselves. Eventually they reached the Cheung Kong, Tai Hoi – Long River and Huge Sea – and there they threw themselves down on the bank and fainted from hunger. Whilst in this coma they had a dream in which the spirits told them that the sand on which they lay might be eaten and would give them strength. Accordingly, when they awoke, they ate the sand and their hunger ceased. After eating, they noticed an object sparkling on the beach and when they examined it they found it to be a three-legged incense pot bearing on the bottom the characters *fan ch'ing*: *fuk ming* – Overthrow Ch'ing: Restore Ming – and on the side the characters *shun tin hang to* – Act according to the will of Heaven. Inside the pot was a sheet of paper bearing a prophetic account of the destruction of the Ch'ing dynasty and the return of the Ming. When they had finished reading this prophecy, they decided to worship the gods and thank them for their assistance and encouragement. They had no joss sticks or other articles necessary for worship but used small tree branches for altar candles and grass for joss sticks. These substitutes burned brightly and sent up fragrant smoke to the heavens.

While they were worshipping, Ch'ing soldiers suddenly came upon them. With the broad waters in front of them and the soldiers behind them, the Ancestors were in great peril and all seemed lost. Suddenly, a grass sandal, being one of a pair they had brought from the monastery, and said to have been the property of Mo Tat, the founder of Siu Lam, turned into a boat and they crossed the waters in it out of reach of the soldiers. They landed and continued to march until they came to the Wu Lung (Black Dragon) River. Here they encountered more Ch'ing soldiers and during the battle with them they lost the precious grass sandals. They escaped from the soldiers and continued to search for a means of crossing the river. Eventually they came to a bridge known as the Yee Pan Kiu – Two Planked Bridge – but found it to be strongly guarded by Ch'ing soldiers. They managed to get under the bridge without being detected and there they saw three large stones floating on the water, each bearing one of the characters *ting, hoi, pau* – calm, sea, floating. Using these as stepping stones, they made their way across in safety.

After crossing the Wu Lung River, the Ancestors met a fruit-seller named Tse Pong Hang who gave them fruit to eat and water to drink and then led them to shelter in the hut of a woodcutter named Ng Ting Kwai. Whilst the Ancestors were sheltering under his roof, Ng Ting Kwai met Chan Man Yiu, the magistrate of Po Ting district, in the woods nearby. Chan Man Yiu enquired of Ng Ting Kwai if he had seen five monks in the area. Ng Ting Kwai sensed that here was an enemy of the Five Ancestors and accordingly he killed Chan Man Yiu with his axe. At a later date, Ng Ting Kwai found one of the grass sandals lost by the monks in a place called Chung Chau and he was afterwards recognized as being the first Cho Hai – Grass Sandal – official of the Society.

Tse Pong Hang led the Ancestors to Kwai Sin Shan, a hill on the border of Wai Yeung district, Kwangtung province, and there they sought shelter at the Po Tak monastery. The abbot of this place introduced them to five of his friends who were living nearby. These men, Ng Tin Shing, Hung Tai Shui, To Pit Tat, Lee Shik Tai and Lam Wing Chiu, were rebel leaders and former officials of the Ming dynasty. They swore to assist the monks and avenge the wrongs done to them by raising forces to attack the Ch'ing. For their devotion and assistance in obtaining recruits for the cause they are now known as the Second Five Ancestors of the Society.

Kwok Yuen, the abbot of Po Tak, urged the little group to go and see Chan Kan Nam who was recruiting followers in the White Stork Grotto and drawing up plans for the overthrow of the Manchus. Only Fong Tai Hung went to the White Stork Grotto, the remainder made their way back to Sheung Yeung city to worship at the grave of Cheng Kwan Tat, their old comrade, who had been executed by order of the Emperor and buried near that city. On arriving at Sheung Yeung city they met the wife and sister of Cheng Kwan Tat as well as two of his good friends named Wong Cheong and Chung Man Kwan. All went to worship at the grave of Cheng Kwan Tat but, while they were doing so, a squad of Ch'ing soldiers, accompanied by the traitor monk Ma Ning Yee, appeared. The worshippers scattered and fled and in the confusion Cheng Kwan Tat's wife and sister lost contact with the others and were trapped by the soldiers on the bank of a river. Rather than surrender to the soldiers, the two women threw themselves into the river and were drowned. Their bodies floated up river, against the current, and were pulled out by Tse King Chin, the son of Tse Pong Hang, who buried them under a peach and plum tree. The other members of the party were pursued for many days by the soldiers and eventually they came upon the graves of the two women. They were struck with anguish at the fate of their two sisters and while they knelt weeping at the grave-sides the peach and plum tree joined together and turned into a sword. With this sword they turned against their pursuers and killed the traitor Ma Ning Yee. Such was the ferocity of their attack that those soldiers not slain fled in confusion from the scene and the little band made their way back to the White Stork Grotto.

The party then returned to the White Stork Grotto and, after discussing matters with Chan Kan Nam, they all decided to go to Muk Yeung city in Fukien province to set up their headquarters and recruit loyal and patriotic citizens to take part in a revolution against the Ch'ing. Tse Pong Hang opened the Yee Hop Tim fruit shop in Tai Ping market near Muk Yeung city and used it as a cover for receiving recruits and arranging for their accommodation, etc., until the time came for revolt. While these preparations were going on two fishermen, Chan Sau Hang and his son Chan Siu Kun, fished Wong Shuen Shan's missing book, the Kam Toi Po Luk, and a jade seal from the sea near Amoy. Being loyal citizens they straightaway took these articles to Chan Kan Nam who recognized the seal as being the Imperial seal of the Ming Emperors.

The recruiting campaign was a great success and thousands of patriots flocked to join the founders. Amongst these recruits was a boy who called himself Chu Hung Chuk and claimed he was a descendant of the house of Ming. He was of noble appearance and produced documents to establish his identity. The founders were overjoyed at his arrival and made him the Crown Prince of their Society. On the twenty-fifth day of the seventh moon in the Kap Yan year, Chan Kan Nam conducted a mass ceremony during which officers of the organization were elected and all persons swore an oath to overthrow the Ch'ing and restore the Ming. Among the officers elected was a General to lead the vanguard of the army. This position was given to a man named Tin Yau Hung who was in reality the reincarnation of Wong Shing Yan, the faithful eunuch of the Ming Emperor Sung Ching. This man had committed suicide with his master when the rebel Li Chi Shing had entered Peking, and his body had been left to rot on the ground instead of receiving burial. His spirit, unable to find rest, had wandered for many years until one of Chan Kan Nam's leading fighters, named So Hung Kwong, had died. The body of So Hung Kwong remained perfectly fresh and warm even three days after death and this was due to the spirit of Wong Shing Yan entering it. After three days the body came back to life and was renamed Tin Yau Hung. At the first mass ceremony, a bright red glow occurred in the eastern sky. This was regarded as a portent since the sound for red (*hung*) is almost identical to the regnal name (*Hung*) of the Ming Emperors so the members decided to refer to themselves as members of the Hung Ka – Hung Family. The character adopted was that of the regnal name of the Emperors, not the character for red. Their Crown Prince, Chu Hung Chuk, changed his name to Chu Hung Ying to show his respect for the members, the character *ying* meaning heroes. The whole organization adopted the society name of Ming Yeun Tong, Kam Toi Shan – Ming Eternal Society of Kam Toi Mountain.

Soon after this the Society launched its attack on the Ch'ing. They captured the whole of Fukien province and marched northwards towards Nanking. It seemed that nothing could halt their victorious progress but then, unfortunately, bad liaison caused their various army groups to lose contact with each other and the Ch'ing were able to concentrate their whole army on each Triad group in turn and destroy them. The rebellion collapsed, and over one hundred thousand Triad members had died in the attempt. Chu Hung Ying disappeared during the confusion of battle and was never seen again. The Triad army retreated back to Muk Yeung city, and shortly after this Chan Kan Nam died. He was succeeded by Sze Kam Ming, the son of Sze Ho Fat, one of the honest Ming officials who had helped set up a patriotic organization and defended Yen Chow during the Manchu conquest. This man went to the Ko Kai temple in Kwangtung province to raise a fresh army against the Ch'ing. When he had raised a large enough force he raised the standard of revolt and within a year had captured seven of the southern provinces. Again it seemed that success would crown their efforts but while encamped near the Pak Fu Kwan – White Tiger Pass – in Szechuan province, the Vanguard General Tin Yau Hung died of illness. This event caused a division of opinion amongst the Triad Generals, some wanting to retreat and others wanting to press forward. While they were so divided, the Ch'ing army attacked and defeated them, and once more the remnants were forced to retreat.

The First Five Ancestors, realizing that a series of simultaneous rebellions in many parts of the country would divide the Ch'ing forces and have greater chance of success than a rebellion originating from one area, decided to scatter to various parts of the country and raise supporters for a fresh attempt. Before parting, they devised a series of secret signs by which they and their recruits might be recognized whenever members met.

Tsoi Tak Chung accompanied by Ng Tin Shing went to Fukien and Kansu provinces where they established the First Lodge of the Society. The Lodge was known as the Ching Lin Tong of the Fung Wong Kwan – Green Lotus Hall of Phoenix District. Its regiments carried a black flag bearing the character *piu* – Glorious. It was also known as the Nineteen Tai – Steps or Ladder – and its seal was rhombic shaped. Tsoi Tak Chung changed his name to Chan Yuen and also used his Buddhist name of Fat Sam and his Triad name of Ching Fong. In the course of his travels he proceeded as far north as Hangchow and there stayed at the Ling Yan monastery where the abbot, Yat Chi, introduced him to another inmate named To Yuen, who was the Third Generation Ancestor of the Ching Mun – Green Family. This association had been formed by Kam Shun putting into effect the principles outlined in the book Ming Yee Toi Fong Luk, written by Ku Ting Lam. Kam Shun was known as the First Generation Ancestor, he was succeeded by Lo Cho who was the Second Generation Ancestor and now To Yuen was leader with the title Third Generation Ancestor. The Ching Mun had succeeded in recruiting most of the boatmen and labourers of the ports and inland waterways in the area of Hangchow, Shanghai and Nanking. On the surface they appeared to be working for the Ch'ing by maintaining communications on the inland rivers and canals but in actual fact they were busy gathering information about Ch'ing troop movements, supplies, and storage depots so that, in the event of a rebellion, they might be able to destroy such stores and also oppose any movement of Ch'ing troops by waterways. To Yuen introduced Tsoi Tak Chung to the leaders of the three main Ching Mun branches named Yung Ngan, Chin Kin and Pun Ching. A general discussion was held regarding collaboration between the Ching Mun and the Hung Mun and it was also decided to change the name from Ching Mun to Ching Pang – Green Party. Tsoi Tak Chung then continued north to Shanghai where he stayed at the Hung Kwan Lo Cho temple. There he met Shing Heung Shan, a notorious leader of mendicants and criminals in the city. Although a criminal, Shing Heung Shan was a patriotic man and, after listening to Tsoi Tak Chung's plans for overthrowing the Ch'ing, he became his disciple and formed his followers into an association called the Hung Pang – Hung Party.

Fong Tai Hung, with Hung Tai Shui, went to Kwangtung and Kwangsi where they established the Second Lodge. It was known as the Hung Shun Tong of the Kam Lan Kwan – Hung Obedience Hall of the Golden Orchid District, and also as the Twelve Tai. Its regiments bore a red flag with the character *sau* – age or longevity. Its seal was triangular-shaped. Fong Tai Hung had the Buddhist name of Fat Mo and the Triad name of Ching Cho. He first concerned himself with raising recruits in the Kwangtung area and then went to Heung Lo To, where he recruited the pirate chief Cheung Po Chai, and went to Wu Lo To where he recruited the female pirate chief Cheng Yat So. The members in the area of Heung Lo To and Wu Lo To called their group the Sam Hop Wui – Three United Association – and Cheung Po Chai also formed an additional group in the Tam Shui/Kwai Chung area which became known as the Yee Lung Shan Tong – Two Dragons Hill Society.

Ma Chiu Hing, with To Pit Tat, went to Yunnan and Szechuan provinces and founded the Third Lodge. It was known as the Ka Hau Tong of the Fuk Po Kwan – Heavenly Queen Hall of the Happy Border (of water) District. It was also known as the Nine Tai. Its regiments bore vermilion flags with the character *hop* – united. Its seal was square-shaped. Ma Chiu Hing, whose Buddhist name was Yan Wai and whose Triad name was Ching Kit, also organized a branch Society in Szechuan known as the Po Ko Wui – Robe of the Elder Brother Society.

Wu Tak Tai, with Lee Shik Tai, went to Hunan and Hupei provinces and established the Fourth Lodge. This was called the Cham Tai Tong of the Lin Cheung Kwan – Great Blending Hall of the beautiful Lotus District, and was also known as the Twenty-nine Tai. Its regiments bore a white flag with the character *wo* – harmonious. Its seal was shaped like a parallelogram. Wu Tak Tai, whose Buddhist name was Lun Hau and Triad name was Ching Shing, also went to the Sam Cho district of Hunan where he recruited a disciple named Kwong Hon who organized a branch of the Society under the name Ko Tai Wui – Elder and Younger (Brothers) Society – which was later changed to Ko Lo Wui – Elder Brother Society – at the suggestion of Fong Tai Hung who also visited the Sam Cho area.

Lee Shik Hoi, with Lam Wing Chiu, went to the
Chekiang/Kiangsi/Honan area and founded the Fifth Lodge
known as the Wang Fa Tong of the Lung Sai Kwan –
Extensive Conversion Hall of the Western Dyke District, and
alternatively, the Forty-seven Tai. Its regiments bore a green
flag with the character *tung* – together. Its seal was circular in
shape. Lee Shik Hoi, whose Buddhist name was Chi Yau and
Triad name was Ching Kwan, also organized a branch of the
main lodge in Chekiang under the name of Hung Cheong Wui
– Red Spear (or Cannon) Society.

Following the formation of the Five Lodges, many
thousands of recruits were initiated into the Society. It had
been decided that recruiting should continue until an army of
several million followers had been raised and the plans drawn
up and studied to determine the most favourable time for a
mass uprising. However, in certain parts of the country the
Ch'ing oppression became intolerable, and the members in
those areas were forced to rise in protest without waiting for
the support of the other Lodges. The first of these rebellions
took place in the fifty-first year of the reign of the Emperor
Kin Lung [1787] in Formosa and was led by Lam Song Man.
The second took place in the fourteenth year of the reign of
the Emperor Ka Hing [1816] and occurred south of the
Yangtse led by Wu Ping Yiu. The third was led by Li Lap Ting
and Hung Chun Nin in Kwangsi province in the twelfth year
of the reign of the Emperor To Kwong [1833]. The fourth was
led by Hung Sau Chuen and Yeung Sau Ching during the
latter part of the reign of the Emperor To Kwong and the
reign of the Emperor Ham Fung [1851–62]. None of these
rebellions was successful and many thousands of society
members were forced to flee the country to escape the
retribution of the Ch'ing. Many went to the goldfields of
America and Australia while others went to the South Seas
and Malaya. Wherever they went they remained true to the
Society and set up new Lodges in order that they might
continue to work for the freeing of China. In 1903, Dr Sun
Yat-sen, leader of the Republican Party, who had also been
forced to flee from China, joined the Kwok On Wui –
National Stability Society – in Honolulu and, because of his
determination to free his country, he was immediately
promoted to the official rank of Hung Kwan – Red Pole
Fighter. Shortly after this, he formed a new branch of the
Society in Honolulu named the Tai Luk Shan – Main Land
Mountain – with himself as the leader. He realized that the
combined efforts of the countless patriotic brothers of the

Society could bring freedom to the country and accordingly he became very anxious to co-ordinate and expand the Society, both in China and overseas. As a result of his efforts, 140 branches of the Hung Mun were established prior to 1911 and 128 branches by the Green Pang. One important branch established was the Hing Chung Wui – Prosperity for China Society – which later changed its name to Kwok Man Tong – National People's Party. Sun Yat-sen, together with other well-known Society leaders such as Chiu Yuk, Wong Wan So, Cheung Oi Wan, and others, went to America to obtain moral and financial support from the brothers there. Others went to Australia, Europe, Malaya, and all countries where the Society had been established, for a similar purpose. With the physical support of those brothers in China and the financial support of those overseas, Sun Yat-sen ordered the revolution to begin in 1911 and within one year the Republic had been established and the Ch'ing driven from the throne of China.

Correlating the events of this traditional history with actual historical events is impossible. As with any folk tradition, the links between the story and the real past are – at best – tenuous, and are likely to have been so at the start. But there are a few identifiable historical links that can be teased out of the mythological and symbolic narrative. Many of the place-names are fictitious, symbolic, or encoded versions of real places. Siu Lam, Muk Yeung, Tai Ping Market (see p. 10) cannot be identified with any actual places. Silu apparently lay between the Altai mountains and the Hoang (or Hwang) Ho River, but this is not certain. On the other hand, many places mentioned in the story are real: Chengtu, Peking (of course), and the various provinces and districts.

Real historical events do feature in Triad history. Sze Ho Fat was the general in command of Yen Chow; Cheng Shing Kung was a real character, and so was Man Wan Lung. As we have seen, lodges were set up in the goldfields of America and in Australia, and Sun Yat-sen (see pp. 14–16) *was* a senior Triad office-bearer.

With this co-mingling of fact and fiction it is impossible to give an exact date for the founding of the Triads. The traditional history even varies, sometimes quite widely. The two versions given in this book demonstrate this, and other extant versions written in Taiwan, in the north of China, and in Shantung province differ on specific points of detail.

The link between all the traditional histories of the Triads, the thread that binds them together, is that they all claim a common origin in the association founded by pro-Ming officials – the so-called Green Party. The patriotic aim of restoring the Chinese Mings to power resounds throughout Triad myth. But though this, too, represents a verifiable aspect of historical truth, patriotism is no longer a motivating force for Triads in the late twentieth century. It, too, has receded into the shadowy world of symbol and myth as the Triads twist history to suit their new criminal purposes.

3

THE CITY OF WILLOWS

Although, at some early stage in their development, the Triad societies may have been administered by a central organization, for most of their history each society has operated as an essentially autonomous unit, self-governing and answering to no authority but the collective dictates of its own officials. In some localities and regions there have been mother lodges, and in some instances lodges have had sub-groups or branches attached to them. But unlike most other secret or quasi-secret societies, the Triads do not have a central administration, or even a single headquarters.

What binds Triad members together is a series of oaths, a common historical *raison d'être* (the now anachronistic 'Overthrow the Ch'ing and restore the Ming'), and a pathological sense of secrecy, the breaking of which usually leads to fatal retribution.

In the past each lodge conformed to a rigid ceremonial and hierarchical structure dictated by tradition and a shared interpretation of the traditional history (see Chapter 2). Triad lodges today – especially those outside the Far East – often do without certain officers and functions, or else amalgamate or redistribute their duties. Certain features, however, appear to be common to most Triad lodges.

Each lodge has an executive hierarchy that presides over its activities. The leader is called the Shan Chu, and there is a deputy leader, the Fu Shan Chu, to assist him and act on his behalf when he is absent. Below them come the Heung Chu, or Incense Master, and the Sin Fung, or Vanguard. These two officers administer the lodge rituals and have the power to invest, initiate, and order retribution against the members.

Beneath them are a number of departmental heads responsible for the everyday running of the society and of any sub-
branches, each of the latter having an internal structure
similar to that of the main lodge except for the Incense Master
and Vanguard. These are only found in principal lodges and
their presence is a sign that a lodge has reached maturity and
achieved power in its own right. Sub-branches are controlled
by a leader, the Chu Chi, and his deputy, the Fu Chu Chi.
Some lodges also have a treasurer, the Cha So, but this is
comparatively rare. All Triad officers are appointed for fixed
periods and are elected by lodge members.

The individual departments of a lodge (the heads of which
form a central council) deal with such things as finance,
recruitment, membership and propaganda, discipline, liaison
with other lodges, the education of members' children and
the welfare of the members' families. Though the Triads
today are first and foremost a criminal fraternity they retain
some aspects of their historical role as protectionist trade
guilds. Particularly in Hong Kong and Singapore, there have
been in fact Triad groups which were principally self-help
groups rather than criminal organizations. A few still exist.

Initiate members are required to pay an entrance fee. They
must also obtain a sponsor, to whom a further fee is payable –
often far in excess of the entrance fee. This is a private
arrangement and is only reached after the initiate's credentials
have been thoroughly checked by the Incense Master and the
Vanguard. A sponsor must also be found, and paid for, when
a member seeks promotion within the lodge. In time,
members can recoup their expenses by acting as sponsors
themselves. A percentage of each entrance fee is officially
shared by the senior officers. All monies earned by an
individual society, from whatever source, are deposited in the
central lodge fund and are theoretically inviolable. In fact
embezzlement by officers is not uncommon and has caused
major rifts in some societies, leading to the formation of
splinter groups and retributory murders.

Within each society there are four ranks of officials. The
first is the Hung Kwan, or Red Pole, who is a fighter and is

responsible for discipline. In the past he was a real fighter, well versed in the martial arts and a skilled weapons man. Today he may be just as skilful at using a computer or modern firearm as a Chinese sword or fighting staff. Formerly the Red Pole was in charge of a fighting unit of up to fifty members. Today, departmental heads are often Red Poles.

The Pak Tsz Sin is also known as the White Paper Fan and occupies a position similar to *consigliere* in the Mafia. He is an adviser and strategist and is usually in line for the job of Incense Master. Traditionally an educated man, he is the society's thinker, often with legal or business knowledge, rather than a man of action.

The Cho Hai or Messenger is a liaison officer who acts as a go-between in lodge affairs. He might be the collector of extorted money, or the lodge's representative in its dealings with the outside world or with other lodges.

All officers' ranks are given a numerical code (ordinary members are known as Sze Kau or 49s), each of which begins with a 4. The system is based on the ancient occult science of numerology in which numbers and combinations of numbers assume symbolic, even mystical significance. Hence the Shan Chu is 489; the Fu Shan Chu, Heung Chu, Sin Fung, and Sheung Fa officers (who are all equal in rank) are 438; the Hung Kwan is 426; Pak Tsz Sin is 415; Cho Hai is 432.

The original numerological meanings have long been lost, though some significance can still be deduced from the 489 of the lodge leader, who is also sometimes known as a 21 (i.e. 4+8+9) − 21 is 3 (the number of creation) multiplied by 7 (both a lucky number and the number of death): in the leader lies the life cycle of the society. The Incense Master, 438, is also a 15 (4+3+8): 3 multiplied by 5, or creation and longevity/preservation, which is appropriate in connection with his responsibility for lodge ritual. The tortoise, an ancient symbol of longevity, is often associated with Incense Masters.

A Triad lodge today rarely has a permanent location. In the past it is known that actual lodge buildings existed: a painting, in the diagrammatical style common to Chinese art, survives of a lodge meeting in progress. The only visual record in modern times is a photograph taken by the Malay Police in the 1930s of a building in Penang stated to be a Triad lodge. Photographs of a lodge interior do not appear to exist.

Short of actually becoming a Triad member it is impossible to be dogmatic on the precise layout of a lodge. The only description of a lodge interior based on primary sources comes from W. P. Morgan's *Triad Societies in Hong Kong*. Morgan, an inspector in the Royal Hong Kong Police in the 1950s, composed his account from personal experience and from statements made by arrested Triad members. His description avoids the usual bland style of police reporting and is both fascinating and of considerable historical importance. Since Morgan's day, lodges have deteriorated somewhat in grandeur and complexity, but certain essential features have certainly remained intact. Interested readers will find Morgan's description quoted in Appendix 3 (p. 170).

The lodge symbolizes the forces and values that bind Triads together, whether criminals or not. The lodge meeting is a coming together of the past and the present. Members are made to feel part of an evolving continuum, and it is on this potent sense of continuity that the oaths of brotherhood are based. The moral and religious precepts of the past hardly impinge on the lives of most Triads today outside lodge ritual. To the criminal brotherhoods that now constitute the vast majority of Triad lodges, ritual and symbols are merely a binding force, imposing secrecy, discipline and, above all, loyalty on each individual member.

The ceremony of Triad initiation is long and complex and can take up to six or seven hours, even longer. The main features include an initial ritual dance; the challenging of the initiate at the East Gate by an official to whom he gives a secret hand-clasp; 'passing the mountain of knives', in which the initiates have to bow below an archway of swords; the entry of the 'fruit seller'; passing beneath the yellow gauze; the burning of the yellow paper which hangs at the entrance of the lodge and the collection of the ashes; the beheading of a cockerel and collection of its blood to symbolize the fate of those who prove disloyal to the society; and the pricking of each initiate's finger to draw blood: the finger is then dipped into a bowl containing wine, spices, the ashes of the yellow paper, and the cockerel's blood, and then licked. Often the bowl is broken, once it is empty, to signify the death of would-be traitors. Throughout the various parts of the ceremony the traditional history of the Triads is recounted, whilst most of the accompanying rubric is incanted in verse. Officials are required to learn the whole ritual by heart.

Amongst other Triad rituals, one of the most important is known as Burning the Yellow Paper, which is carried out when the members of two Triad societies decide to come together for a specific mission or common purpose. It is also held when a new sub-group is founded, to combine weaker societies into a stronger unit, and to pledge allegiance to a mother lodge or senior society. Often it forges a bond between Triads from different societies or groups who operate in the same area: for example, those running protection rackets in a city may burn the yellow paper with those who control the street narcotics trade, thereby ensuring that neither group poaches on the other's business. The ceremony is based on an ancient Chinese contract-making custom: each party to the contract would give the other a piece of yellow paper on which was written their name and address, a brief summary of the agreement, and a statement of their intention to honour it. The papers were then burnt, signifying that each party would be true to the other. (The practice was still used in the nineteenth century in the Hong Kong law courts in much the same way as the Bible is used in the West.)

To the Triads, the yellow paper also relates to the yellow gauze quilt which is hung on the lodge altar and to the sheet of paper at the lodge entrance on which the names of the initiates and the thirty-six oaths are written.

Triad ceremonial dress is similar in style to the costume traditionally worn by Buddhist monks and priests. The lodge leader wears a red robe, the Incense Master a white one. Only the leader's robe is allowed to be decorated, and only the Incense Master is permitted to wear prayer beads. All the

other ranks wear black. The robes are made of cotton since –
ironically in the light of the Triads' well-deserved reputation
for violence – Buddhism disallows the taking of life.

Headbands, or loosely woven semi-turbans, are worn with
the ends hanging over the front of the shoulders. Officers roll
their trouser legs up over three folds: the left folding
outwards (in the Western masonic manner), the right
inwards. They also remove their shoes and put a grass sandal
on their left feet. The Vanguard carries a whip and an
umbrella, to signify that he has travelled from afar, and
carries a pack on his back which symbolically contains the
ashes of the thirteen monks who died escaping from the
monastery of Shao Lin.

Triad members recognize each other by hand signs. Within
the confines of the lodge these are overt and unequivocal.
They are used in the ritual dance during the ceremonial
opening of the lodge, and also when objects are given or
received. Outside the lodge there are a vast number of hand
signs used to signify membership and rank. The manner in
which a cigarette is taken from an offered packet; the way in
which a tea-cup or chopsticks are held; the way money is
offered in payment; the manner of holding a pen – all these
actions, and many more, can indicate membership and status
to other Triads. As with Freemasons in the West, the most
common form of signal is the handshake: the way a person
stands also communicates the same message.

Coded phrases also serve the same purpose: 'Where were
you born?' – 'Under a peach tree.' 'Have you a mother?' – 'I
have five.' 'Do you not owe me some money?' – 'I paid you, I
recall.' 'When?' – 'In the market [i.e. Tai Ping market].'

Triad society documents are traditionally marked with a
seal, of which there are several orders: primary seals,
secondary seals, and a variety of others used for specific types
of documents. Senior officials use one set of seals, junior
officials another. The system is exceedingly complex, and
today few Triads – if any – know its complete symbolic
significance.

One interesting footnote to Triad ritual relates to the

humble willow pattern plate, which is in fact a symbolic interpretation of the Hung Society story. The conventional version of the willow pattern story is well known. Two lovers are forcibly parted by the girl's father. The girl is imprisoned and forcibly betrothed to a man she does not love. She is rescued by her lover and flees from the wrath of her father to an island, where the two live happily together for a time. But their whereabouts are discovered, the lover is killed, and the girl sets fire to their house and dies in the flames. But the gods take pity on the star-crossed pair and turn them into doves.

But there is another interpretation. The willow tree that is central to the plate's design stands behind a wall: this is Muk Yeung, the City of Willows, a central symbol in Triad ritual. On the island there is a temple which does not feature in the traditional fairy tale: is this the memorial shrine to the Five Ancestors? The burning of the house at the end of the tale may refer to the burning of the Shao Lin monastery, whilst the trees in the pattern are recognizably all peach trees. The whole willow pattern design, in fact, can be related to Triad ritual and traditional history.

One wonders also if the man holding his hand in the Hung Society symbol of fire on the 1917 issue American dollar bill knew something we do not.

4

A CENTURY AND A HALF OF CRIME

The Triads' transition from patriotic secret society to an international crime network began in Hong Kong, which today has the unjust reputation of being 'Triad City'. Hong Kong had long been a refuge for pirates and malcontents from all over China south of the Yangtse: it was both geographically and symbolically far from the Manchu court, and it offered a good all-weather harbour for pirate vessels. For the Triads it was ripe for exploitation. Even before the ceding of Hong Kong to Britain by the Treaty of Nanking in 1842 Triad members had made their way to the nascent port. As soon as Hong Kong became, in effect, a foreign country, the Triads saw it as a protected haven and moved there in droves, along with the coolies, fishermen, and tradesmen from whom they recruited members. The new immigrants established trade associations and guilds to protect their interests under a foreign government. The Triads, ever resentful of central authority, also banded together and quickly took over control of many of the guilds. By 1845 they had made their presence felt to the extent that a law was passed for their suppression. By this time Hong Kong effectively had two governing authorities: the British and the Triads.

From the start the Triads stirred up disaffection against the British – an uncharacteristically foolish move since the British provided protection against the Chinese emperor. As early as 1844 the embryonic Hong Kong police raided a lodge, founded two years earlier, and arrested seventeen members. By 1847 Hong Kong was seen as the nerve centre for Triad activity all over China, and Triad membership in the colony was estimated to be as high as three-quarters of the local Chinese population.

The 1845 prohibition made Triad membership illegal. The punishment for membership was three years' imprisonment and branding on the upper arm. Deportation back to China was at the discretion of the individual judge, and if a defendant could prove that he had been forced into membership charges were dropped.

The legislation was impotent from the start and did nothing to slow down the growing power of the Triads. Within three years of its introduction Triad members threatened to attack the town of Victoria when the garrison there was temporarily depleted. But the authorities were tipped off and the police, supported by a small army unit, rounded up some two hundred men who had gathered in the hills behind the town. A number of those arrested were found to be Triads.

A decade later, in the 1850s, the Triads had the Hong Kong labour market in an iron grip – extorting money from coolies, controlling specific types of employment, and whipping up strikes and disputes. The Hong Kong authorities regarded these developments with increasing concern in view of what was happening in China, where the Taiping rebellion and, reportedly, Triad-inspired uprisings were reducing the country to anarchy. But then the Triads in Hong Kong began to back off from direct confrontation with the British. In the Canton region and the coastal areas of Kwangtung province they now decided to co-operate with the British authorities, and throughout the second half of the nineteenth century, and up to the founding of the Chinese Republic, Triad activity in Hong Kong was comparatively muted. The Triads continued to exploit the Chinese community, but they withdrew from direct action against colonial settlers or the British administration.

By being in Hong Kong, which attempted to maintain a neutral position with regard to China, the Triads were also constrained in their political opposition to the Manchus. And so they turned their energies more and more to crime within the Chinese community of the colony, controlling everything from rice shops to meat and fish markets – in fact the whole trading economy of Hong Kong was soon under their influence.

With this power base established, the societies were able to bail out arrested members and also penetrate the Hong Kong Police, which by the 1880s had a substantial Chinese constabulary commanded by European officers. In 1886 gang warfare broke out amongst rival Triad factions in the boarding-house business. These doss-houses were transit stops for coolies heading overseas. All were Triad controlled. The gang riot that flared up in connection with them led to a series of internal government inquiries, which revealed that the Triads had successfully planted men, not only in the police, but in most government departments where Chinese were employed in clerical posts. One of the two Triad societies concerned (the Man On Society) had a Chinese police detective as its leader. He was arrested, granted bail, and then fled to China, where he was later killed in combat against Imperial forces. The society subsequently changed its name and continued to operate for some years before almost disappearing; it was revived in 1949 by former members as a small narcotics dealership known as the Man Shing Tong. Their opponents in the boarding-house riot, the Fuk Yee Hing, still exist.

Throughout the second half of the nineteenth century increasing numbers of Chinese fled to Hong Kong from China. Many of them were Triads on the run from Imperial forces. At the end of the century the Republican Party established a regional headquarters in Hong Kong and in 1901 founded its own Triad society, the Chung Wo Tong, to liaise between all the Hong Kong Triads. After the declaration of the Republic in 1911 this society evolved into the Wo group of Triads, which became – and remains to this day – one of the most powerful of all Triad groups, both within and outside Hong Kong.

To avoid the kind of internecine struggle that had broken out between the Man On and the Fuk Yee Hing, the Triads divided Hong Kong up into territories, with each society being responsible for a specific geographical area or ethnic group. By 1931 eight main Triad groups were operating in Hong Kong: the Wo, the T'ung, the Tung, the Chuen, the

Shing, the Fuk Yee Hing, the Yee On, and the Luen. Each had its own headquarters, sub-societies, and central administration. They maintained various public covers. The Fuk Yee Hing became a registered society, the Fuk Yee Industrial and Commercial General Association (it was also registered as the Kiu Kong Hoi Lok Fung Workers' and Merchants' Benevolent Association). It had twelve branch offices throughout Hong Kong and a membership of ten thousand (the subscription fee being one Hong Kong dollar a month), of whom three and a half thousand were oath-bound Triads.

Despite their criminal base, these societies also operated as welfare societies for their members. When occasion demanded the societies would educate members' children, pay doctors' bills, find jobs for unemployed individuals, and in general look after their own in the best traditions of trade unions the world over. One effect of this systematized benevolence was that genuine trade unions and guilds had to become more like the Triads by setting up a system of rituals and oaths to ensure the loyalty of their members. In time they inevitably became subsumed into Triad societies to whom they turned for protection. The Tung Society, originally founded for hospital coolies to protect themselves from the Wo group, expanded its activities and became a full blown Triad society. Government sanitary department coolies formed a boxing and martial arts club to protect themselves physically from Triad interference, and this developed into a Triad society called the Ching Nin Kwok Ki Sh'e.

Others followed the Fuk Yee Hing example. The Yee On registered as the Yee On Commercial and Industrial Guild. The Chuen established street hawker associations. The Luen founded ironworkers' associations that were active in the commercial shipyards, and even in the Hong Kong Royal Navy dockyard, HMS *Tamar*. The Wo operated Death Gratuity associations.

Clubs dedicated to the martial arts were – and still are – numerous throughout Hong Kong and in expatriate Chinese communities overseas. Not all were Triad societies *per se*, but many had Triad allegiances. Other apparently innocuous

benevolent societies may also have had Triad connections, as
is the case today.

Also allied to the Triads were the Bomb Associations – less
alarming than they sound. Traditionally, the Goddess of
Mercy and the God of the Earth were honoured annually by a
major festival which drew vast crowds. The climax was the
explosion of a large 'bomb' – actually a firework containing a
bamboo bar engraved with the name of the deity and the local
temple. Officers from all the local guilds and associations, not
only those with Triad affiliations, lined up and tried to catch
the bar as it fell back to the ground. The association
represented by the person who successfully caught the bar
was allowed to keep the talisman for a year and had to
maintain a shrine to it. Both deities were traditionally
worshipped by the Triads, and so Triad involvement in the
festival was obligatory. Members even paraded publicly with
their banners. But by 1948 the struggle for possession of the
bamboo bar had become so violent that this aspect of the
festivities was banned.

The gradual fragmentation of the eight main Triad groups
weakened their structure and (by the early 1950s) the Triad
underworld was disunited. Older societies had to struggle to
maintain their grip, whilst younger groups had no qualms
about trying to usurp power from their seniors. The result
was gang warfare – perhaps not on the scale of the Mafia, but
ferocious enough – beginning in the late 1930s and still
continuing. Inter-Triad rivalry – then as now – involved
serious woundings, often fatal. The punishment mentioned
in the Triad oath-taking ceremony – of dying by a myriad of
swords (see Appendix 3) – is frequently carried out. The
victim is slashed with a razor-sharp butcher's knife across all
his main muscles – in particular, the calfs, thighs, forearms
and biceps. He may also have his scalp slashed. The Triads'
other favourite weapon is the meat cleaver, which is used to
inflict similar damage.

By early 1941 the Japanese had advanced mercilessly
through China and were threatening the south of the
country. The Triads were split – internally fragmented and

divided by two incompatible responses to Japanese aggression. One section of the Triad community was prepared to resist the Japanese by throwing their weight behind the Kuomintang (KMT), the Nationalist army of Chiang Kai-shek (himself a senior Triad officer of many years' standing). An opposing section of opinion elected to support the Japanese attack on Hong Kong. Others played a game of 'wait and see'.

The pro-KMT faction was led by the Nationalist Admiral Chan Chak. When the Japanese attacked Hong Kong in 1941 his followers roamed the streets wearing Triad armbands to prevent sabotage and, when they could, furtively murdered collaborators – many of whom were fellow Triads from rival societies. But once the Japanese had seized the colony their supporters amongst the Triads had the upper hand and began persuading the pro-KMT faction to take a pragmatic view of the matter. The Japanese, understanding the power wielded by the Triads within the local community, wisely set about harnessing that power by organizing the Triads into what was called the Hing Ah Kee Kwan, which roughly translates as the 'Asia Flourishing Organization'. Now officially recognized and supported, the Triads felt secure. So did the Japanese. The prime movers amongst the Triads who set up the Hing Ah Kee Kwan were the Wo group. They policed the new status quo and provided intelligence information on un-Japanese activity: so far had the old Triad patriotism deteriorated. Other Wo members were recruited into Japanese military intelligence and – irony of ironies – into the police force, where there were already a number of Triad spies from pre-war years. For its part, the Japanese administration did nothing to restrict the Triads' criminal activities; indeed up to a point it encouraged them.

Under the Japanese the Triads became revitalized and soon recovered from their fragmented pre-war state, quickly cornering those few remaining criminal markets they had failed to monopolize before the war. After the Japanese surrender in 1945, during the interregnum before the re-establishment of a British civilian government, the Triads made the most of a chaotic situation and took advantage of the war-weakened police force by initiating a campaign of looting, robbery, and burglary. As social order was gradually restored these sources of income began to diminish for the Triads; but then the temporary British Military Administration played right into their hands by banning narcotics in the colony. Opium had been yielding the Triads a substantial revenue for forty years or more, but now they had the opportunity to reap vast profits. It was an opportunity they were not slow to grasp.

Opium is a drug obtained from the sap of a certain species of annual poppy (*Papaver somniferum*) that grows wild throughout much of Asia and Asia Minor, from the eastern reaches of China, through Tibet, the USSR and central India to Turkey, and that can be grown easily from seed. The sap is harvested by milking the seed pod in much the same way, but on a tiny scale, as rubber is collected: the outer layer of the plant is scored and the oozing sap collected. With the poppy, the sap congeals on the surface and can then easily be removed.

Opium has been known as a narcotic agent since prehistoric times (traces of its cultivation have been found in Switzerland dating to 4000 BC). The Assyrians used it as a medicine, whilst to the Sumarians it was 'the plant of joy'. Opium is a potent painkiller, inducing narcosis and a dream-rich, relaxing sleep. It was traditionally prescribed as an antidote for a wide range of ailments and conditions – including poisoning, snake-bites, headaches, vertigo, deafness, epilepsy, asthma and coughs, jaundice, leprosy, melancholia, and dropsy. At the same time, its addictive properties and the fact that it could be used as a poison in its own right were clearly recognized. Cases of opium abuse are many: Hannibal kept a lozenge of opium in his ring and was reputed to have committed suicide by taking it, whilst Britannicus, son of the Roman Emperor Claudius, was murdered by his stepmother using opium.

Opium, however, was not a widespread problem in China until it was introduced by Europeans towards the end of the eighteenth century. The East in general, and China in particular, had much that the West desired: tea, silk, cotton, rice, spices. Yet China required little of what the West had to offer, and Britain – the West's major mercantile trading nation – had to pay for her goods in silver bullion, the price of which fluctuated widely and was often in short supply.

So the British looked for something China wanted. They found it in the opium grown by the East India Company. Once shipped to China, demand inevitably increased quickly and continued until 1907, when the British agreed not to export any more opium and the Chinese undertook to stop poppy cultivation within China. But the damage done to China had been incalculable, whilst on the British side vast fortunes had been made from the trade. Banks sprouted up in Hong Kong between 1843 and 1863, though financial crashes in 1865 and 1866 wiped most of them out, along with opium frauds (most notably in the case of the National Bank of India). Nevertheless, the big *hongs* (the commercial institutions of the Far East) survived and throve: Dent and Co., Butterfield and Swire (now the Swire Group), Hutchison and Co., and – most famous of all – Jardine, Matheson and Co. (still central to Hong Kong's economy), amongst others, grew and prospered. All these firms were founded on opium.

The extent of opium addiction in China as a result of the enforced import of the drug was horrifying. All social classes, from coolies to the Imperial court, were affected. By 1891 the opium poppy was being cultivated in twelve of the eighteen provinces of China. Szechuan produced the best quality opium, Yunnan the lowest and the cheapest. Such was the demand that cereal crops were abandoned in favour of growing poppies. The number of addicts is exemplified by the figures for the city of Wenchow in 1891. The city had a population of 80,000. Within the city limits were 1,130 opium dens patronized mostly by the working and middle classes. Besides these, there were many other addicts who smoked opium in their own homes but seldom visited a den.

The tax revenues accruing from the legitimate sale of opium were enormous and of immense importance to the Chinese government. But taxation also led to smuggling, illicit trading, unregistered poppy cultivation, and a thriving black market that inevitably and swiftly came into the clutches of the Triads. Over the next century and a half they became experts in cultivating, distributing, and what we should now call marketing the drug, though today opium has given way to its even more dangerous derivative, heroin.

In Hong Kong, before the Second World War, opium could be smoked legally provided that the drug was obtained from official distribution points and smoked only in the privacy of the addict's home, the intention being to discourage dens, divans and street pedlars. Supplies were plentiful, and consequently criminal involvement was minimal, except at street level, in comparison with what it has since become. As ever, the Triads exploited the situation, but on a relatively small scale and amongst coolies, rickshaw pullers, stevedores, and the poorest social level of addicts, for many of whom opium was the only escape from a wretched existence.

Throughout the 1920s and 1930s international pressure began to mount for the prohibition of addictive drugs like opium. In China addicts began to move on from plain opium. As early as 1912 in the *yang hangs* (opium shops) of Tientsin, a number of more powerful alternatives were on offer: heroin powder (smoked in tobacco cigarettes), morphine, imported cocaine, and an assortment of other drugs, mostly opium based, called White Powder, Yellow Powder, Golden Pills, Black Plaster, and *k'uai shang k'uai* ('quick up quick'), which was smoked in a pipe and had, as the name implies, an extremely rapid effect.

All these drugs were smoked or inhaled. The intravenous injection of drugs was unknown to the Chinese. Opium was smoked in a pipe heated over a small oil lamp, or burned in an elaborate pipe containing a piece of glowing charcoal. Heroin was also smoked, either by inhaling the fumes through a special pipe, or by breathing them in from a heated metal plate suspended over a flame. This process was known as 'chasing the dragon'. Raw opium, a brownish substance which is malleable rather like beeswax, melts when heated and in this mobile form was known as 'dragon's spit'. Few Western addicts use the 'chasing the dragon' method today, whilst Chinese addicts, in their turn, have adopted the injection procedure, which has a far more immediate and powerful effect than smoking.

Chinese government action against opium dealing was ineffectual. In 1917, it was discovered that the Vice-President of the Republic of China had diverted £4 million of public revenue, purchased Indian opium with it, and sold it at an enormous personal profit on the black market. He was aided and abetted by a Triad society in Shanghai which controlled the illicit drug trade there.

In 1928 China banned the sale, possession, importation and exportation of opium, opiates, and cocaine and made it a capital offence to be convicted of drug crimes. Eight years later Chiang Kai-shek set up a commission for the suppression of opium. Since Chiang was himself hand-in-fist with the Triads it is perhaps not surprising that this measure was only partially successful. Other steps were taken, both within China and internationally, in an attempt to eliminate the drug problem, but inevitably prohibition only drove the trade underground.

As soon as opium was prohibited in Hong Kong the Triads moved into the market in force. They established large numbers of opium dens and divans and monopolized the importation and sale of the drug. The scale of their profits brought about an irreversible shift in their criminal status. Up till now they had been operating as bootleggers supplying opium alongside the legal outlets. Now they were sole dealers on a grand scale. The die was irrevocably cast.

After the Second World War the Triads continued to prey upon their own people. All vestiges of an honourable, patriotic ideology had disappeared, and with the cessation of hostilities in the Far Eastern theatre they returned with a vengeance to manipulating and exploiting their fellow countrymen.

Prostitution was added to their growing list of criminal activities, and with the influx of new expatriate Europeans and large numbers of military personnel (swollen even more in the 1950s during the Korean War) sex became big business for them. There were still cat-houses providing cheap prostitutes for working-class Chinese, but the big money was to be made from Europeans. Wan Chai, the eastern water-front area of Hong Kong Island, close to the naval dockyards and the main military barracks, became the most infamous red light district in the Far East – possibly in the world.

Large numbers of girls were imported from China and elsewhere in the Far East, their ranks increased by the many refugees escaping ahead of the Communist advance. The prostitution market in Hong Kong was totally controlled by the Triads, and individual societies were fiercely protective of their particular establishments. Brothels as such did not exist. Girls were picked up in bars, either Triad-owned or paying heavy protection money to them, and clients were taken back to the prostitute's own tiny room. The Triads supplied the girls, charged for their 'sale', and took a percentage of their gross earnings, as well as often charging them extra for the rent of their room if it was in a Triad-owned or -controlled building. When the girls became too old, too diseased, or too ill to work they were thrown out to fend for themselves. Many turned to opium – and thus contributed even more to Triad profits.

Manipulating the labour market was even more lucrative. Coolies were hired from firms which specialized in providing labour for specific types of work – bricklayers, dockworkers, and so on. As Hong Kong prospered, as war damage was repaired, and as investment increased, so did industry and trade, and coolies were in great demand.

Each hiring firm, the management of which were Triad members or officers, employed an overseer, who was himself often a junior Triad office-bearer. Each morning the overseer would appoint coolies for the work available on that particular day. It was therefore essential to stay on the right side of the overseer: it was also extremely costly. An overseer would often take 50 per cent of a coolie's wages at source, sometimes as much as 75 per cent. This would then be shared with the firm's management. To offset his loss of income the coolie would steal from his place of work, and if he was unable to dispose of the goods himself he would arrange for them to be fenced through Triad channels – a rather elegant though corrupt system of symbiosis.

The coolie tenements, in which the unfortunate inmates were packed cheek-by-jowl, often sleeping in the beds in a rota system, were – of course – Triad owned. The coolies ate Triad-supplied food (at inflated prices) and, like the whores, smoked Triad-supplied opium. The only way of breaking out of this vicious circle of exploitation was to join the Triads. And so the coolie tenements provided the perfect recruiting conditions for '49s', rank-and-file Triads.

Extortion, protection rackets, prostitution, labour manipulation, opium dealing – these became the Triad stock in trade. Staff employment agencies supplying the expanding hotel trade were run by Triads, whilst hotel owners themselves were 'squeezed' for protection money. Even lowly street hawkers had to pay protection to avoid beatings or having their goods confiscated or their stalls destroyed. Licences for street sellers were often hard to obtain, especially in the case of streetside food stalls; but as always the Triads could oblige, for a price, since every government department had its Triad members.

And so it went on. A vast labyrinth of corruption and exploitation feeding a criminal fraternity that was growing ever richer, ever more powerful, ever more ruthless. Against the expanding power of the Triads the police could do little or nothing. Their efforts were seriously hampered by the presence of Triad police officers and non-Triad policemen who were open to bribery; hampered, too, by the code of terrified silence that victims of Triad crime maintained (this is still often the case). It was better to pay 'the squeeze' (or 'tea-money', as it was also euphemistically known) than go to the police.

But then in the late 1940s the Hong Kong Triads, as well as

the government of the colony and the local Chinese population, came under threat from an unexpected source. Amongst
the massive influx of refugees to Hong Kong from
Communist China came members of northern Chinese Triad
societies, in particular the Red and Green Pang Societies, and
also a number of Chinese criminals unconnected officially
with the Chinese Triads but forming a loose alliance with
them.

The Green Pang soon established themselves in Hong
Kong. Through other northern Chinese already in the colony
they rapidly gained influence at government level whilst
concentrating their attention at the same time on wealthy
refugees and criminals in exile, who were obliged to succumb
to Green Pang pressure. The technique was simple and
effective: the Green Pang would make it clear to the victim
that they had the power to arrange extradition back to China
through its police and government contacts if sufficient
protection money was not forthcoming. The more wealthy
refugees were also persuaded to invest in Green Pang business
ventures.

Areas of Hong Kong became semi-ghettos of northern
Chinese, particularly from Shanghai, which the local Triads
were unable to penetrate. The Green Pang established dance
halls, brothels, restaurants, and illegal gambling dens. They
also introduced into Hong Kong something new and deadly:
heroin.

In 1952, Li Choi Fat, outwardly a pillar of the community
but in fact the leader of the Green Pang Society, was arrested
and deported. This was a serious blow to Green Pang morale
and the society lost much 'face' to the local Triads, but it
continued its operations and even branched out into the
developing tourist industry. Other Triad groups also came into
Hong Kong from Communist China until the colony was
literally awash with them. Often ethnically based, these groups
represented practically every region in China – the Hakka, the
Cantonese, the Chiu Chow, the Hoklo, the Shanghainese, the
Foochow . . . In retrospect, it is astonishing that the Hong
Kong police managed to keep the lid on it at all.

Amongst this mêlée a few societies were naturally dominant. Some of these have disappeared over the years, amalgamated with other societies, changed their names, died out only to be resurrected in a new form, or have been broken up by the police. Three societies in particular, however, survived intact. Today they wield awesome power in an international arena of crime. They are the Wo Shing Wo, the Sun (sometimes San) Yee On, and the formidable 14K Triad.

The Wo Shing Wo originated in the Wo groups of Triads which grew out of the Republican Chung Wo Tong. Before the war, Wo group societies, whose bases were in the Western District of Hong Kong and Yau Ma Tei in Kowloon, had been heavily involved in the labour market. In Hong Kong they controlled coolie firms and tenements and through them dock- and market-coolies. In Kowloon they controlled wharf-coolies and building labourers. They were also important in the 'Bomb' associations.

When the Japanese occupied Hong Kong the Wo group consolidated their power under the aegis of the Japanese administration. After the war they began to diversify whilst at the same time tightening their grip on the dock-coolies in their traditional domain of the Western District, where three Wo societies – Wo Shing Tong, Wo Yung Yee, and Wo Hop To – struggled for dominance. One police investigation during this period revealed that several Wo Shing Wo members were earning a conservatively estimated $HK 15 million a year from initiation fees and the control of street hawkers, rickshaw pullers, shoe shine boys, illegal gambling, dance hall hostesses and prostitutes, illegal taxis, black market theatre and cinema tickets, restaurant protection rackets, pickpockets, and of course the local narcotics trade.

By the late 1950s the Wo group comprised forty-one affiliated societies, more than any other Triad grouping. The size of these affiliations varied considerably. Some were small and largely inactive, many had no criminal connections. But some were huge: the Wo Shing Wo had a membership of over six thousand (some estimates double that figure), which included not only civil servants and corrupt police officers but even British army personnel. Their power base was divided between Kowloon Walled City and the Portuguese colony of Macau, forty-five miles to the west of Hong Kong. Other important Wo group societies included the Wo On Lok, which at one time had as many as twenty thousand members and which – as well as the usual list of Triad crimes – ran an extensive loan sharking operation; the Wo Shing Tong, which in 1958 had some five thousand members; and the Wo Shing Yee, which controlled large numbers of dock-coolies and had a membership of up to ten thousand. Today, the Wo Shing Wo is by far the most powerful of the Wo group Triads.

The Sun Yee On – aka the Yee On Commercial and Industrial Guild – was originally a society for Hong Kong Chinese of Chiu Chow origin and its leaders were reported to have been prominent members of the Red Pang Society. It began its operations under the guise of the To Shui Boxing Club (Chinese martial boxing, not fisticuffs) and the Tai Ping Shan Sports Association. Based in Kowloon, it had branches all over Hong Kong and an original membership of over ten thousand. In 1953, after its leaders were arrested and deported by the police, the society split into two main groups, the Chiu Kwong and the Chung Yee, and these in turn fragmented into other smaller groups. But in the last decade the society has re-emerged as one of the most powerful of the Hong Kong criminal Triads and now has extensive international interests.

In January 1988 history repeated itself when nine of the Sun Yee On's leaders, including 'Dragon Head' Heung Wah-yim, were arrested and imprisoned on a variety of serious charges. During the following spring and early summer, in a massive operation, the police raided a total of seventeen hundred premises and arrested 179 people, including eleven men on their wanted list. In all over thirty thousand people were interrogated. This has resulted in a considerable reduction in the local crime rate and fighting between rival factions – in particular between the Sun Yee On and the Wo Hop To over control of protection rackets in the

Wan Chai area, where eleven Triad groups are said to operate – has lessened. But the Sun Yee On remains firmly entrenched in Hong Kong despite the police success.

The Sun Yee On's main lair was Kowloon Walled City, which has been a bolt hole for Triads for many years. Originally it was a small, walled mandarin's *yamen* and village, in size a mere two hundred by three hundred yards. In fact Kowloon Walled City is a misnomer for an anachronism. Its actual walls were demolished by Japanese occupying forces, using British prisoners-of-war as labour, in 1942–3, the stone being used as hard core for what is now the apron of Hong Kong's international airport only a few hundred yards away. When the New Territories were ceded to the British in 1898 (for ninety-nine years) the Walled City, as a result of a poorly worded agreement, became disputed territory with both the British and the Chinese claiming sovereignty over it. And so, ever since, Kowloon has existed in a kind of administrative limbo, making it a perfect haven for Triads. Within the Walled City the Hong Kong police have been virtually powerless and the city has developed into one of the most notorious criminal ghettos in the world.

There are no streets as such. Over the years – unencumbered by planning regulations and restrictions – the city has grown into an almost solid mass of buildings. New storeys balance precariously on old; sanitation is non-existent. Water and electricity are tapped illegally from the mains. There is no lighting in the narrow fetid alleys, which remain pitch dark even at noon, and the pavements continually run with water (leaking from overhead pipes, around which hissing and sparking electricity cables are wrapped) – and worse: sewage and the guts of animals being 'processed' in the one-room factories that turn out pork balls, fishcakes, and sweetmeats. Other aspects of Kowloon Walled City's economy include cheap shirts, hair oil, cooking utensils, bicycle spares, and sex toys for Western sex shops.

The occupants – at one time it was estimated that fifty-eight thousand people lived in the Walled City – are packed into 'flats' only a few feet square, with shared cooking and toilet

facilities. The buildings are twelve storeys high but there is
virtually no space between them. What space there is can be
only inches wide and is certain to be filled with garbage up to
a height of thirty feet from ground level. Only two 'court-
yards' exist. One is around the original *yamen* building (the
former residence of a nineteenth-century mandarin famous
for his public executions: the chopping spot before his gates
still remains), the other around the main temple (which is
netted over to keep garbage off the roof). In the cellars of the
Walled City is another temple. Both are of great importance
to the Triads.

In this human warren drugs – first opium, and then heroin
– have always been in plentiful supply. The main alleyway
through the city is correctly called Lung Chung Street: the
locals know it as Pak Fa'an Gai – White Rice or Powder
Street, slang for heroin. Opium and heroin dens existed here
until the early 1960s, and continued to exist in a few
particularly inaccessible places. It was a no-go area for
Europeans, as well as for the police and for anyone
unconnected with the Triads. Only one non-Chinese
outsider has lived in the Walled City: Jackie Pullinger, an
evangelist missionary who for over twenty years has run a
drug rehabilitation programme in the city. Her success rate –
using only the power of her faith – has been staggeringly high.

But the character of Kowloon has changed and it is no
longer a diplomatic anomaly. In anticipation of 1997, the
Chinese authorities have asked the British government to
raze the Walled City to the ground. Police now patrol the
alleys. The residents are being moved out and rehoused
locally; others are emigrating. The buildings are now rapidly
emptying and are having to be guarded against being taken
over by squatters. The Triads have fled. One centre of Triad
infestation, at least, has been destroyed.

Besides the Wo Shing Wo and the Sun Yee On, the third of
the great Triad societies of modern times is the 14K Society.
Like the Wo group, it was originally founded on a patriotic-
cum-political ideology. Towards the end of the Second

World War, when the Triads were fragmented into partisan fighters, pro-Japanese collaborators, and those who simply chose to keep their heads down, a senior Kuomintang official (probably Chiang Kai-shek, though possibly his mentor, Big-Eared Tu) ordered that a league should be set up to include every Triad society in China. The result was the Five Continents Overseas Chinese Hung League, based in Canton. Towards the end of 1945, at an elaborate ceremony in Canton, a new Shan Chu, or ultimate leader, was appointed from amongst the military leaders of the Kuomintang.

In the immediate post-war years Chiang Kai-shek's Nationalist government was losing ground to the Communists, and in an effort to gather support, and to try and halt Communist infiltration, the government enlisted Triad help, Chiang himself being a senior Triad office bearer. The aim was to recruit as many people into the Triad ranks as possible using a variation of the old rallying cry: overthrow the foreign invader (the Communists) and restore the Chinese (Nationalist) government. China was divided into administrative districts for this purpose. One of these, the Kwangtung region, came under the authority of Lieutenant-General Kot Siu Wong, who was suddenly precipitated into the leadership of the Five Continents League.

Kot Siu Wong was without doubt a dedicated patriot. There is some doubt as to how long he had been a Triad, or indeed if he had been one at all before being initiated in a ceremony that deviated radically from accepted Triad practice. He did, however, believe that the only way to stem the tide of Communism was to enlist massive popular support, and to do this it was necessary to mobilize the power of the Triads. Kot Siu Wong was not a criminal, but primarily a soldier. He cherished a naïve vision of the Triads as essentially a patriotic movement and deplored the degeneration into crime and gangsterism. He was not alone in this. Well into the 1960s old men who had been Triads since their youth lamented this decline. 'Squeeze' was allowable, indeed had existed for centuries. The gross shaking down of poor coolies and the calculated exploitation of opium addicts was something else; but even in the 1940s the tide had begun to turn irrevocably and the Triads were committed to their criminal interests.

By 1947 Kot Siu Wong had succeeded in bringing all the Triad groups in his region under the umbrella of a single organization, the Hung Fat Shan branch of the Chung Yee Wui Society, and he established a regional headquarters at 14 Po Wa Ching Chung Yeuk, Po Wah Road, Canton. Soon the Hung Fat Shan Triad Society was renamed the Hung Fat Shan Loyalty Association, or Hung Fat Shan Chung Yee Wui.

Within months of his appointment rivalry broke out amongst older members of the one-time Five Continents League, and Kot Siu Wong was ordered to improve his standing by carrying out initiation ceremonies of his own. These took place in the state-owned Kwok Man University in Canton, and huge numbers of Nationalist troops were initiated, along with thousands of civilians – many of whom had no idea of Triad tradition – in a brief mass ritual that bore little resemblance to the established ceremony. In the case of military initiates, the Five Ancestors were replaced by a picture of Sun Yat-sen, and the oaths were pared down to obedience to the Kuomintang, dedication to the ideal of a united and Nationalist China, and oath 35: 'I must never reveal society secrets when speaking to outsiders.' Many of the members recruited in this way had no idea what kind of organization they were joining. They were motivated primarily by fear – of the Communists, on the one hand, and of being seen as Communist sympathizers if they did not join on the other.

For purposes of identification, the new quasi-Triad recruits, which some estimates put at upward of a million members, gave their individual groups (forty-four of them in all) separate names, each of which included the number 14 (after the street number of the organization's headquarters). In time the Hung Fat Shan Chung Yee Wui became known simply as the 14. The sheer size of the organization made it unwieldy, and jealousies inevitably erupted. For this reason, the 14K has never been a fully integrated and united society, but rather an umbrella name for a large number of small societies and groupings.

After the defeat of the Nationalist cause, Kot Siu Wong fled to Hong Kong with a large number of 14 members. Both the colonial administration and the existing Triad societies in Hong Kong took a dim view of this massive influx. But despite opposition and outright attacks from local gangs, including a major battle in Kowloon in the area controlled by the Yuet Tung Society, the Hung Fat Shan (as it came to be known) successfully established itself, gained the respect of the local Triads, and began to pursue its own criminal enterprises.

It also started to expand, taking in disaffected members from local Triad societies and recruiting strongly amongst the rapidly growing refugee community. It was at this time that the Hung Fat Shan formally changed its name to the 14 Society and took on the 'K' suffix – possibly derived from the initial letter of Kot Siu Wong's name, but more likely from the letter 'K' (for karat) stamped on Hong Kong gold, which was harder than Chinese gold. Kot Siu Wong himself was deported from Hong Kong in 1950, the authorities fearing that such a powerful figure was capable of uniting both patriots and criminals into a single organization. He slipped back into the colony the following year but was unable to bring about the kind of unity the authorities feared. Though Kot controlled many Triad members through a chain of command (there was even a lodge, the Shun, or Faithful, Society, for former Nationalist troops) he failed to establish a centralized power structure, and on his death in 1953 internal power struggles broke out with each society attempting to out-muscle the others by initiating more and more members. All but two of the lodges put all patriotic pretensions behind them and turned instead to crime.

By the late 1950s the 14K, as it was now universally known, was the second biggest Triad society (after the Wo group) with a membership of over eighty thousand. Utterly ruthless, it was constantly the object of police attention and several spectacular arrests were made – the biggest being a round-up of 148 members in 1955 that included Kot Siu Wong's son. But these were only temporary setbacks and the 14K continued to expand. Today it is one of the most organized – and most feared – of all Triad societies, both within Hong Kong and elsewhere.

Politics were by no means completely subsumed by the Triads' criminal activities. In 1946 a secret meeting was held in the New Territories of Hong Kong attended by senior officers of the main Hong Kong Triad groups. A high-ranking Nationalist army officer addressed the meeting and reminded it that the Kuomintang – as Nationalists and therefore, by proxy, Republicans – had overthrown the Ch'ing dynasty only with Triad assistance. Claiming Triad support in areas of China already under Communist control, he requested that the Hong Kong Triads unite their memberships (estimated at some three hundred thousand) and back the KMT. The Communists were, he implied, the new Ch'ing, not entirely foreign but motivated by foreign ideology and therefore to be overthrown.

The proposal was to bring all the Hong Kong Triads together within an organization to be called the Kuomintang New Society Affairs Establishment Federation, Hong Kong Division, which he would head. Local Triad leaders agreed to the plan in principle, but few rank and file members were keen to implement it. They were growing fat off the proceeds of crime, and as the Nationalists suffered further defeats at the hands of the Communists enthusiasm for the idea faded.

At about the same time the Americans began to finance the so-called Third Force, which was intended to remove both the Communists and the Kuomintang and establish a democratic Chinese government. It called itself Man Chi Tong, or Overseas Chinese Democratic Party, and was a registered society in Hong Kong. Amongst its founders was Chiu Yuk, who had been setting up Triad groups in the USA for some time. Anyone wishing to join the Third Force was more or less obliged to become a Triad member – a fact the Americans were either ignorant of or deliberately chose to ignore. By late 1947 Man Chi Tong was in alliance with Wo Group societies and controlled several areas of Hong Kong. But as the Communist victories multiplied, so the Third Force faded, Man Chi Tong was absorbed by the Wo Group, and the influence of the patriots amongst the Triads diminished even further.

Though Hong Kong is the Triads' main base they have also been active elsewhere in Asia. Their presence in Malaya is of particular interest. In China, their historic homeland, their numbers have been drastically reduced as a result of effective policing and severe legal penalties; but in Malaya, Triads have existed in force for well over a century and a half.

The first record of a Triad society operating in Singapore is in 1830, before Hong Kong existed as a British colony. The Malayan Triad groups, made up of political refugees from China, were known as Thian-ti-hui – the last word, 'hui', giving rise to the nickname 'Hueys' or 'Hooeys'. They soon set up protection rackets, which affected Europeans as well as local people. Indeed Singapore is the only place where Europeans are reported to have joined a Triad, though this has not happened since the 1880s. Like the street hawkers of Hong Kong, European settlers were forced to join the Triads for their own protection. Living on plantations with little or no police protection, they needed not only to protect their property but also to maintain their labour force, which, being predominantly Chinese, was open to exploitation and intimidation by the Triads.

By 1843 the Singapore Triads, who operated under the cover of apparently benevolent societies, had so terrorized the local Chinese population that a public meeting was held at which two resolutions were passed:

> That it is an understood fact that many of the Chinese shopkeepers and traders in the town, particularly the native-born subjects of China, pay regular sums to the *Hueys* or Brotherhoods (organized associations of Chinese, often for unlawful purposes) as protection money for their own property, or as a contribution in the nature of blackmail, and

that it rarely or never happens that the Chinese are themselves sufferers from the depredations complained of . . . That it is highly expedient a law should be passed having for its object the suppression of these brotherhoods . . .

Over the next two decades riots and discontent amongst the Chinese population were common, fuelled sometimes by inter-Triad rivalry, sometimes by anti-British feeling. Legislation was totally inadequate – in spite of the 1843 resolution – to deal with the Triads, whose grip on the local population simply grew tighter. This brought them into direct conflict with the Roman Catholic Church, which began to gain large numbers of converts in Singapore. The Triads' opposition to Christianity originated partly in what was happening in mainland China, then in the throes of the Taiping Rebellion; but it soon developed from attacks on Chinese Christian converts to all-out confrontation with Europeans throughout the Malay peninsula. Serious rioting broke out in 1851 and again in 1854. A contemporary report of the 1851 riot indicates clearly the scale of the problem:

A volley was then fired [by the police] amongst them, which caused them to advance with more caution, and allowed the officers to continue their route; but repeated attacks, which required continual repulses, caused the march to be very slow. The rioters were most determined, and the firing lasted during an advance of more than two miles. Finally the death of three of their leaders, who fell at a distance of about twenty feet from the police force, stopped them, and the officers were able to reach their station with their prisoners and the goods. All the ammunition except a few cartridges had been expended. It has since been ascertained that five of the attacking Chinese were killed and a great number wounded.

The authorities on being informed of these facts sent the gunboat of the steamer *Hoogly* with twelve men of its crew to reinforce the police, and the crew of the gunboat and thirty convicts were directed to join this force, but by some misunderstanding only seven of the last reached the station in the early morning of Sunday. The force consisting now of thirty-eight men, of whom twenty-eight were armed with muskets, it was resolved to make a round to the sea to look after the gunboat, which was left with only seven or eight men in the Old Straits, to exchange some of the men and to take provisions and ammunition. The detachment, leaving a small reserve at the station, arrived a little after sunset at the Old Straits, without meeting anything; but returning home, and approaching the village, the road was again found barred by a numerous band of Chinese, while the signals of alarm were again heard. Necessity again compelled the police to fire into these dupes of the Hoe [i.e. secret societies], after all peaceful means to disperse them had been unsuccessful. They rushed on and were rewarded by the death of two of their number . . .

A Christian planter named Tan Ah Choon, who had been informed that his plantation was to be attacked and robbed, took all the money he could collect, amounting to more than $80, and two piculs of white pepper, and departed for the town with two or three coolies, but was stopped near Amokiah by some Chinese, who seized and carried him into the jungle with the decided intention to murder him after having robbed him. The coolies escaped and reported the fact; on which Mr. Dunman with a number of peons went himself in search. On the road a man informed him that Tan Ah Choon had been carried to Loh Siah's plantation. The chase was continued, some bangsals were passed, where Chinese were gambling to their hearts' content; and Mr. Dunman finally succeeded in delivering Tan Ah Choon, who was in the custody of three of his captors in Loh Siah's premises, who himself was secured. The other criminals escaped, having been informed by the calls and cries of the nearest neighbours of the approach of the police. Here is a most visible proof of the effects of the power of the Hoe. A man is kidnapped, carried through some crowds of Chinese, without any person interfering to prevent the crime, and these same men save the criminals by their calls and signals. Tan Ah Choon's plantation has since been robbed of nearly all its contents.

The 1851 riot left the Singapore Triad leaders suffering from severe loss of face. Not only had they been defeated militarily; they were also forced to come to terms with the Chinese Christians, who received an enforced payment of fifteen hundred Malay dollars from the Triads.

The collapse of the Taiping Rebellion swelled the number of expatriate Chinese throughout the Far East, and in Malaya their arrival was greeted with disquiet by the authorities.

Over ten thousand Chinese a year began to pour into Singapore alone (the figure for 1853 was over eleven thousand). How many entered illegally is beyond estimation.

The riots of 1854 were the result of factional rivalry. They began after an argument about rice weights but soon escalated. The disturbance was so bad that the Royal Marines had to be called in to support the police. In October 1863 another outbreak of Triad rivalry resulted in several murders. This time the cause was the control of Chinese prostitutes. (There were 75,000 Chinese living in Singapore at this time, of whom only 12 per cent were female. Women were therefore in demand as a marketable commodity and some Triads began 'importing' them from China, thus upsetting the delicate balance of power amongst the Triad groups.) The riot was put down with some ingenuity by a British magistrate called Read, who swore in two dozen local Triad leaders as special constables. At first the Triad constables thought it was all a joke; but after a day and night on continuous patrol they complained to Read of fatigue and requested that they should be allowed to return to their businesses. Read responded by saying that he would relieve them of their duties only after peace was restored in the Chinese quarter of the town. He later informed them that if rioting broke out again each Huey member would receive two dozen lashes across the buttocks: the loss of face caused by this would far exceed the physical pain. Read's tactics paid off. But within two days an announcement appeared in the newspapers to say that one of the Triad leaders, Tan Wee Kow, who had been amongst those who had agreed to become special constables, had been expelled from all societies. The same strategy was used by the police four years later, and legislation was introduced that compelled registration of all Triad societies. The authorities noted that the Hueys were 'believed to have their origin in praiseworthy and benevolent motives, but, after a little time, are apt to degenerate into unlawful combinations'.

Triad disturbances were not confined to Singapore. In 1867 severe rioting flared up in Penang, and this soon developed into an all-out inter-society war, involving some 35,000 men, between the Ghee Hin Society, who were Cantonese Chinese, and the Toh Peh Kong, who were primarily Hakka or Hokkienese Chinese. (The Ghee Hin Society can be interpreted as Heaven and Earth Society, and can therefore be seen as a branch of the Hung League.) To add to the confusion, two Malay (i.e. non-Chinese) secret societies were also involved: the Red Flag Society and the White Flag Society. After ten days of disturbance, peace was restored by the arbitration of the Governor of the Straits Settlements, Colonel (later Major-General Sir) Archibald Anson, who imposed fines of $5000 on each society and used the money to construct fortified police posts in the native quarters of Penang. Further compensation was obtained from the societies for the damage caused by the rioting.

As a result of the Penang riots a commission was set up whose report provides some fascinating insights into Triad activities in Malaya in the nineteenth century (it is reproduced at length as Appendix 4). It includes descriptions of Triad rites and oaths and shows the degree of rivalry that existed between various groups. Amongst its conclusions were that 'the riots had their origin in a trifling quarrel between two rival Muhammadan Societies . . . and that they were fostered by two other rival societies of Chinese . . . That the organization and discipline of the Societies appear to be as complete as any disciplined force of the Government.' The committee recommended the suppression of the societies, or at least their registration, the prohibition of oaths, the imposition of legal liability on the leaders in the event of any criminal action being proved, and the banning of processions.

A later list of those Chinese secret societies in Singapore that were officially registered with the authorities prior to their proscription in 1890 makes interesting reading. The leaders are named, together with their lodges, addresses, and occupations. The latter include: gambler-shopkeeper (i.e. bookmaker and general gambler in games of chance, cock-, dog-, and cricket-fighting); doctor and theatre manager; opium shopkeeper (i.e. divan operator); gunsmith; geomancer and coffin-maker.

Just how much power the Malayan secret societies wielded, despite government restrictions on their activities, was shown by the Larut Wars of 1872–4. As tin mining increased in Malaya large numbers of Chinese arrived looking for work in the mines, often Chinese-owned. In 1871, with a work force some forty thousand strong, the mines produced over a million dollars'-worth of tin and generated vast profits for the owners. Inevitably, inter-Triad rivalry resulted, with factions struggling for the right to 'squeeze' mine owners, the supply of opium to the coolies, and such subsidiary rackets as provision of food and liquor to the labour camps.

Once again, the two protagonists were the primarily Cantonese Ghee Hin and the Hakka/Hokkien Hai San societies. Each supported a different local ruler (who received royalties from the tin mines) and, when the question of succession to a local throne came up, open warfare between the groups broke out. The Cantonese Ghee Hin built stockades on the Larut River, blockaded the area, and severely hampered the movement of tin and ore, as well as raiding passing vessels.

The conflict might have rumbled on indefinitely had it not been for the arrival of Captain Speedy of the Straits Settlements Police. Speedy quit his job and entered the employment of a local ruler who was supported by the Hakka Hai San Society. Whereupon he went to India, recruited a mercenary force of Sikhs and Pathans, and returned to overrun the Ghee Hin stockades. In the meantime, the British had sent in the gunboats whilst the Triads had called on reinforcements from China. The troubles were eventually brought to a conclusion when the British established a state council, on which sat Speedy (now Assistant Resident for the area) and the leaders of the two local secret societies, the Chang Keng Kwee and the Ch'in Ah Yam, which became officially registered and recognized and remained part of the local process of government for several years.

There was, however, a distinct anti-British feeling amongst the Malayan Triads, and this continued to brew until the peninsula gained its independence in 1957. The political situation in Malaya was very different from that in Hong

Kong, or indeed in other British possessions with substantial Chinese populations. For one thing, Malaya was a confederation of separate states, each with its own ruler. It was also racially mixed, with the Chinese by no means the dominant group. Indeed, to the local Malays of broadly Indo-Chinese stock, the Chinese were – historically speaking – intruders. They had come into the peninsula in large numbers with the British, who needed coolie labour, and were predominantly Buddhist or Taoist, whereas the local population was primarily Muslim.

The British became cast in the role of tyrants by both the Chinese, who believed they were being exploited, and by the Malays, who objected to being colonized. The Triads took up the cause of the minority Chinese from whom they 'squeezed' their income. As the independence movement gained momentum the Triads did what they could to destabilize the situation. After the Second World War they even allied themselves with the Communists - their traditional enemies. With hindsight, their opposition to the British and espousal of the independence cause worked to the Triads' disadvantage. Today, although the Triads continue to operate widely throughout Malaysia and the independent state of Singapore – for instance, smuggling large quantities of opium and heroin from production areas in Thailand and Laos – their position is far less secure than it was in the days of British rule, since drug dealing in Malaysia and Singapore now commands a mandatory death sentence.

In the late nineteenth century, although Triad activity was centred on Penang and Singapore, where there were large concentrations of Chinese, it was also rife throughout the Malay states and increased as the Chinese population grew. Once the British had calmed the situation on the west coast, large numbers of Chinese began to migrate to the Malayan peninsula, so that in many areas they outnumbered the native Malays. This potentially inflammatory state of racial imbalance was described in 1876 by W. A. Pickering, a colonial civil servant, in *Fraser's Magazine*:

We cannot shut our eyes to the fact that peace in the Malay States means a large influx of Chinese; this involves our interference to keep the peace. The men who find the capital for mining or agricultural purposes are, for the most part, born or naturalized British subjects, and the labourers are all connected with our colonies by the secret societies, so that any disturbance in the Native States injures the trade of our people, and endangers the good order and tranquillity of our Settlements. Furthermore, we have a moral duty to protect the Malays from majorities of Chinese, and to protect the turbulent Chinese from massacring each other.

Two months after Pickering's article appeared, a British official, a Captain Lloyd, was found murdered with a hatchet. It was established that the murder had been ordered by a Triad society, the Ho Seng, and eventually a Chinese (almost certainly a scapegoat) was hung. Hugh Low, British Resident of the state of Perak where Lloyd was killed, reported that:

The whole coast of Perak is in possession of the Ho Seng Society, from the Krian to the mouth of the Bernam River, and they have an idea that having established themselves, as they allege, without the assistance of Government, the Government has no right to tax them or impose regulations for their guidance. The Government of Perak was defied by two of these communities in 1877, but successfully vindicated its authority, and the belief is current in Larut that discontent at the dues charged at Pangkor has engendered a feeling of resentment which has encouraged the perpetration of crime.

It was unusual then – indeed it still is – for a Triad society to murder a European, or anyone not in direct conflict with them. Clearly, the Ho Seng Society saw Lloyd and the British interest he represented as a serious threat to their continuing, but unofficial, rulership of coastal Perak.

In 1884 the Chinese in Perak were given a Protector by the British, a Captain Schultz, who set about trying to liaise with the secret societies, persuading them to register where he could. But this had little effect, and the riots, assaults, and murders continued, due – as Schultz noted – to 'the pernicious influence of secret societies which through their perfect organization for evil have caused petty quarrels and jealousy between individual members of rival societies to develop into serious breaches of the peace resulting in murder, arson, and destruction of valuable property.'

The authorities, in fact, were powerless. The jungles even harboured secret groups of which they were utterly ignorant. In 1884, the year of Schultz's appointment, the Hok Beng Society of Malacca established a sub-branch in Selangor and two thousand members were initiated before the police were even aware of what was going on. Schultz came to the conclusion that registration was not the answer and that far more drastic measures were necessary if the societies were to be controlled. He wanted them outlawed and the carrying of a 'Triad ticket' (a membership document) made an offence. As Schultz wrote:

These secret societies consider the Native States, especially Perak, as a happy hunting ground from which they derive a very considerable portion of their exceedingly large income: so tempting is this to them that notwithstanding the considerable risk to their emissaries and agents in carrying on their work here, any number of these latter over-run the State secretly inducing their countrymen to join their societies. Not content with doing this, in order to increase their numbers and their revenue, they have lately, I understand, relaxed their own rules with this object in view, by not making it a condition any more that the candidates from the Native States who are willing to enter the Societies must come over to Penang to be initiated. Their travelling agents or Secret Masters have power to hold lodges in the State and there to make the candidates acquainted with the necessary signs and take the oath from them.

In August 1889 the kind of measures advocated by Schultz came into force. It was now an offence to be a Triad member, to use Triad flags and signs, or to be in the possession of Triad membership documents. The penalties ranged through fines, caning, imprisonment, deportation and confiscation of property. But even these new powers failed to check the growth of the secret societies and membership figures amongst tin miners continued as high as before. In one area, of 222 miners all were members of the Hai San Society. In Perak, 9447 miners were Ghee Hin members and 5394 were Hai San followers. The number of unaffiliated miners was negligible.

The Malays had their own 'Flag Societies' (a *jema'ah*, meaning an assembly, particularly one of a religious nature). In their own way, these too caused problems for the colonial administrators, though not to the same extent as the Triads. After secret societies were proscribed, the Flag Societies began to amalgamate and by the turn of the century there were two main *jema'ah*s, both based in Penang: the Red Flag and the White Flag (the former based in Acheen Street). In 1915 a Triad society proper appeared in Sitiawan with – for the first time – a multi-racial membership of Malay and Chinese.

A decade later the situation was even worse. Secret societies proliferated and their membership now included many Malays in positions of authority and influence in the community. One nocturnal ceremony, reported to the police, took place in a forest clearing and involved the killing of a cockerel on an altar, after which its blood was drunk by the members from cups which were then broken. Not a single Chinese was present at the ceremony, but the Chinese Triad ritual was clearly followed. The Darul Ma'amur Football Club was founded in Penang in 1920. By 1925 it was recruiting members in the tradition of the White Flag Society, but again used Chinese rituals. Triad phrases and ranks were translated into Malay: the Incense Master became *tembaga* or copper (out of which the incense pot was made); a *kipas* (fan) was an officer of White Fan rank; a Straw Sandal was a *kasut* or shoe; whilst a Red Pole was a *tongkata*, a literal translation of rod or staff.

From this time onwards the Malayan Triad societies were multi-racial in composition – mainly Chinese and Malays, but also Indians and, from the 1960s, Filipinos and Indonesians. As in Hong Kong, crime had become the societies' main *raison d'être*, due in part to Sun Yat-sen's drive to raise funds for the Republican cause from overseas Chinese communities. Sun had visited Singapore in July 1905 and eight months later, having set up the T'ung Meng Hui in Japan, returned to start a Malayan branch and made Singapore his base. He soon began to reap profits from the Chinese community, which, unlike its counterpart in Hong Kong, was comparatively wealthy. Amongst other things, he offered mining rights in parts of mainland China to local mining magnates and, for two dollars each, sold passes that would supposedly provide safe conduct on the mainland when the revolution came. This was protection money by another name.

Sun Yat-sen moved to Penang in 1909 after enthusiasm for his revolutionary ideals began to wane in Singapore. But in southern Malaya patriotic feelings still ran high, supported by the Chung Wo group whose meeting places included the Chinese Commercial School and Chinese Free Dispensary in Perak and the Chinese YMCA in Singapore. After the success of the 1911 Wuchang Rising in China there was a huge inflow of members to the T'ung Meng Hui in Malaya as the sense of national identity amongst the Chinese population began to increase.

In other parts of the world Triad societies proliferated wherever there was a Chinese community for them to prey on. Though from time to time Triad gangsters came up against foreign police forces, even government agencies, in the main they restricted themselves to operating within the Chinese communities, where they functioned not just as criminals but also as welfare groups and patriotic rallying points. Inevitably, some Triads began to wield considerable political muscle. One Triad leader in particular typified the fusion of crime and politics – a man as fascinating as he was powerful, as terrifying as he was clever. His name was Tu Yueh-sheng.

5

A PAIR OF MR BIGS

The top men in the Triads – those who wield the real power – are seldom known outside the Triad societies themselves. They never court publicity, as some Mafia godfathers have done. And yet they have succeeded in manipulating social and political conditions – both locally and internationally – to an astonishing degree, and none of their opposite numbers in other criminal organizations can now match them in the range and extent of their activities.

There have been a number of these men in the present century. Some have been patriots or soldiers; others were petty criminals who rose through the ranks, achieving power by their ruthless criminal strategies. This chapter looks at two such men: Tu Yueh-sheng and Ng Sik-ho.

Tu Yueh-sheng, commonly known as Big-Eared Tu, was the leader of the Green Gang, a Triad syndicate operating out of Shanghai in the early 1900s. Tu's gang dominated the heroin and opium trade in Shanghai, then a bustling seaport of several million people and the gateway to China. Tu was known to the Shanghai police, but they were unable to catch him. Had they been successful the history of modern China might have been different; for Big-Eared Tu was Chiang Kai-shek's secret sponsor. Through his control of the Shanghai drug trade, through the proceeds of extortion and prostitution, and through political coercion, Tu helped Chiang Kai-shek to power and supplied the Kuomintang with much-needed funds. He also arranged for the murder of thousands of Communists and Communist sympathizers – a fact still remembered today in Peking.

In many ways, Tu was the archetypal criminal Triad. He

was born in 1887 or 1888 in the village of Kaochiao in Pootung district, across the Yangtse River from Shanghai – a derelict place of poverty and destitution listed by the authorities in Shanghai as the worst slum in China. His father was a coolie in a rice shop which he owned, his mother was a washerwoman. Tu's mother died when he was three years old and, as was the custom, his baby sister was given away (Tu later spent much time and money trying to trace her, but without success). On his father's death in 1892 or 1893 Tu went to live with his stepmother (though his father never actually married her) until 1895, when an earthquake and cholera epidemic hit Shanghai. His stepmother was then kidnapped and sold either into slavery or to one of the innumerable Shanghai brothels.

Tu then passed into the guardianship of an uncle who abused him. As a teenager he was described as a sinewy specimen, with long arms, yellow teeth, and the eyes of a rat. By the age of twelve Tu was a hardened delinquent and an inveterate gambler with a tough reputation. When he was fifteen he ran away from his uncle and worked for a while as a fruit vendor's assistant in the French Concession in Shanghai, at the same time running illicit opium across the Yangtse into the city and acting as a contract killer in the underworld of the Shanghai docks.

His physical appearance was both distinctive and un-settling. His head was shaved, throwing into even greater prominence the huge ears that had given him his nickname. His broad-nosed face, supported on a thick neck, was covered in strange bumps as a result of the savage beatings he had received from his uncle; his lips were full and tight over protruding teeth that gave him a permanently scornful and vicious expression. A photograph of him has survived: the eyes were completely without emotion, like those of a reptile – an effect enhanced by the fact that his left eyelid hung down in a permanent semi-wink.

Before he was fifteen Tu had been introduced to a Triad society called the Red Gang by an itinerant gambler and pimp known as 'Lot Drawer', for whom Tu worked. Once a member of the Red Gang he began to frequent the house of its leader, Huang Chih-jung, known as Pock-marked Huang – not only a formidable Triad leader (arguably the most powerful in the Yangtse valley), but also the chief detective for the French Sûreté in Shanghai.

Through Huang's mistress, who was an opium dealer in her own right and for whom Tu recovered – after a rickshaw chase through the streets of Shanghai – a quantity of pilfered opium, Tu was formally introduced to the leader. Huang quickly saw that Tu had qualities he could put to good use and soon Tu became his main opium-runner.

Before long Huang began to take Tu into his confidence and the younger man suggested an amalgamation of the three gangs – the Red (their own gang), the Green, and the Blue – that were then running Shanghai's illicit opium trade. Huang agreed, and authorized Tu to carry out his plan. The leader of the Green Gang, unfortunately, saw no virtue in amalgamation, and so Tu simply killed him and assumed the position of leader himself. The leader of the Blue Gang, Chang Hsiao-lin, wisely decided to co-operate, and the new association was duly formed under a triumvirate of Chang, Huang, and Tu. The territory controlled by these three was extensive, comprising the criminal underworld of Shanghai and the opium trade of the whole city, the provinces of Chekiang and Kiangsu, and the entire Yangtse River system for a thousand miles – well into China's poppy-growing regions, giving them control of a large sector of the raw opium market.

Within the International Settlements of Shanghai – essentially individual foreign ghettoes, each with its own police force and garrison – the opium trade had traditionally been run by the Three Harmonies Triad, a society of Chui Chow Chinese whose leader was Wong Sui, a Cantonese. Using his undoubtedly effective powers of persuasion, Tu forced Wong to agree to amalgamation with the Green Gang, and then promptly set about disbanding the Three Harmonies Society. By 1910 the Green Gang had subsumed all the local Triad groups, except for a peasant league outside the city which remained autonomous under the Green Gang flag and a patriotic and social group who retained the name of the Red Gang but had little or no criminal interests.

Pock-marked Huang was the supreme leader of the gang; but Tu was the activist and head of operations. He grew fabulously wealthy, with a personal fortune estimated at the time (probably conservatively) of something like forty million US dollars. Shanghai was his private fiefdom. In 1915 Tu married, but his wife was infertile. The couple adopted a son and Tu acquired two fifteen-year-old concubines. All three women lived in a luxurious colonnaded house on the Rue Wagner in the French Concession, the two concubines bearing Tu six sons whose safety was secured by the services of White Russian bodyguards. Later in life the vigorous Tu took on two more concubines. Tu had Shanghai sewn up. The Triad soldiers under his command controlled virtually everyone, from dock-coolies to bank tellers in the Hongkong and Shanghai Bank. Tu himself had access to the mail (which he read when he needed to), whilst the press and the foreign police forces were in his pocket. Nothing happened without his knowing of it – and that in a city of millions.

Through extortion Tu exercised control over major import/export houses as well as casual labour hirers. As a result of the system whereby foreign business houses employed Chinese agents or 'compradors' he had a large measure of influence over foreign business interests, making him in many ways the first 'godfather' figure of the criminal world – years ahead of the American Mafia.

It followed that Tu did not take kindly to the political threat to his empire posed by Communism. In July 1921, meetings were held at 106 Rue Wautz and in the girls' school on Rue Auguste Boppe (Joyous Undertaking Street) at which the Chinese Communist Party was founded. Tu had undercover agents present at all the assemblies. In due course he became responsible for murdering thousands of Communists and Communist sympathizers, for breaking Communist-inspired strikes, and for attacking ordinary Chinese workers' societies and groups with Communist connections. His actions have never been forgotten by the People's Republic – one reason for the present Chinese government's implacable hatred of the Triads.

In this virtually unassailable position of power, Big-Eared Tu met all kinds and conditions of men. And women. One of these was Ai-ling Soong, the daughter of Charlie Soong, a Chinese runaway brought up and educated in the American Methodist Church. His real name was Han Chao-shun and he was educated at Trinity College, Durham, North Carolina, at the personal expense of the millionaire Julian S. Carr, one of the richest men in the American South and a former soldier in the Confederate army during the Civil War. Carr saw in this apparently devout young Chinese strong missionary material and intended that he should return to China to preach the Methodist cause.

Charlie Soong subsequently attended Vanderbilt University at Carr's expense from 1882 to 1885. However he seems to have had little interest in the religion he was baptized into on 7 November 1880, when he took the name Charles Jones Soon. He returned to China in January 1886, ostensibly to begin his missionary work, but it was not long before he began to pursue other interests – including revolutionary politics, running a printing company (from which he made a substantial fortune), publishing bibles, and secretly sponsoring the Republican activities of Sun Yat-sen. Through the latter, Soon (who now called himself Charlie Soong) made contact with the Triads and became an office-bearer. His own former sponsor, the gullible Julian S. Carr, still believed that his protégé was strong for Christ and Methodism and funded Soong's first successful company, the Sino-American Press, which also received financial backing – unknown to Carr – from Soong's Triad group. The SAP received contracts from Carr to print, publish, and distribute bibles, Methodist tracts, hymnals, and prayer-books for Chinese missions, as well as textbooks. At the same time Soong printed revolutionary broadsheets, inflammatory political broadsides, and Triad initiation certificates and other documents. In 1892 Charlie Soong did the decent thing and finally resigned from the Southern Methodist China Mission, to which he was attached as a missionary. He was, to put it charitably, a shining example of a Christian pragmatist.

Soong had six children, all of whom distinguished themselves in their various ways. Perhaps the most brilliant was his daughter Ai-ling Soong, who combined ruthless cunning with an astute financial sense. She married the banker and businessman Kung Hsiang-hsi, a friend of Sun Yat-sen (who was himself married to one of Ai-ling's sisters). On her way home from the Young J. Allen Methodist Church to her house in the French Concession (where her father was living under the protective wing of Pock-marked Huang) she would often meet Tu Yueh-sheng – though how exactly she became acquainted with him is not known. In due course Tu became a regular visitor to Ai-ling's house.

As a direct result of this friendship, the Kung banking empire, controlled by the Soongs, was amalgamated with the Triad Green Gang. For twenty-five years, until 1940, this alliance amassed a staggering fortune from banking, stock market dealings, and company takeovers. The Soongs' veneer of Christian respectability gave them an entrée to the foreign business community, whilst Tu had his own methods of dealing with the local Chinese. Between them they had the Chinese economy before the Communist takeover firmly under their control.

Not all Big-Eared Tu's friends were so well connected – at least not at first. He was fond of frequenting the upmarket brothels operated by the Green Gang, his particular favourite being the so-called Blue Villa, where he would often be found in the company of a Green Gang soldier well-known to the police – especially in the British-administered International Settlement – as an alleged murderer, extortionist, and armed robber. His name was Chiang Kai-shek.

Tu and Chiang visited brothels together regularly (their tastes ran to boys as well as young girls) and generally collaborated in various areas of Triad business. When Chiang's mentor and co-revolutionary, Ch'en Ch'i-mei, was murdered, Tu offered support and protection. He also saw to it that Chiang avoided arrest in the International Settlement, to where he had fled during the revolution of 1913. Tu supplied Chiang with mercenaries, and Chiang in turn sent these to support Sun Yat-sen in Canton; and it was Chiang who helped bring together Tu, Sun Yat-sen, and the crippled millionaire Chang Ching-chang (also known as Curio Chang as a result of his art dealerships in Paris and New York which handled Chinese works of art often stolen by Green Gang members or Chiang Kai-shek's followers). Out of this triumvirate came the founding of the stock and commodities market in Shanghai, which became a source of funds for the revolutionary cause. Chang Ching-chang became one of Chiang Kai-shek's closest allies and most trusted adviser and played a crucial role in the realization of Chiang's political ambitions – to the extent that Chang became known as Chiang Kai-shek's 'evil genius'.

Tu of course made handsome personal profits from the stock market he had helped to set up, and for his political services he was made a major in the Kuomintang army. Other Green Gang leaders also became high-ranking Kuomintang officers, whilst Chiang Kai-shek, who had been employed as a clerk on the Shanghai stock market before becoming politically involved with Sun Yat-sen, lined his pockets from his activities as a broker (it was an in-joke at the time that he was called a broker because he broke the arms and fingers of those who crossed him).

Chiang Kai-shek and Big-Eared Tu were not just business partners. They had an even closer relationship. Chiang's second wife, Ch'en Chieh-ju, whom he married in a Buddhist ceremony in November 1921 (having divorced his first wife and dismissed his concubine in order to do so), was literally owned by Big-Eared Tu, for whom Ch'en had formerly worked as a prostitute. Within a month of this marriage, Chiang Kai-shek fell in love with May-ling Soong, Ai-ling's sister. In due course, with Tu's help, he married her.

During the second Sino-Japanese War of the 1930s, Tu left Shanghai for the comparative safety of Hong Kong. He sailed there on a French passenger liner and on arriving in the colony rented a suite in the Peninsula Hotel, then considered one of the best hotels in the world outside London or New York. He was accompanied by one of his concubines; another was in Britain, where her sons by Tu were receiving a public-school education. Tu remained in Hong Kong in semi-exile for some years; he bought a house there as well as maintaining a suite in the Gloucester Hotel. From time to time he would make trips to Wuhan to look over his business interests there and to liaise with Chiang Kai-shek and his senior officers. One small footnote to Tu's time in Hong Kong is worth recording. In February 1938 he was interviewed by W. H. Auden and Christopher Isherwood on the activities of the Chinese arm of the Red Cross, of which Tu was a director.

Chiang Kai-shek's political career continued to be sup-ported by Big-Eared Tu, who provided him with both funds and strong-arm support where necessary. Even after Chiang fell from power Tu went on helping him. In 1949, with the Communists closing on Shanghai, Chiang called on Tu to help rob the Bank of China. Chiang had attempted to shore up the Chinese yuan by issuing a gold coin with an exchange rate of four to the US dollar, but this attempt had failed owing to the fact that there was no gold to back it up. Half the gold reserve had been spirited away by the Soongs and the Kungs. The rest lay in the vaults of the Bank of China in Shanghai. (The day before Chiang announced his 'gold yuan' reforms, Tu's third son, Tu Wei-ping, dumped thirty million shares on the market, selling short. He was tried for this audacious piece of insider dealing, though the charge was merely share dealing outside the stock exchange and he received only eight months' imprisonment.)

Chiang arranged for a freighter to be moored alongside the Bund, Shanghai's waterfront, opposite the Cathay Hotel. Its 'coolie' crew were actually hand-picked naval ratings dis-guised as shabbily-dressed stevedores. Heavy bribes to the bank's officials, laced with Tu's not-so-veiled threats, opened the doors to the vaults and the contents were loaded on to the freighter by the supposed coolies aided by Green Gang members.

Just a few days before the Communists took Shanghai, Tu fled to Hong Kong, where he lived in an apartment on Kennedy Road. He lived on, paralysed and debilitated from decades of opium and heroin abuse, for another two years. He died on 16 August 1951, leaving seven sons and three daughters. Chiang Kai-shek issued a laudatory tribute praising Tu's loyalty and integrity. Tu's body was refused burial in Hong Kong since he had not been a resident there for the statutory eight years. In October 1952 his coffin was finally shipped to Free China (Taiwan, then Formosa) and interred in a tomb in the hills above Taipei.

As a final, supremely ironic epitaph on this extraordinary master criminal, the following entry in the Shanghai *Who's Who*, written in the 1930s when Big-Eared Tu was known as the Right Honourable Tu Yueh-sheng, would be hard to better:

> At present most influential resident, French Concession, Shanghai. Well-known public welfare worker . . . councillor, French Municipal Council. President, Ching Wai Bank, and Tung Wai Bank, Shanghai. Founder and Chairman, board of directors, Cheng Shih Middle School. President, Shanghai Emergency Hospital. Member, supervisory committee, General Chamber of Commerce. Managing director, Hua Feng Paper Mill, Hangchow. Director, Commercial Bank of China, Kiangsu and Chekiang Bank, Great China University, Chinese Cotton Goods exchange, and China Merchants Steam Navigation Co., Shanghai, etc. President, Jen Chi Hospital, Ningpo.

On second thoughts, perhaps the irony of this *can* be bettered. In 1936, when Tu was baptized as a Christian in Charlie Soong's own church in Shanghai, May-ling Soong commented: 'Tu Yueh-sheng is becoming a real Christian because ever since he was baptized there has been a marked decrease in kidnapping cases in Shanghai.'

There has never been a Triad leader quite like Tu Yueh-sheng. Succeeding Triads have tried to build a power base as extensive as his, but no single person has yet come close to rivalling his personal wealth and influence. Tu was a Chinese criminal through and through. Apart from his periods of exile in Hong Kong, it is doubtful whether he ever left China. Ng Sik-ho was different. As with many Triad leaders, Ng (known later in life as Limpy Ho) started life in poverty and degradation. He rose quickly through the Triad ranks to become, in the 1960s and 1970s, arguably the most powerful drugs baron in the world.

Ng Sik-ho was born in 1929 in a village near the seaport of Swatow. He was poor and semi-literate, but naturally quick-witted and likeable. As a child and young teenager he ran errands and took messages for the local Triad society, saving his earnings with one ambition in mind: to become a senior Triad member himself.

At the age of 21 he fled from China and went to Hong Kong, with thousands of other refugees from Communism. Once in the British colony he was lost. He spoke no Cantonese (the local language), knew no one, and was penniless. He naturally gravitated towards other refugees from his home region, and because of his former Triad connections he was granted entry to a Hong Kong Triad consisting of Swatow Chinese. He rose rapidly through the hierarchy and within a year was made a 426 Red Pole in charge of the society's operations. His seniors appreciated the fact that he was a hard worker and that he was keen, efficient, and ambitious. He was 'hungry', and this could be turned to the society's advantage. The more he earned, the more the society reaped. And Ng continued to earn, accumulating power and influence as he did so. Soon he was a dominant figure in the Hong Kong underworld. He was even made an honorary member of two of the major Triad groupings, the 14K and the Wo Shing Wo.

Because of his powerful position and ruthlessness, Ng became both respected and feared. But despite this, and the ties of Triad brotherhood and the collective protection Triad leaders generally enjoy, some Triads resented his rapid rise to power. He was ambushed, and his right leg was savagely beaten with a four-pound teak pole. The attack left him crippled and gave him his nickname of 'Limpy Ho'.

Ng Sik-ho began dealing at first in street narcotics, selling No. 3 heroin (the less strong variety) from a fruit shop. He prospered and took on two partners, Lo Shing (a Triad comrade) and Lo Shing's wife. In June 1960 the fruit shop was raided by the police and Ng Sik-ho was sentenced to twelve months' imprisonment, whilst Lo Shing, who had a previous record for narcotics dealing, received three years. After his release, Ng lived with Lo Shing's wife, Cheng Yuet-ying. (Lo, addicted to his own drugs, was sexually inactive. Ng scorned the use of drugs.) Though Cheng was an experienced drug dealer, she was soon caught red-handed packaging heroin for sale and was sentenced to three years' imprisonment. Observing the strict code of Triad loyalty, she firmly refused to implicate Ng Sik-ho (it was also part of the Triad code of honour that no brother should molest another's woman, or have sexual relations with her, but this seems to have been disregarded by Cheng and Ng).

After her release Ng was waiting for her. In the interim he had established himself with two fronts, a tea shop (a kind of café) and a rice shop next door. Deals were struck over the tea bowls and the merchandise distributed in bags of rice. The couple were under regular police surveillance and Ng was arrested again early in 1965, but he could only be charged with membership of the Triads and was bound over for two years.

As a result of police interest in him, Limpy Ho (as he was now generally known) kept his head down whilst still managing to continue his drug dealing. But he was dissatisfied with the limited rewards of street dealing. That was for Triad rank and file. Limpy Ho wanted more. Much more. In collaboration with other Triad members he set about forging a drugs empire, funded by Triad money and by loans from members of the Chinese business community for whom the risks involved were outweighed by the enormous profits to be made.

Outwardly Limpy Ho was a prosperous and legitimate businessman who wore expensive European clothes – indistinguishable from many other middle-class Chinese merchants during the boom years of the 1960s. But this outward respectability was a cover for massive criminal ambitions. During the Cultural Revolution (1966–7) China was in chaos, and the Royal Hong Kong Police – occupied with the civil troubles this unleashed – eased up on their surveillance of petty criminals and Triads who no longer seemed active. Limpy Ho seized his chance. In a matter of months he set up a number of partnerships to deal in heroin. Cocaine, the scourge of the next two decades, was not then such big business as it has now become, whilst the heroin market was rapidly expanding in the USA and Europe.

Limpy Ho's plan was to buy prepared morphine and opium base from Thailand (where it was manufactured from poppies grown in the so-called Golden Triangle in the inaccessible mountain regions of central Indo-China), transport it in his own fleet of vessels to Hong Kong, and there set up his own heroin laboratories in the teeming suburbs of Kowloon and in the hills of the New Territories. The aim was to produce as much No. 3 heroin as the Hong Kong market required and then to process the remainder into No. 4 heroin (three times stronger) for export to the USA and Europe.

Ng Sik-ho's main partner was another Swatow Chinese, Ng Chun-kwan. By 1970 their profit from this operation was estimated to be in the region of £15–20 million a year. Once the opium base was purchased it was transported to Hong Kong in two stages. First, Thai cargo ships carried it to international waters off Hong Kong where it was transferred to ocean-going fishing junks. Once in Hong Kong waters, the base was transferred again to sampans, of which there were thousands fishing in the off-shore waters, making detection almost impossible. What did not travel by sea came overland. Each person in the chain had a cut-off so that no one could betray the next, whilst payments were made through itinerant cashiers who never met each other or the representative of Ng Sik-ho who in turn paid them. It was a brilliantly conceived and executed system and virtually invulnerable. It was only through betrayal at the highest level that Limpy Ho was brought to justice.

Before his arrest, however, Ng Sik-ho and Cheng Yuet-ying (now his wife) had invested his vast income from drugs in property and real estate: flats, houses, factories, commercial buildings. They retained three homes for their private use, all of which were registered in Cheng's name. The grandest of these was in Kent Road, Kowloon Tong, set in walled gardens and heavily guarded by men, dogs, and electronic equipment. Ng also owned four restaurants and founded the Hong Kong Precious Stone Company, ostensibly to deal in gemstones imported from Thailand, but in reality a 'laundry' for his drug income. As a further financial cushion, Ng and Cheng invested in illegal gambling casinos, the most luxurious of which – in Prat Avenue in the heart of Tsim Sha Tsui, the tourist shopping area of Kowloon – was managed by Cheng herself. (It operated round the clock and members had their own pass keys.) At the other end of the economic scale Ng owned unlicensed street stalls, which remained largely free from police interference as a result of the fact that, before the crackdown in the early 1970s on police corruption, a number of police officers were in Ng's pay.

At the height of his criminal career it was estimated that Limpy Ho was the direct source of income for over a thousand people who depended on him for their livelihood. By 1970 he had achieved his ambition of being one of the wealthiest and most powerful drugs barons in the Far East. But success also brought him enemies, especially amongst Hong Kong Triad societies who also operated in Thailand. On a number of occasions his couriers were murdered and the shipments they were carrying disappeared without trace. In spite of this, Ng Sik-ho was determined to expand his empire even further. He was, beyond doubt, the 'Mr Big' of the Far East drugs trade. He now saw himself to be powerful enough to deal with the American Mafia on equal terms. The breaking of the so-called French Connection gave him the opportunity to do so.

The potent No. 4 heroin was much in demand in the USA, and Ng could supply it. In 1970 and 1971 meetings were held in Japan between Ng and Mafia representatives. A deal was struck and for a few months the association operated profitably. But the Mafia felt uncomfortable with Ng Sik-ho – especially his arrogance – and withdrew from the deal. Yet as a result of his contacts with the Mafia, Limpy Ho was now known to the United States Drug Enforcement Administration (DEA), and the DEA immediately informed law enforcement agencies in Hong Kong, Tokyo, Bangkok, Singapore, and elsewhere of Ng's Mafia dealings.

The DEA were particularly interested in the Singapore Triads, who operated in Holland, then a distribution centre for heroin throughout Europe and on to the USA. But these groups did not have either the finance or the expertise to refine the drugs, nor did they have the organization for supplying the base opium from Thailand. Limpy Ho had both the finance and the organization and set up a network through Dutch-based Triad groups for supplying heroin to dealers throughout Europe: amongst the users were US servicemen in Germany, some of whom were also dealers.

But the net was closing in on Ng Sik-ho. In 1972 a police raid uncovered seven hundred kilos of raw opium and eighty kilos of morphine in a tunnel connecting flats rented by Ng on Pearl Island in the New Territories and a duck farm owned by Ng on the mainland. Arrests were made, but no one implicated Ng. A year later his illegal casinos were closed down, but still he was unindictable.

In February 1974 a seaman called Leung Fat-hei was murdered after double-crossing Limpy Ho. He had foolishly stolen half a shipment of drugs from Thailand and then sold it under the market price. Three of Ng's close associates were arrested on suspicion of murdering Leung. Ng Sik-ho himself was living in Taiwan – then, as now, a safe haven for Triad criminals from Hong Kong, since many members of the Nationalist government were also senior Triad office-bearers. When the three suspects for Leung's murder were eventually released, unconvicted, Ng returned to Hong Kong.

Back in his old haunts, Ng re-established his gambling

businesses, though he avoided drug dealing for the time being. But while he seemed secure from attack by outsiders he was becoming increasingly vulnerable to betrayal from within. He was unpopular with other Triad leaders, who saw him as muscling into their territory; more importantly, he had antagonized people within his own organization. One of these, Ng Ping, had broken with him after an argument. Another, a senior aide, had been the object of three murder attempts instigated by Limpy Ho, who believed the aide to be a traitor. In retaliation, he went to the police and gave them statements implicating Ng Sik-ho in drug trafficking.

In late 1974 Ng was questioned for some hours in the Royal Hong Kong Police headquarters in Arsenal Street, Wai Chai. Naturally, he denied all the charges that were put to him but he was taken into custody for trafficking in dangerous drugs. Twenty of Ng's premises were then raided by a specially chosen squad of detectives. Though he had been exceptionally cautious about keeping paperwork relating to his criminal affairs, Ng had not been cautious enough. Documents were found relating to the purchase of base drugs from Thailand and to his former partnership with Ng Chun-kwan, who had since set up his own drugs syndicate. The police could not believe their luck.

The police then began rounding up Ng Sik-ho's followers, many of whom, realizing that Ng's time was up, agreed to testify against him in return for lenient sentences or, in some cases, freedom from prosecution. In May 1975, Ng Sik-ho, along with eight others, was convicted and was sentenced to thirty years' imprisonment. His wife, Cheng Yuet-ying, escaped immediate arrest by moving from one safe house to another; but eventually she was brought to trial and sentenced to sixteen years.

Though from different eras, Big-Eared Tu and Limpy Ho shared a background that was typical of other Triad bosses, and which is still typical of many Triad street fighters today. Both were from peasant backgrounds; both were poorly educated. They rose to power through the ranks by a sheer determination to succeed, no matter what. Power was all, and crime offered the means to achieve it. Tu was one of the greatest crime bosses of all time – the dominant figures of the American Mafia included – whose criminal activities supported his political ambitions. (In the case of Tu Yueh-sheng, the lines of Bob Dylan come to mind: '*Steal a little and they throw you in gaol/Steal a lot and they make you the king*'.) Ng Sik-ho was a gangster, pure and simple, but on a grand scale. Both had a natural criminal instinct that combined astuteness and a capacity for organization with ruthlessness. Membership of the Triads gave them all the opportunities they needed to use these misguided talents to the full.

6

THE MEN OF PAK FA'AN GAI

In many ways it was with Tu Yueh-sheng that the Triad ethos was finally purged of all pretence of patriotism and altruism. Until Big-Eared Tu's rise to power there were many Triad groups who still held to the old patriotic ideal of overthrowing foreign domination (whether in the form of genuine foreign oppression or Communism) and restoring authentic Chinese rule to China. But Tu was motivated by pure self-interest. In spite of the political effects of his wealth and influence, he remained primarily a mobster, and since his time the Triads' commitment to crime has been absolute. Triad societies now have little interest in the cause of Chinese nationalism. Where once the Triads produced Robin Hood-like folk heroes and patriots who waged just war against oppression and injustice, they now breed gangsters and thugs. Ng Sik-ho was perhaps the first Triad leader of this type, for unlike Tu he had no political connections and he extended his criminal organization far beyond Hong Kong – a sinister omen of things to come.

Today the Triads form an international criminal fraternity, but their roots remain in street-level crime. The men of Pak Fa'an Gai, the main alleyway in Kowloon Walled City, have their counterparts now throughout the world. On the street, Triads operate opportunistically, making the most of every situation they encounter. Exploitation is their main activity, since protection rackets are easy to set up and enforce. To see how the Triads operate at street level one has only to spend a little time in Hong Kong. Their activities there are more or less duplicated in every overseas Chinese community – whether in London, Sydney, or San Francisco.

Few Europeans, other than the police, come into contact with the Triads at street level. One who has is the remarkable Elsie Elliott. Born in Newcastle-upon-Tyne and married to a Chinese (ironically, her surname is now Tu), she has served on the Hong Kong Urban Council for a quarter of a century. Throughout that time she has championed the cause of the ordinary Chinese, and by so doing has come into direct conflict with the Triads. In her autobiography she vividly describes her brushes with the Triads. Of particular interest is her account of the intimidation of taxi drivers, which demonstrates how the Triads impose and maintain their authority on the streets.

In Hong Kong's dense urban environment public transport is essential and complex. There is an underground railway network, huge fleets of public buses, sea-going ferries, an urban railway system, innumerable minibuses, and the biggest concentration of taxis in the world. And yet, with a population well in excess of five and a half million people, the public transport system is inadequate and has led to scores of illegal taxis and minibuses.

In the 1970s these illegal vehicles formed a vital part of Hong Kong's public transport. Known as a *pak pai*, the illegal taxi was ripe for exploitation. Some were operated by Triad groups, others by ex-policemen, some by a joint ownership of Triads and police. It was not long before the illegal taxis began eating into the business of the legal drivers, who were afraid of operating in some areas of the city. Beatings-up and threats became commonplace. Taxis were bound by law to pick up their passengers at taxi ranks, but they were losing business because the police were allowing illegal taxis to pick up fares in front of the ranks.

Elsie Elliott was approached by one of the legal taxi drivers, who asked her to expose the scandal. Elsie took the matter up with the Hong Kong Police, but only met with prevarication and evasion. (The traffic division of the police was notoriously corrupt at the time. Its senior English officer, Chief Superintendent Peter Godber, was later con-victed on wide-ranging corruption charges and was extradited from Britain back to Hong Kong, where he was tried and sentenced in 1975 to four years' imprisonment for bribery and conspiracy.) Elsie Elliott saw for herself how the Triads openly extorted money from legal taxi drivers. She even photographed the Triads concerned, but her evidence was ignored by the police, many of whom had a personal stake in the taxi racket.

Street hawking is another major area of Triad exploitation. The streets of Hong Kong teem with cooked-food stalls and vendors selling everything from live snakes to cheap enamel bowls. In order to set up a stall, traders have to obtain a licence and are then allocated a set pitch in a particular street. But as with the taxis, police officers and trade department officials turn a blind eye to illegal hawkers, often as a result of bribes. The Triads offer 'protection' to the hawkers: in return for payment (a fee for the service plus a percentage of the sales revenue) they will keep a look-out for approaching police or officials. If payment is not forthcoming they simply report the illegal hawker to the authorities, a measure they often augment with a beating-up and the destruction of the hawker's stall.

Since its inception, the Royal Hong Kong Police has had to deal with the endemic problem of Triad infiltration. With a preponderance of Chinese officers, Triad affiliation amongst a significant percentage of them has always been inevitable. The situation has undoubtedly improved considerably, though one still hears cynics refer to the RHKP as 'the best police force money can buy'. Part of the problem has been that the police have been obliged to maintain contact with the Triads for intelligence purposes – just like any police force does with its particular corner of the criminal underworld. And it is undeniable that the Triads have been useful to the police. Since the earliest days of the colony, the Triads have passed on invaluable information – not only on rivals and enemies (the Triads always take a pragmatic view of their oaths of brotherly loyalty) but also on political subversives.

Since the 1920s the Triads have been politically right of centre. Both socialism and Communism are inimical to their way of life. They thrive best in a free market democracy. When China fell to Mao Tse-tung, and the Nationalists – along with huge numbers of Triads – fled to Hong Kong, the Triads' political antagonism towards Communism was complete. On the other hand, once settled in Hong Kong, they set about imposing their criminal rule on the Chinese community there, which of course brought them into direct conflict with the colony's administration. Once again they bit the hand that fed them, as they had done in the early years of Hong Kong's existence.

For a time political activism commingled with their criminal expansion. The Nationalist General Kot Siu Wong, for instance, was the founder of the 14K Society and was largely responsible for the development of Triad-organized crime in Hong Kong in the 1950s. (He is sometimes credited with the dubious honour of being the man who introduced heroin manufacture into Hong Kong.) At the same time he set up a pro-Nationalist political movement with an efficient intelligence-gathering network.

In 1956, when rioting broke out in Hong Kong, the Nationalists and their Triad allies tried to take advantage of the situation, but this only resulted in a severe crack-down by the authorities. Over the next four years some ten thousand Triads were arrested and convicted, and six hundred were deported. It was the last time that the Triads committed themselves to overt political action. Henceforth they concentrated their energies on extending and developing their criminal interests, though during the pro-Communist riots of 1967 they supplied the authorities with information on Maoist activities and sympathizers, Communist meeting-places, leftist trade unions, and on the location of bomb-making factories.

At this time the Triad Bureau (temporarily transformed into the Bomb Investigation Unit) was headed by Super-intendent Ernest 'Taffy' Hunt, one of the senior European officers later to be indicted on serious corruption charges. It was alleged that Hunt had received huge sums of money from the Triads, and he himself said that he had earned enough never to have to work again. At the trial of Peter Godber, Hunt (who was then serving a gaol sentence for corruption) admitted that he had received regular bribes for eighteen years from 1955. In his view, a divisional superintendent could reasonably expect to earn an annual income from bribery of between $HK 700,000 and $HK 1.2 million. Elsie Elliott maintains that Hunt – allegedly on Triad orders – deliberately tried to discredit her attempts to publicize the extent of Triad exploitation on the streets. This has never been proved, but it is certain that Hunt (of the Triad Bureau) and Godber (of the Traffic Division) were close friends and that both had interests to protect.

In the early 1970s, when corruption was at its height in the Hong Kong government, it was estimated that 35 per cent of all Chinese policemen were Triad members or affiliates, and that most police stations had at least one senior Chinese NCO who was a Triad office-bearer. Some estimates were even higher. The precise figure is immaterial. The only thing that mattered – that still matters – is the iron grip the Triads had over what went on in Hong Kong: the police, immigration, housing, resettlement, education, public works, transport – every area of the colony's administration was corrupt, with key figures in each owing allegiance to the Triads.

Corruption, 'squeeze', 'tea money', the custom of kickbacks and 'presents', bribes to smooth one's way with officialdom – these things were well established in Chinese life for they were often the only means of speeding up the notoriously sluggish Imperial bureaucracy. Though not quite so lethargic, the colonial administration of Hong Kong was infested with such practices from the start, and once established they were almost impossible to root out. (The sceptical view is that, in the last analysis, the sheer power of Triad money and influence is unassailable and that there will always be individual police officers who will be vulnerable to bribery and intimidation.) Whether the administration itself was fully aware of how rotten it was at the core is not clear. Senior police officers on the take simply ensured that information on the extent of infiltration went no further up the chain of command than themselves, whilst more junior officers kept quiet for fear of jeopardizing their chances of promotion, or of being given risky assignments by their seniors, or simply of being permanently silenced. Those in the Royal Hong Kong Police who refused to succumb to temptation, and who are still in the force, will privately admit that they were told to keep quiet or get out or face the consequences. More blatant threats of physical reprisal were made to Chinese officers. The rule of fear that the Triads imposed so implacably on the streets had penetrated to police station messes and locker-rooms.

This atrocious state of affairs was only alleviated by the establishment in 1974 of the Independent Commission Against Corruption (the ICAC), which began its work by a close examination of police officers' personal backgrounds and lifestyles. It became a crime for officers to live obviously beyond their means, and there were mass resignations and arrests. In spite of strong resistance – including a near mutiny of officers – the stranglehold of corruption was weakened and, to that extent, the power of the Triads reduced.

The drive against police and government corruption continues to the present day, but, like the situation on the streets, it is a battle in which vigilance can never be relaxed. Nevertheless, the Royal Hong Kong Police today is, by and large, clean and in this, the final phase of the colony's existence before being handed back to China, there are signs that the police are making some headway in their battle against the Triads on the street. The gains may be small, but they are gains nonetheless, where before the Triads' rule was absolute. With the near-eradication of Triad infiltration, and the continuing work of the ICAC, the police are now in a far better position to hit the Triads hard when an opportunity to do so presents itself. Two such opportunities occurred in 1987 and 1988. The first was extensively reported in the Hong Kong *Sunday Morning Post* of 13 December 1987, from which the following account is drawn.

The report begins:

Police are locked in a protracted war against Triads where the battle lines rarely move. Advances and retreats are sometimes barely noticeable in this war of attrition, as each time an enemy pocket is overcome another trouble spot flares on the front. But a recent all-out assault on one gang has driven a salient deep into Triad territory.

The gang in question was the 14K Ngai Triad faction, and as a result of sustained police and legal assaults over two years, successful convictions in the Wan Chai District Court helped shatter the myth of Triad invincibility. The Ngai, or 'Resolute', faction was a particularly vicious group that was targeted by the police after its members were linked to brutal choppings in gang battles over illegal gambling rackets. In August 1985 a top secret task force was set up under the leadership of Superintendent Steve Vickers.

Vickers was then heading up the Special Investigation Unit and set about planning a long-term campaign against the Ngai group. The carefully-picked team consisted of Chief Inspector Roger Booth, Inspectors Michael Yu Shi-cheung and Henry Chan Tai-ling, and four NCOs. Each member of the team was rigorously vetted and the operation conducted with the utmost secrecy. The task force started its assault on the Ngai with a major tactical advantage. In 1980 two undercover policemen, code-named Rodney and Sandy, had infiltrated the Triad and over a three-year period had collected damaging evidence against its leaders. The evidence of Rodney (Constable Ma Chi-man) and Sandy (Constable Yu Kam-cheung) was to be crucial when the Ngai bosses were eventually brought to trial.

These two agents had been recruited in 1979 and had been selected by a senior Triad Bureau officer to take part in the undercover operation against the 14K in Mongkok. The two men formally resigned from the force and grew their hair before moving into an apartment in Mongkok. They then set about becoming part of the street life of the area, first as hawkers. It was after they joined the Ying Fat Sports Association, a known breeding ground for Triads, that they met leading members of the 14K Ngai group. Eventually Ma

Chi-man gained access to the 14K itself and even struck up a relationship with one of its top men.

Intelligence information from these two undercover agents was crucial in planning the Task Force's three-phase attack on the Ngai. First of all the team set about investigating the Ngai's violent chopping attacks. This was done publicly and several members of the Triad were prosecuted. But this was merely a front for the task force to build up a dossier of information on the Ngai's membership and on its multi-million-dollar illegal bookmaking business.

The Ngai operated a highly sophisticated telephone bookmaking network with some fifty centres located throughout the New Territories, Kowloon, and Hong Kong, many of these in secluded areas. In at least one village in the New Territories, a householder's telephone line would be diverted to a hut where operators manned a bank of phones on race day. The Ngai bookmakers would take large bets from major punters who wanted to avoid changing the odds on the official Royal Hong Kong Jockey Club tote: off-course betting is illegal save in a few Jockey Club centres. The police also believed that the network was linked to race fixing. A few of these illegal operations were raided to test the water, though the raids were carried out by other police units so as not to compromise the task force's security. A massive strike was then planned that aimed to deal a death blow to the Ngai's gambling income.

On Monday 31 March 1986, some two hundred detectives from the Special Investigations Unit, the Organized and Serious Crimes Group, the Narcotics Bureau, and the Commercial Crimes Bureau arrived for work on what they thought was just another day. By the end of the third race at Happy Valley they had been assigned to special teams for simultaneous raids on 43 bookmaking centres. Each team was given a detailed briefing – delayed until the last possible moment so that the Ngai bookmakers could not be warned of the raid. Even so, as one detective who took part in the raids admitted, the Ngai had simple but effective measures to destroy evidence. 'When we hit them,' he said, 'we found many had magnets for erasing tape recordings. The magnets were standing next to the telephone tape recorders. They would just be knocked on to the recorder and the [magnetic] field would erase the recorded bets. The bets were also written on soluble paper and there were buckets of water at the end of each desk. These guys would just sweep all the papers on the desk into the buckets if there was any trouble. Fortunately, we had some advance warning and were aware this might happen, but in a few cases they were able to ruin the evidence.'

This assault crippled the Ngai gambling ring and more raids over succeeding weeks kept the pressure on the Triads. Thirty-three people were charged with gambling offences. The task force found that the Ngai network was interlinked with similar rings operated by other Triads, but inquiries into these connections were dropped so that police resources could be concentrated on the main target: the 14K Ngai members.

The police had one name, that of the faction's leader, Dai Bei-tang, or Big-nose Tang. But Tang was an old man in failing health (he died in 1987) and was only a figurehead. The real power lay elsewhere. The task force began detailed investigations into Ngai protection rackets, trying all the while to identify the group's active leaders. (As far as the Ngai themselves were concerned, the task force was merely an anti-bookmaking squad.) By July 1986 the task force was ready to launch a final blow against the Ngai aimed at rounding up its leadership.

At midnight on 13 July, the police headquarters in Arsenal Street was sealed off. Hundreds of search warrants were issued and a holding area for prisoners set up, complete with catering facilities and even mobile toilets from the Urban Services Department. 'This time we really turned on the muscle,' said one officer. 'We used all of those units who had taken part in the gambling raids, plus a whole 160-strong company from the police tactical unit. There were 500 officers all up. Raiding teams of all these units hit all the addresses. Starting at 3 a.m. and for the next 48 hours, they went on non-stop.'

The raids netted 53 suspects who, shocked and disbelieving, were kept in the holding area before questioning by the task force. The police were disappointed to discover that one key figure they had wanted to question had left Hong Kong for Taiwan shortly before the raids. But in spite of this, convictions on serious charges against five men and two women were a major blow to the Ngai. Tai Chi-kwong, Leung Hung, Lam Wing-kei, Ma Man-chuen, Tsui Ping-wing, Mak Mei-kiu, and Sung Hueng-lan – all in their twenties and thirties – were charged with a total of nine offences, including helping to manage an unlawful society, conspiring to traffic in dangerous drugs, committing assault causing bodily harm, wounding, damaging property, and incitement to commit assault causing bodily harm. They all pleaded Not Guilty, but had reckoned without the evidence of star witness 'Rodney' – Constable Ma Chi-man.

The court heard how, while working undercover in 1981, Constable Ma had met a man called Chui Shun-kwok who told him that he was a 14K member and a follower of Ng Wah-hei, whom the Crown alleged was a 14K Ngai group leader. Through Chui, Constable Ma met the seven defendants and joined the 14K himself on 25 November 1981. He had been asked by Lam Wing-kei to become his follower and he had agreed to this without undergoing a formal initiation ceremony. Through Lam he met Ng Wah-hei in a restaurant on 4 July 1981. He testified that Lam, Leung, and the others called Ng 'Tai Lo' – Big Brother. Tai and Leung were also present at another gathering in To Kwa Wan, attended by both Constable Ma and his associate Yu Kam-cheung, on 20 July. At this meeting the group discussed an attack on a nearby mah jong school.

Constable Ma also told of a plan to attack a rival Triad gang, the 'Big Circle Boys', who had argued with one of the Ngai group. At another meeting in December 1981 which took place in a waiters' changing-room at a Mongkok restaurant, Constable Ma met a man nicknamed Hak Chai, who indicated that Tai, Leung, Lam and the rest were his 'cousins' – which Constable Ma understood to mean followers of the same 'Big Brother' in a Triad society. 'He said Hak told them they would pick about ten members to take charge of various districts. This meant that if anything happened in these districts the chosen members would negotiate with opponents. If anyone in that district refused a call for help they would get no aid in the future.' The court also heard of how the gang beat up a girl for testifying against another woman and how Constable Ma had himself taken part in a Ngai attack on a sauna, using a water pipe to smash up the furniture and fittings: 'Gang members were told that they were to kill anyone who resisted,' reported the *Sunday Morning Post*.

After a seventeen-day trial, the jury found all seven defendants guilty. But after appeals had been made, the drug charges were quashed and the sentences reduced. The 14K Ngai had been dealt a severe blow, but they were far from being beaten.

Another major crackdown on Triad activity took place in 1988 and was reported in the *South China Morning Post* of 3 July that year. In the early hours of the morning police searched nearly 800 premises and rounded up over 13,000 people for questioning. From this they made 70 arrests, including eleven men who were on their wanted list. The eight-hour operation, under the command of acting Assistant Commissioner John Sheppard, concentrated on known Triad haunts, Mongkok and Yau Mai Tei – home of the 14K – and Wan Chai, where the Sun Yee On is based. There had been a similar crackdown a few months earlier in March, when 17,000 people had been brought in for questioning and 109 people arrested for various offences. The police had raided night-clubs, ballrooms, and vice establishments in a concerted bid to disrupt burgeoning Triad-related crime. The follow-up raids in July were part of this continuing effort to try and curb the power of the Triads on the streets.

At least eleven Triad groups had been identified operating in Wan Chai. Besides the Sun Yee On these included the Wo Hop To, which enforced protection on over two hundred premises. Sun Yee On boss 'Dragon Head' Heung Wah-yim was jailed in January 1988, along with nine other high-ranking members; but though the Triad continues to be a potent force, especially in the districts of Tsim Sha Tsui, Sau Mau Ping, and Tuen Mun, the police action against them has had an effect, as the *Post* reported:

> Police enforcement in Wan Chai has resulted in closing down the majority of massage parlours and 'fishball stalls' ... Liquor lounges catering to young men are now being targeted because of increasing violence caused by drunken customers. There has only been one homicide in Wan Chai district, which has a population of 250,000, in the first quarter of this year [1988]. In the same period there were nine woundings and 82 serious assaults. These figures are regarded as low for such a densely populated area with a heavy concentration of bars and entertainment spots.

The optimism of such press reports, however, is misleading. There have been, and will continue to be, police successes against the Triads; but officers admit that it will be impossible to stamp them out altogether. Battles are being won, but the war goes on. And the secrecy surrounding the setting-up of special units like the 1987 task force that smashed the Ngai gambling network reveals the ever-present danger of Triad infiltration into the police.

In some areas of Hong Kong, the power of the Triads has been visibly curtailed: for instance, the girlie bars of Wan Chai are mostly gone, or reduced to a few tame tourist attractions. In other areas, however, the situation is as bad as it ever was, with the streets dominated by Triad gangs who rule with absolute authority. For hoodlum Triads like these, tradition means nothing. As recently as twenty years ago, Triad lodges in Hong Kong (and elsewhere) still held traditional initiation ceremonies. Even at mass initiations, when over a hundred candidates at a time might be introduced, the ritual stressed the traditional history of the Triads and gave members a sense of their historical identity.

Today things are very different. Initiation ceremonies are often truncated versions – partly for security reasons, but partly because the old ways are increasingly irrelevant to the new generation of Triad street thugs with their designer clothes and expensive Western cars, who require no other encouragement to be loyal to their Triad than the threat of violent death if they betray their brothers. The shortened ceremony is called 'Hanging the Blue Lantern' and consists of the reciting of a few poems or even just a simple affirmation. (The name derives from the Chinese custom of hanging a blue lamp outside the house of a recently deceased person and signifies that an initiate has died to his former life and has been reborn a Triad.)

When longer ceremonies do take place – as they still occasionally do in Hong Kong or, more often, in nearby Macao – they usually involve internal promotions as well as the induction of new members. But even these no longer follow the traditional forms. Over the last thirty years, less than half the initiates taken into Triad societies have undergone the complete traditional ritual. Today there is rarely a full complement of presiding officials and many elements of the old ritual, like the burning of the yellow gauze, have been dropped. Even when longer initiation ceremonies take place the procedures are often inaccurately followed. There is a Chinese saying which, loosely translated, states: 'When history dies, the future has no children.' For the Triads, history has long been buried.

In spite of police crackdowns, the Triads' street power remains formidable in Hong Kong and they have woven themselves into the very fabric of life amongst the Chinese community there. Take religious festivals, for instance. These are always major events for the Triads, who organize 'donations' from shopkeepers and members of the public, as well as publicly taking part in parades – often in front of visiting dignitaries. The Cheung Chau Bun Festival was for long presided over by the Wai Chow and Chiu Chau Triads. (The most important public festival for the Triads is in celebration of the god Kwan Ti, the Hung Society's governing deity.) In 1982, at the Tin Hau Festival, one of the largest public religious festivals, two groups of the 14K Triad and a

500-strong contingent of the Wo Shing Wo society attended the celebrations defiantly sporting their own T-shirts – a brazen flouting of the law which prohibits public advertisement of Triad membership.

Public services are another lucrative area for the Triads. When areas were set aside by the government for the erection of temporary shanty accommodation, the local Triads charged the squatters for constructing the houses. When the authorities responded by laying down foundations for each house and putting the building work out to an official contractor (who in any case was probably paying the Triads protection money) the Triads promptly set up decorating and utilities companies. The same scams were set up in the huge resettlement blocks, and these still continue.

In squatter areas – the shanty towns that cling to the hills surrounding Hong Kong – Triads often build the dwellings and charge for them. They also supply electricity from illegally tapped supplies. In one instance, when the electricity company provided power to an area in an attempt to thwart the Triads, the cables were dug up, replaced with Triad cabling, and the road resurfaced overnight. Water in these squatter areas is provided by stand-pipes which are swiftly commandeered by Triads who then either charge for its use or pipe it off to a tank and charge for connections.

Triad ticket touts will sell anything from football match tickets to members' badges for the prestigious Royal Hong Kong Jockey Club meetings and ferry tickets.

In the construction business, Triads control labour and extort protection money from firms. With manual labourers now in short supply, the Triads have started importing labour from China and elsewhere. They charge the labourer for finding him a job as well as charging the building site overseer for providing workers. In the markets and abattoirs the same kind of system operates. The Triads also maintain a variety of 'legitimate' front businesses, typically restaurants, nightclubs, and bars.

Gambling is a major source of Triad revenue and earns them millions of dollars annually. Their operations in this area include mah jong clubs, illegal casinos, card schools, and of course horse betting. As the operation against the 14K Ngai revealed, illegal bookmaking can turn over immense profits in a single race. Some Triad bookmakers have now moved their premises to Macao, forty-five miles from Hong Kong, where they can take bets on mobile radio-phones outside the jurisdiction of the Hong Kong authorities. Some bookies have even established themselves over the border in Communist China.

Loan sharking is also a standard Triad activity, though its incidence has reduced somewhat in recent years since the government gave its approval to the setting up of Deposit Taking Companies (DTCs), which lend money on less collateral than a bank might demand. But there will always be prey aplenty – inveterate gamblers in particular – for the Triad loan sharks.

In Hong Kong, of course, sex is big business, and most of that business is Triad-run. The legalized brothels, massage parlours, ballrooms, dance-halls, and escort agencies throughout the colony are largely Triad-owned and operated. With the rise in the general standard of living and the buoyancy of the employment market in Hong Kong, there are now fewer local girls so desperate for a job that they have to turn to prostitution; so the Triads are importing girls from Thailand, Burma, and the Philippines. Triad pimps also operate one-girl brothels using Filipino women who come to Hong Kong for work as domestic servants, waitresses, and a variety of other low-paid jobs.

Many of the traditional vice establishments run by the Triads have been closed down by the police, including the infamous 'fishball stalls' which were plentiful in Hong Kong in the 1970s and up to the early 1980s and so called because the girls' breasts were tiny, like the fishballs placed in soup, and because the act of kneading fishballs had its sexual equivalent. These were essentially under-age brothels whose punters could obtain girls as young as thirteen or fourteen. (During the heyday of the fishball stalls it was not uncommon for the full-time whores to be joined by girls from some of

Hong Kong's best schools seeking to augment their pocket money. It was not unknown for some school girls to offer 'quick time' services during their lunch break.)

Though the number of fishball stalls has been drastically reduced it is still possible to obtain under-age sex in Hong Kong, usually through establishments ostensibly calling themselves 'health clubs' or 'recreation clubs' which openly advertise in local newspapers as *hong lok chung sum*. In the Triad-run brothels of Yaumatei, an urban district largely dominated by Triad groups, even worse perversions are catered for. There, in the area around Temple Street, sex with 'freaks' – hunchbacks, blind or mute girls, and amputees – can be arranged. Pornography, especially videos, is another massive revenue earner for the Triads, whilst many of the sex toys sold in the West are Triad-made in Hong Kong. In the squalor and filth of Kowloon Walled City vibrators and dildos are turned out in vast quantities for export. In one small 'factory' they manufacture over a thousand surgical-pink latex penises a day.

Whatever entertainment Hong Kong has to offer, there will always be a Triad connection, from billiard halls and bars to night-clubs and electronic games halls. Not all of these are Triad-owned, but all of them are targets for Triad 'squeeze' (night-clubs, for instance, are forced to employ Triad bouncers). Down on the waterfront, the market known as the Poor Man's Night-Club is a favourite tourist haunt. Four Triad societies operate the market, though few tourists wandering amongst the cooked-food stalls and the fortune-telling finches realize this.

Hong Kong also has a thriving film and music industry. One well-documented case of Triad exploitation involved a famous Hong Kong film star who was working on location in the USA. He was contacted by the American Chinese crime syndicate, the Ghost Shadows, and was told that he had been chosen to star in a film to be financed by them, which he refused to do. The San Francisco offices of the company for which he was working were shot up and, on returning to Hong Kong, the actor received threats from a local Triad group. The incident demonstrates the links between Chinese gangsters overseas and Triads in Hong Kong, and there have been other examples where Chinese artists wishing to perform abroad have had to pay off local gangs to avoid having their bookings disrupted or cancelled altogether. Film and video distribution companies also fall prey to Triad pressure. Some are taken over completely by Triad management; others are used as a means of distributing Triad-produced pornography or pirated films. As always, few victims of Triad extortion actually go to the police. The prudent course is always to pay up and keep quiet. The penalties for resistance or disclosure vary from being beaten with heavy bamboo stakes or iron bars to being – literally – chopped to pieces with a meat cleaver and dropped into Hong Kong harbour.

The Triads also have a host of other money-making activities: illegal immigration documents, counterfeit currency, coin (now using sophisticated hydraulic stamping presses), and identity cards; and producing excellent replicas of Dunhill, Cartier, Hermès, and Rolex wrist-watches that are indistinguishable from the originals until the backs are unscrewed. (They keep excellent time.) Then there is tax evasion, money laundering, insurance and credit card fraud, and a multitude of other financial frauds.

All these activities bring in millions of dollars for the Triads – and that is without their income from drugs. The profits from Triad heroin dealing run into billions of dollars – larger than the gross national product of many Third World nations. This enormous financial muscle is what makes the Triads, in many people's eyes, so formidable a threat. The pessimists regard the Triads as being invincible, so entrenched are they in the life of Chinese communities all over the world. They are, indeed, part of the Chinese cultural fabric and, despite everything, ordinary Chinese everywhere are mostly resigned to Triad influences in their lives. Only when this attitude changes will law enforcement agencies stand a fighting chance of eradicating the Triads.

The criminal structure of Hong Kong consists of four main

groups: the Triads, other organized crime groups, youth gangs, and street gangs. The latter three are each manipulated by the Triads. The youth gangs are streetwise thugs and delinquents, the same as any urban environment engenders – petty criminals who are used by the Triads to bring in recruits and as temporary muscle. The street gangs are similar but are typically into more serious types of crime. Again, they provide the Triads with freelance muscle when the need arises. The organized crime groups are syndicates of criminals who are not affiliated to the Triads and who are engaged generally in fraud and other forms of white collar crime. Often, however, these groups have Triad members who act as liaison points between the two organizations.

Current estimates put the number of Triad societies operating in Hong Kong at between fifty and sixty, of which twenty are related in some way to the 14K group. (Not all of these are active societies, and only about a third figure regularly in police reports.) The single biggest Triad operating in Hong Kong is now the Sun Yee On, which has about 33,000 members divided into several hundred street gangs and youth groups, as well as some separate organized syndicates. (The Sun Yee On actually has a membership list: many others do not.) The number of members seems alarming, but it includes elderly Triads who may not now be involved in crime and the figure of 33,000 must be seen against the total population of Hong Kong, currently just over five million.

The fortunes of individual Triad groups in Hong Kong rise and fall with barometric speed. At one time the 14K predominated. Then came the Wo Shing Wo. Now the Sun Yee On seems to be in the ascendant. Shifting loyalties, the imprisonment or death of leading members, the emigration of other leaders to set up operations abroad – all these factors contribute to the power a particular society is able to wield. Today there are three main types of Triad societies in Hong Kong: those operating on an unstructured, unilateral basis with no established leadership or 'parent' Triad to oversee their activities; those structured on traditional lines with large numbers of office bearers each with an assigned role; and those organized on radically new lines. The latter type is particularly dangerous. Each has a designated leader and a small, closely-knit central committee. These Triads approach their criminal activities with a calculating, business-like efficiency. They are particularly adept at specialization – allocating specific types of crime to members who have particular skills or aptitude.

The complexion of Triad crime is now changing. Members from different societies are coming together to form syndicated groups in which the old Triad loyalties take second place to new priorities. Some of these syndicates may also include non-Triad members. The old ways are being rapidly forgotten as the Triads gear themselves up to expand their operations on a global scale. In the past, they have largely confined themselves to exploiting expatriate Chinese communities. Not any more. For the Triads, business is business.

7

TRIADS INTERNATIONAL

In Hong Kong the Triads are an integral part of the community and permeate virtually every aspect of life in the colony. On the face of it, it might appear that in other countries, where concentrations of Chinese immigrants are isolated from the indigenous culture, and therefore easily identified, it would be much easier for law enforcement agencies to curb Triad activities. In fact this is not the case, since local police forces, even international agencies, do not yet have the resources for coming to grips with the Triad threat.

Within Chinese communities abroad – London, Manchester, New York, San Francisco, Amsterdam, and elsewhere – the Triads' pattern of operation is the same as in Hong Kong: extortion, protection, gambling, vice, opportunist crime in general, and profit-turning sidelines such as the distribution of Chinese videos, books, and newspapers. They 'squeeze' their countrymen in Soho just as they do in Mongkok or Shamshuipo. But though their *modus operandi* remains the same, abroad it is far more difficult for police to infiltrate individual Triad groups and gather intelligence. For instance, London's Metropolitan Police has few ethnic Chinese officers (the 'Met' is understandably cautious about revealing the exact strength of its anti-Triad force), and those it does have tend to concentrate on areas like narcotics dealing and large scale fraud rather than comparatively petty street crimes such as protection rackets, even though these may often lead to assault or murder. As I write, there is still a dearth of properly trained police officers in central London, although there are at least two who have received training in anti-Triad policing by the Royal Hong Kong Police. But both of them are British, not Chinese, and can do little more than maintain a physical presence in London's Chinatown and attempt to gain the confidence of the local community there. This is minimal policing, to say the least, and will have no effect on increasing Triad activity in London.

The Triads no longer confine themselves to sucking the lifeblood from Chinese communities. As we have seen, they are now major players in international syndicated crime – indeed they are *the* major players, the scale of their operations making the Mafia look like amateurs. The key to this power is not street crime, lucrative though that is. Street crime provides the Triads with bread and butter income. The real money comes from drugs – heroin in particular.

Before the Second World War, cannabis and related drugs like hashish and marijuana were confined to small circles of users. Cocaine was the main illegal drug in the West and developed a glamorous image from its association with film stars, artists, and fictional characters like Sherlock Holmes. The public at large, however, especially in the affluent USA, settled for booze. During Prohibition, the demand for alcohol – easy to produce and distribute – made huge profits for organized criminals in America, and when opium was declared an illegal substance in Hong Kong after the Second World War the effect was the same, only this time the suppliers were the Triads and the use of opium soon led to the introduction of its more dangerous derivative, heroin.

As demand for heroin increased, so the power of the Triads as international suppliers grew, helped by the American Mafia who, with the ending of Prohibition, were looking for new sources of income. Drugs were the perfect answer. It was comparatively simple to set up a trafficking network: the drugs themselves were readily available; the business was self-generating as addiction amongst users increased; and the capital investment, measured against the final profits, was negligible. Even today, raw opium which costs a thousand dollars at source can be refined into heroin with a street value fifty times that, and this level of profit is continually increasing.

For the Triads, too, extending their opium operation was both logical and desirable. They had traditionally supplied the drug for opium dens and divans in the Far East, had operated large numbers of their own dens, and controlled the growing of opium poppies. Supplying heroin, both to local users and to satisfy an accelerating demand in the West, was the obvious next step.

Their supplies came from mountain areas in the so-called Golden Triangle (the four northernmost provinces of Thailand, the western boundary of Laos, and the Shan states of Burma), which is the source of at least 60 per cent of the world's heroin. This area has an indigenous population of around half a million, made up of the Meo, Yao, Lisu, Akha, and Lahu tribes, which are predominantly of Tibetan/Burmese stock (though the Meo and Yao are of Chinese ancestry). The economy of the region is based on agriculture, stock herding, hunting, and, over the last forty years, growing opium.

The Golden Triangle region has been the major Far Eastern source of the drug for centuries. In the 1930s, annual production was about forty tons, much of it channelled through Triad societies in China into the legitimate market but avoiding the tax levies. A decade or so later, the rising demand for heroin increased this output dramatically, since heroin requires more raw opium to produce (one kilo of opium refines into only ten grammes of heroin).

In 1950, after the Communists came to power in China, the Kuomintang General Li Mi (a former colleague of General Kot Siu Wong) fled to the mountains of the Golden Triangle with the routed 93rd Division, of which he was commander. Li quickly realized the commercial potential of the region's poppy fields and set about corrupting Thai officials to obtain control of the mountains. At the same time the US government, via CIA agents, were providing Li's Nationalist forces with money, supplies, and military advisers in an attempt to halt the growing Communist influence. In April 1951, Li's 93rd Division – now known grandly as the Yunnan Province Anti-Communist National Salvation Army – crossed into

China. It was resoundingly driven back into the mountains, and from then on Li Mi abandoned nationalism for the rewards of growing and marketing the opium poppy.

In collaboration with the commander of the Thai military police, General Phao Sriyanonda, Li Mi set up a distribution system for the raw opium, which was transported out of the tribal hill country by caravans of donkeys and coolies, escorted by his soldiers. The business prospered and after Li Mi's death was run by another Kuomintang general, Tuan Shih-wen, who claimed that the opium profits were being used to support anti-Communist resistance. There seems no evidence that this was so: Tuan and his men simply consolidated their own power in the Golden Triangle region. In the 1960s another Kuomintang officer, General Li Wen-huan, set himself up in the opium business, quickly followed by yet another, Lo Hsing-han. By this time the market for raw opium was so big that it could comfortably support three drugs barons in the Golden Triangle alone.

The political instability of Indo-China since the 1950s has meant that the production of raw opium and its derivatives has gone virtually unchecked, with the result that the Golden Triangle is now the world's major source of heroin – producing some 1500 tons of raw opium a year. The hill tribes who cultivate the opium poppies are, tragically, themselves consumers, and have no share in the vast profits being made. Opium has long been part of their lives – as a medicine, a component of religious ceremonies, and as a form of currency. Now they are often paid by the opium barons for their work in refined heroin, the resulting addiction ensuring a docile and undemanding labour force. Thirty years ago the raw opium was shipped out of the region for refining in laboratories in Thailand or Hong Kong – principally by Triad chemists. But by the late 1970s heroin was being processed at source, shipped out, and then distributed through Triad-operated networks known as 'mule-lines', the so-called mules being carriers who smuggled the drug overseas from distribution points in the Far East (such as Hong Kong, Bangkok, Singapore, and Kuala Lumpur) to London,

Left: The traditional Triad Society motto: Overthrow the Ch'ing and Restore the Ming – or overthrow the Manchu dynasty and restore the Chinese to the throne of China

Below: A seventeenth-century painting of a Triad ceremony, the lodge depicted as an entire building

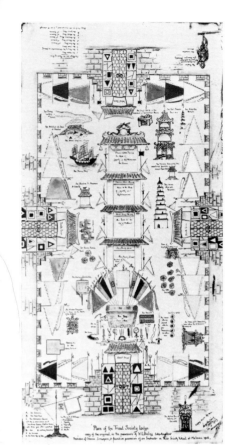

Left: A diagrammatic plan of the mystical journey of a Triad joining member, portrayed as a traditional Triad lodge: few lodges today are this detailed

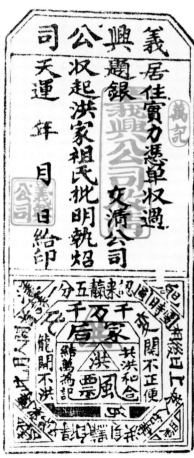

Right: A membership diploma from the Ghee Hin Society, dating from the 1870s

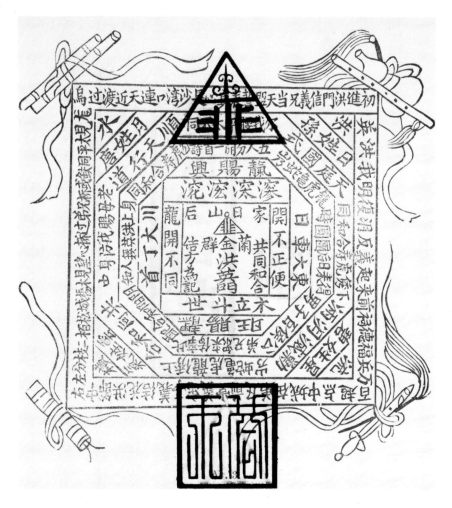

Above: A nineteenth-century Triad Society membership certificate: the overprinted seals are in brilliant scarlet

Right: A seal for the Ghee Hin Society, dating from the 1870s

Above: A legal Triad Society march, photographed in Hong Kong early in the twentieth century. Note the Indian Hong Kong Police constable escorting the parade

Left: Tu Yueh-sheng, *aka* Big-Eared Tu, the ruthless and brilliant leader of the Green Gang in Shanghai and the sponsor of Chiang Kai-shek, one of the most important, if shadowy, figures in modern Chinese history

Right: Kot Siu Wong, the Kuomintang Lt. General who was the founder of the 14K Triad Society in Canton

Below: Ng Sik-ho, *aka* Limpy Ho, being escorted from court in Hong Kong during his trial

Above: Chang Si Fu (Khun Sa) together with the deputy commander of his Shan United Army (10 January, 1982)

Left: The altar in a lodge, with two society officials, photographed by arresting police officers in the mid-1970s

Above: A Triad Society altar in a lodge. The photograph, taken in the 1950s and staged by the Hong Kong Police, shows a real altar captured in a raid. Note the complexity compared to the simple affair used in a ceremony in the 1970s

Right: Triad Society members discovered in a meeting by Hong Kong Police officers

Above: Hand signs at an altar

Left: Hand signs during a Triad ceremony. Notice the grass sandal on the left foot of the officer and the stance of the man on the left and the similarity of this to the craft Freemason's stance

Left: A police officer dressed in the uniform of an Incense Master

Right: The Incense Master at the altar

Left: Traditional Triad Society street-fighting weapons

Right: A Triad Society dismissal notice, excommunicating a disloyal member. Such a letter often precedes execution

Right: The Triad Society deity, Kwan Ti, photographed in the temple dedicated to him in Kowloon

Left: One pound of heroin artfully hidden within a tin of lychees

Above: Forty-two condoms, each containing 4 grams of heroin, removed during autopsy from the stomach and lower intestine of an American courier *en route* through Hong Kong in February, 1982. One condom burst whilst the courier was aboard an incoming jet, killing him

Below: A packet of opium, from the mid-1970s. Many drug shipments were made in brand name packaging

Right: A ship's fire
extinguisher and the
consignment of drugs it
contains

Below: A stuffed toy turtle
and its stuffing – Thai
sticks

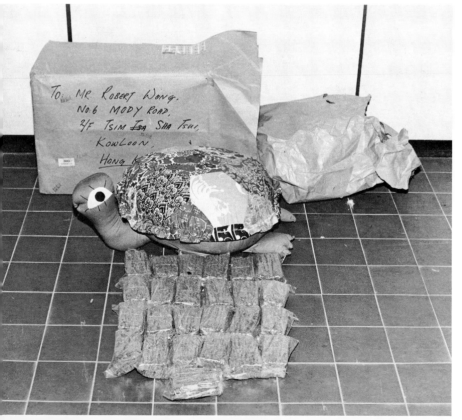

A street poster discouraging membership of Triad Societies

Above: Spectators at the ceremonial opening of a Chinese restaurant in Manchester in 1988. The T-shirts allegedly display membership of the Wo Shing Wo Triad society

Below: Edmund Louey, Cheung Yin-ng and Mr Poon, present-day members of the non-criminal, patriotic Mun Ji Dong Triad Society, in Melbourne in 1988: 'We are not a secret society, we are a society with secrets.'

Above: Old traditions resurface: protesting students in Tiananmen Square in Peking, shortly before the massacre of 1989, wear headbands just as the Red and Yellow Turbans did 2,000 years before

Below: A pro-democracy protester in Peking in 1989. As throughout history, the army was sent in to ruthlessly quell rebellion in the masses, organized by patriots threatening the 'throne'. The protester's shirt and headband are red. Does this man represent the birth of a new, patriotic system of Triad-like societies?

Amsterdam and Rotterdam, Hamburg, Marseilles, and the major cities of North America. The mules ranged from Chinese seamen and airline cabin crews to immigrant workers. Some were professional drugs couriers, others unknowing dupes.

The drug routes used were numerous and were constantly changed (they still are). In Hong Kong, for instance, the raw opium would arrive in bulk by sea, on a fishing junk or small coastal steamer, then be off-loaded into inshore vessels and run ashore in small loads. These would then be taken to a laboratory, usually situated outside the city. (Refining heroin in a built-up area is always a risky business because of the tell-tale smell the opium gives off in the process.) Often this is a temporary facility, perhaps set up in a forest clearing or a cave, which is closed down after a set weight of heroin has been prepared.

A variety of ingenious methods were developed for smuggling both processed heroin and raw opium in the early days before demand soared and bulk shipments became essential, including hollow shoe-heels, toothpaste tubes, wrist-watches, and bottles of soya sauce. Another well-known method was to wrap the drugs in condoms, which the courier then either swallowed or inserted into some other orifice – there have been several well-publicized cases of couriers suffering terrible deaths on inter-continental flights when the condoms in their intestinal tracts burst. For today's bulk shipments the traffickers use false-bottomed or false-sided cargo containers, the hollow centres of plastic toys and the packing of stuffed toys (of which Hong Kong is the world's greatest volume producer), double bulkheads in seagoing vessels, sealed air cargo containers, and, in some cases, diplomatic bags. An example of the last method occurred in 1971, when the new Laotian ambassador to France, Prince Sopsaisana of the royal house of Xieng Khouang, arriving at Orly airport in Paris, was discovered to be carrying sixty kilos of pure heroin (worth, at that time, over £8 million). The prince, who was also vice-president of the National Assembly of Laos, President of the Alliance

Française, and Chairman of the Laos Bar Association, had his credentials revoked and was sent back to Laos.

The key to the Triads' distribution system, once the heroin is safely landed, is the presence of expatriate Chinese communities, within each of which, regardless of where they are situated, the Triads operate virtually as they wish. Holland is one major example. After the Second World War, due to the widespread use of Chinese seamen on Dutch cargo vessels, several small Chinese communities sprang up in Rotterdam. These were composed mainly of Chinese from Malaya, Singapore, and the Dutch settlements in the East Indies. As ever, the Triads quickly colonized these communities and exploited them in the usual ways. After the War, when Indonesia gained its independence from the Dutch and as the Dutch colonial empire disintegrated, thousands of Chinese migrated to Holland and a Chinatown was established in Amsterdam. It was from there that the Triads controlled the distribution of heroin into Europe and beyond. Holland was ideally situated for their purposes. The Dutch police had only a small narcotics squad, and the legal penalties for drugs dealing were derisory: the maximum sentence for a serious conviction was only four years' imprisonment.

Heroin was first imported into Holland in 1965 and the trade expanded rapidly. From Amsterdam in particular it was redistributed throughout Europe. The main target, however, was American servicemen stationed in West Germany. Many of the two hundred thousand personnel had become heroin addicts whilst serving in Vietnam, where Laotian and Vietnamese criminals had made vast sums of money supplying drugs to the American troops. (There is even uncorroborated evidence that the Communist Chinese government, whilst overtly proscribing Triad societies on the mainland of China and taking stern measures against their activities, actually used Triads to supply drugs to the Americans in an attempt to undermine their military effectiveness.) US garrisons in West Germany and neighbouring cities – Heidelberg, Ulm, Frankfurt, Munich, Stuttgart, and

Wiesbaden – were flooded with high-grade heroin. Some US addicts also acted as couriers, shipping the drugs back to North America in military baggage.

As we have seen, this trade was controlled by the Mafia, who received their supplies from Chiu Chow Triad groups in Malaya and Hong Kong, who were in turn supplied by Thai sources. The kingpin was Limpy Ho, who established legitimate business as fronts and organized what was commonly known as the Dutch Connection. His withdrawal from the Dutch trade and subsequent imprisonment led to a bitter inter-gang struggle in Amsterdam to gain control of the immensely lucrative heroin business.

For several years, Amsterdam was the centre of Triad activity in Europe. Inevitably, one man emerged as top dog. Chung Mon – dubbed the 'Unicorn' – was a Cantonese, born in 1921. At the age of 16 he joined the Kuomintang, but after a year's service he left and, in 1938, arrived in Hong Kong. Within a few months he found a job as a cook on board a cargo vessel bound for Rotterdam. Once in Holland he either jumped ship or was signed off; at any rate, he lived in the Chinese community as an illegal immigrant throughout the German occupation of the Netherlands and married a Dutch woman. After the war he moved to Germany and opened a restaurant, but this venture failed, as did his marriage, and he returned to Amsterdam in 1969. There he opened another restaurant, the Si-Hoi, and a gambling establishment called the Yeun Wong, both financed by local Chinese businessmen – either because of Triad connections or because the investors were being 'squeezed'.

Shortly after the Yeun Wong opened there was a shooting incident and Chung Mon was arrested on suspicion. After being held for three months he was released for lack of evidence: the police were unable to find any witnesses prepared to testify against him. Despite his arrest, Chung Mon's relationship with the Amsterdam police was generally good and from time to time he turned informer on petty criminals and drugs traffickers within the Chinese community. He travelled widely using five passports – British,

Malaysian, Republic of China (Taiwanese), Indonesian, and even a Corps Diplomatique passport, all in fictitious names. In 1973 in Nevada (where he obtained a divorce from his first wife), he married a young Chinese woman called Chen Hsen, using a false name.

By this time Chung Mon was running several businesses. Besides the restaurant and gambling establishment, he owned a trading company and the Overseas Chinese Travel Service. All Chung's concerns had the same head office in Amsterdam: 105–6 Prins Hendrikkade. Within a short space of time Chung became conspicuously wealthy – far wealthier than these legitimate businesses could have made him. The Dutch police suspected him of being a Triad but had no proof (it seems probable that he was in fact a member of one of the 14K groups). The fact of Chung's having been in the Kuomintang is strongly suggestive of Triad connections, as is his role of arbiter in the inter-gang squabbles that broke out from time to time in Amsterdam's Chinatown. The respect he was given by the Chinese community is shown by his nickname, Fu Kee Lang – the Fearless One. This kind of respect is only given to a senior Triad leader.

The source of Chung's wealth was almost certainly the importation of heroin and the business was well established when Limpy Ho set his sights on Holland as a major distribution centre for the drug. Three of Ng Sik-ho's henchmen arrived in Amsterdam and set up a luxuriously appointed casino in competition to Chung, who tried to get the police to close it down. When this failed, a tip-off from Chung resulted in a police raid on the casino during which they discovered heroin hidden inside mah jong tiles imported from Hong Kong. Several arrests were made, but Limpy Ho's three representatives were not amongst them.

Annoyed at their escape, Chung took a trip to Hong Kong and is supposed to have gone to the police there to inform on Limpy Ho. This move supports the idea that Chung was not a lone operator, as the Dutch police believed, but was acting with the support of the 14K, which was strong in Amsterdam at this time and had crossed swords with Limpy Ho in Hong Kong. But retribution was swift and Chung Mon was gunned down outside his own restaurant in March 1975. He succeeded in naming his three assassins before he died, but the police were unable to gather any evidence against the killers. The only fact they could establish was that they were members of Ng Sik-ho's syndicate.

Chung Mon's murder finally forced the Dutch authorities to move against the Chinese gangsters and illegal immigrants began to flee overseas, some back East, but many Hong Kong Chinese with British passports moved across the English Channel to centres in the UK where the 14K Triad, in particular, was well established.

In Britain, as elsewhere, Triad societies have existed as long as there have been communities of Chinese immigrants. In the 1890s Triad societies were operating in Limehouse, in the dockland area of London's East End, where there was a substantial Chinese population mostly connected with the merchant navy, and by 1921 there was a lodge of the Ghee Hin Society in Liverpool, another seaport with a large Chinese community. These communities, and others like them, were self-contained and largely closed to outsiders. In Limehouse the Chinese had their own brothels, eating- and gambling-houses. Many Chinese seamen – the majority of which came from Hong Kong, Canton, and the Malay peninsula – were addicted to opium, which was not then an illegal substance in Britain, and indeed was still commonly used as a pain killer in the form of laudanum. But opium was not easy for expatriate Chinese to obtain – except through the services of the Triads.

For several decades, the Triads restricted their activities to within the expatriate communities. It was only with the expansion of the drug culture in the 1960s, and the appearance of heroin on the streets of Western capital cities, that the Triads began to reap substantial financial rewards from other sources. In the 1960s, too, there was a massive influx of Chinese, particularly from Hong Kong, into Britain; and with them came new Triad groups only too aware of the profits to be made from drugs.

The 14K was already in existence in Britain, though it is not known when or where the first lodge was set up. Today, it has three main centres of power: London, Liverpool, and Bristol. There are few hierarchical or organizational links between the 14K in Britain and in Hong Kong – or anywhere else, for that matter. A 14K group in London, or Bristol, or New York is not a splinter group of the parent organization in Hong Kong (unlike a Mafia 'family' in Las Vegas, which may be related by command structure and blood ties to a 'godfather' in Chicago): it is a self-sufficient body in its own right. A 14K Triad from Hong Kong cannot simply arrive in London and expect to be welcomed by the local 14K brotherhood unless he becomes a member. There is no automatic fraternity between Triads as there is, for instance, between legitimate organizations like the Freemasons. Links between Triad groups in Hong Kong or Malaya and those abroad are founded purely on self-interest. The 14K in Hong Kong may supply heroin for 14K groups in London; but this is not a case of brotherly support, merely dealer selling to dealer for the mutual financial benefit of both parties.

Pure No. 4 heroin began to arrive in London in significant quantities in 1971. Previously heroin had been available in a less pure form known as Brown Sugar (made famous by the Rolling Stones' hit record of that name), which was smoked widely within Chinese communities but was not common on the streets. It is still not known which Triad group was responsible for the introduction of the purer form. Possibly it was the 14K, though it may have been the Wo Shing Wo, which was also well established in the UK by this time. What is certain is that it came to Britain as a consequence of Limpy Ho's drive to control the world trade in the drug.

The British police were completely unprepared for what was to come, despite being vigorously forewarned by the American Drug Enforcement Administration (DEA), then known as the Federal Bureau of Narcotics and Dangerous Drugs, and by the FBI. These agencies knew that much of the heroin now pouring into the USA was passing through Britain. The US government had even established an officer at the

American Embassy in London whose role was to infiltrate drug trafficking operations and track down couriers. Though he worked with the full co-operation of the UK's minuscule Drug Squad, the British authorities were shocked by his methods, which included paying informers to pose as buyers and, using large sums of federally-provided money, actually buying quantities of drugs in order to establish their *bona fides* with the suppliers.

In 1973 the Drug Squad's senior officer was charged with conspiracy to pervert the course of justice in a drugs case brought against a Pakistani family. Though acquitted, the officer resigned from the force on grounds of ill health. Several others were found guilty of perjury and still others were transferred to other units. In the space of a few months the Drug Squad, never a substantial unit, had lost its most experienced officers. It took two years to rebuild the squad, during which time the Triads took full advantage of this disarray.

In Hong Kong during the same period the anti-corruption drive was in full swing. This resulted in large numbers of corrupt Chinese officers being arrested or fleeing the colony. Many senior Triads also decided this was an appropriate time to leave Hong Kong and head for Britain. In order to enter the UK, the passports of Chinese seamen were 'borrowed', sent to Hong Kong, where false photographs were inserted, and brought back to Britain by the new Triad holders. The photographs were then replaced and the seamen had their passports returned, allowing them to return to work. The logistics of this operation were simplified by the fact that the Hong Kong seamen's union had been run by the Triads since the nineteenth century.

The 14K leaders who settled in Britain soon established lodges with a full hierarchical structure, including all the traditional office-bearers, in every major city where there was a Chinese community. In many of these they came up against the already established interests of the Wo Shing Wo, and the inevitable gang wars broke out. This conflict came to public attention in February 1976 when a 14K revenge squad broke into a basement flat in Gerrard Street, Soho, used as a gambling den. The attackers were looking for the killers of a certain Kwok Li, from Holland, who, it was rumoured, had been involved in the murder of Chung Mon. The men they were looking for were not there, but the father of one of them – a restaurateur from Essex called Kam Wong – was. He died as a result of a kung-fu kick.

As usual the police could make little progress in their investigations. No one would speak. (The dead man was supposed to have fallen down the stairs.) Eventually, however, the police established the names of the attackers: one was Kwok Shui-li from Burnham-on-Sea; the other three, all with the surname Kwok, came from the Home Counties. But catching them was another matter. Through family connections the gang made their way first to Belfast, where they stayed in a safe house owned by a restaurateur, and then to Dublin, where they were bankrolled. Two then travelled to Belgium and subsequently on to Holland, whilst the others kept their heads down in Larne for a month. Eventually they gave themselves up and were found guilty of manslaughter.

This case, with its arabesques and intrigues, was an eye-opener for the British police. Here was a professional gangster unit operating in Britain from within a supposedly quiet and law-abiding community; that was able, moreover, to escape into a network of safe houses and be supported financially by apparently respectable members of that community. It was soon after the Kam Wong murder that the British realized that they needed to recruit Chinese police officers to combat the growing problem of Triad crime. A Royal Hong Kong Police detective, Superintendent Douglas Lau, was flown in, but by the time his plane touched down in London a Triad-affiliated police officer had tipped off British Triads of Lau's arrival, which was made much of in the press. In spite of this, Lau brought with him extensive knowledge of Triad organization and activities and emphasized the crucial role of infiltration. Lau's plan was to train Metropolitan policemen disguised as 'hippies' to become part of London's underground drugs scene and thus put them in the best position for meeting Triad dealers. This strategy of infiltration remains a key part of the Hong Kong police's fight against the Triads. (Undercover officers in Hong Kong are known irreverently amongst their colleagues as *fai jai* – Cantonese slang for a spiv. In London during the late 1970s the hippy undercover officers were nicknamed The Unwashables.)

In Britain, however, infiltration is far more difficult than in Hong Kong. In a relatively small, tightly-knit community like London's Chinatown, a new Chinese face is quickly noticed and a background story easily checked with sources in Hong Kong or Singapore. A European face is even more obvious, although the end-user or buyer of Triad-supplied drugs is generally non-Asiatic and so some degree of acceptance is possible. But actually penetrating the supply network itself is both difficult and dangerous.

The British authorities do now have established modes of infiltration, though they are understandably reluctant to disclose them. They probably involve a combination of paid informers, Chinese undercover agents, and a small network of intelligence gatherers within the Chinese community. One of their early successes was the downfall of May Wong – the leader (highly unusual for a woman) of a Triad group, a Malaysian society called the Guat San Sih.

With their land access to the Golden Triangle, the Malaysian Triads have convenient supply routes for their heroin stocks, though this geographical advantage is offset by the risks they now run. The once utterly corrupt Thai government has become a byword for severity in relation to drugs-related crimes, whilst the Singapore authorities regularly impose the death penalty on dealers and traffickers, regardless of their nationality – in recent years, Chinese, Malays, and Europeans have all received the death sentence.

In 1976 the Guat San Sih sent two dealers to Britain to establish a niche in the expanding market for heroin. One was Li Jarfar Mah; the other was Mrs Shing Moori Wong, known by the European name of May Wong. The society's drugs operation had been run by another Malay Chinese, Chin

Keong Yong, who had been running a street narcotics trade in London. Chin had come over from Amsterdam in 1972 and his supplies came from Thailand via Singapore or Kuala Lumpur through Amsterdam. He had made a lot of money but he was also a gambler. When he gambled away a significant amount of the society's funds it was decided to replace him. Since he had broken his Triad oaths, replacement was virtually a death sentence, and to protect himself Chin committed a series of robberies in the hope of getting caught (he reasoned that he would be safer in a British prison than on the streets). He was duly arrested and, in 1976, was sentenced to fourteen years for importing narcotics. For a time this put a stop to the Guat San Sih's drugs business in London, but within months of Li and Wong's arrival it was thriving once more.

Li Mah was an experienced and skilled street operator, and an equally accomplished smuggler. May Wong was a more enigmatic figure, the daughter of a wealthy bullion dealer allegedly assassinated by a Triad group in 1971. At her trial she claimed in her defence that she became a drugs dealer in order to discover the identity of her father's murderers and avenge his death. Educated at Roedean, she was a pretty and intelligent young woman. After leaving school she set up a successful beauty salon and a boutique in Singapore and then became a night-club hostess. Li Mah, handsome and capable, was said to be her lover.

They travelled regularly to Amsterdam together to arrange for supplies to be delivered – cash on arrival – in London, which cleverly spared them the necessity of arranging for mules from the Far East and then couriers from Holland. Once safely delivered, the drugs were distributed – the pair used a few of Chin Keong Yong's street pushers but relied mainly on their own Singaporean Chinese pushers, who were unknown to the police.

The police, however, soon began to keep tabs on the pair as a result of a former associate of Chin Keong Yong, a London boutique owner called Molly Yeow. For some time before his arrest the police had been maintaining close surveillance on

Chin and had built up a large dossier of information on him and his activities. Once Li Mah and May Wong were seen with Molly Yeow and another of Chin's associates, Chi Sang, the conclusion was obvious. A raid on Molly Yeow's flat in Kentish Town produced notebooks of names, addresses, and dates. The notebooks indicated substantial earnings from drugs and also gave the address of the distribution centre in Islington from which the heroin was issued to the street pushers. Molly Yeow, Li Mah, and other members of the group were arrested, but May Wong was in Singapore at the time and had to be tricked back to the UK with a message that her two associates had been badly injured in a car crash. She was arrested on arrival in London and a search of her flat revealed that she possessed two handguns, one of which had been recently fired. In all, fourteen people were brought to trial. Li Mah and May Wong received sentences of fourteen years, Molly Yeow received ten years, an Australian associate five and a half years.

The Triad control of the UK heroin trade was by now well known to the police, but the arrest rate of major offenders remained – and remains – low. Large amounts of the drug still flood into Britain, in spite of anti-drugs campaigns, the fear of AIDS, and increasingly effective police and customs seizure operations. One reason is the adaptability and increasing sophistication of the Triads' smuggling operation. They no longer use Chinese airline staff or passengers as mules, but Europeans – either knowingly or unwittingly (the latter have their bags tampered with in hotel rooms or at airports). Some are persuaded by Chinese 'friends' to carry supplies; some mules are addicts themselves; others are young people hoping to make a fast buck, or holidaymakers willing to take a risk in order to recoup their vacation costs and make a profit. The men – and women – who organize these smuggling operations are a new breed, no longer streetwise Chinese from the alleys of Kowloon Walled City or the backstreets of Hong Kong or Singapore, but educated, highly intelligent and commercially astute, with the same qualities of mind and outlook that might otherwise make them successful bankers or stockbrokers.

Despite the increasing effectiveness of police and customs undercover work, large quantities of heroin are still being imported into the British Isles by the main Triad groups – the 14K, which has a number of active societies in the UK; the Wo Shing Wo, whose headquarters are in Manchester but which has allied groups in London, Liverpool, Birmingham, and Glasgow; and the Shui Fong, another powerful society based in London and Southampton. Rivalry between these groups over the division of territory is intense and there have been several Triad gang murders in recent years (in 1987, for instance, a Triad hit man based in Nottingham was arrested and convicted). The gang battles and killings are carried out by trained Triad fighters brought over from Hong Kong as illegal immigrants, usually arriving via Eire. Some are Chinese, some Vietnamese. (Hong Kong is home for large numbers of Vietnamese refugees, and in some parts of the colony over 60 per cent of street crimes are committed by Vietnamese – a staggeringly high figure in view of the small proportion they form of the total population.)

In Cardiff, Nottingham, Glasgow, Bristol, and Belfast, the struggle between rival Triad gangs is particularly bitter, with the once dominant Wo Shing Wo being challenged by the Shui Fong. As police reaction to the Triads intensifies, the societies 'squeeze' local Chinese communities all the harder in order to maintain face and income from street crime. The Wo Shing Wo, for instance, controls many aspects of life in the Chinese community of Manchester, their members known to openly flaunt T-shirts emblazoned with the society's insignia. Their grip on the market for Chinese labour bites particularly hard: many young Chinese cannot find employment without Triad membership, and the Wo Shing Wo can easily ruin a firm by withholding workers or by terrorizing employees into resigning.

The same pattern is repeated elsewhere. Triads control at least 50 per cent of the lucrative Chinese video and music market; they own shops, restaurants, and a wide variety of legitimate businesses, as well as running an equally wide range of illegal interests – from gambling, franchise frauds, and copyright infringement to labour and immigration rackets (the latter providing them with a source of drug couriers), protection rackets, prostitution, and, of course, drug dealing.

Except for drug trafficking, which impinges seriously on those outside the Chinese community, most Triad crime in Britain is carried out at street level within the ethnic enclaves. But this is changing. Triad groups in Hong Kong are transferring more and more funds to British banks, not only to avoid detection by the Hong Kong authorities but also in preparation for 1997. In 1985 a parliamentary committee reached the unequivocal conclusion that the Triads posed no significant threat in the UK. How wrong they were is now becoming frighteningly clear.

The history of the Triads in America follows a similar pattern to its development in the UK and shows an inexorable expansion into organized crime over the last forty years. Before the Second World War, as in Hong Kong, Amsterdam, London, and elsewhere, Triad societies flourished solely within the Chinese communities from which they drew their members and on whom they relied for their funding. At this period they still operated as welfare organizations with patriotic as well as criminal undertones. The American expatriate Chinese population is far larger than any other in the world, and generally wealthier. It thus provided the Triads with even greater opportunities both for applying 'squeeze' and for securing donations in support of patriotic causes. It was to the American Chinese communities that Sun Yat-sen looked for funds, and Chiang Kai-shek also made appeals to American Chinese (and to the US government) to support the Nationalist Kuomintang forces.

With the global increase in narcotics trafficking in the 1950s and 1960s the Triads came into their own. The drug trade in the USA was firmly under the control of the Mafia, who relied on two sources for their supplies: the Golden Triangle and Asia Minor, then a key area. But the Mafia were outsiders and needed local agents or go-betweens –

sometimes Europeans or Australians with specialist knowledge and the right contacts, but more often Chinese, Thai, or Malay Chinese gangsters. For all their muscle, the Mafia were unable to purchase direct from the prime sources.

In 1972 the whole system was badly hit when the growing of the opium poppy was banned in Turkey. Until then crime syndicates in Corsica had purchased opium base in Turkey to be shipped to Marseilles, where it was refined prior to its being smuggled into America. This was the celebrated 'French Connection', eventually smashed by American and French agencies. The opium base was then shipped from Turkey through the Lebanon, where it was refined in Beirut. The proceeds of the trade were responsible for financing the sectarian factions that have torn that country apart ever since, though the fighting that closed Beirut airport has at least severed another drug route to the West.

It was the Corsican syndicates who introduced the Mafia to the Triads. Corsican criminals had long had interests in what was then French Indo-China (Vietnam), and they remained in the region after the French withdrawal in 1954 in an unsuccessful attempt to control the drug routes from Thailand through Saigon to Hong Kong and Malaya. Their failure to do so was due to the intervention of Chiu Chau Triad societies in Vietnam. The arrival of American troops provided an enormous on-the-spot market, as well as easy access back to America. In the theatre of war itself drugs of every kind were available to US service personnel: cannabis, marijuana and opium for smoking, heroin for injection – much provided by Chiu Chau Triads operating in Saigon and even within military installations outside the capital.

Hong Kong was a favourite 'Rest and Recreation' (R & R) destination for American servicemen and the Triads there made vast profits from brothels and bars. The latest *Billboard* Top Ten records drew in custom as effectively as the pimps and bar touts who worked the streets by the US Navy landing pier, and a rating would often get his drinks, his girl for the night, and his drugs in exchange for records 'liberated' from the mess-deck jukebox. With the cessation of hostilities in

Vietnam heroin continued to pass through the country from Burma and Thailand en route for the USA (today almost all the heroin consumed in America is of Thai origin), supplied to Mafia importers and distributors by the Triads. The route used was via the Philippines and South America (especially Paraguay, Panama, Colombia, and Venezuela), sometimes through Europe. The South American route was organized by a Corsican called Auguste Ricord, a Nazi collaborator who had fled to Argentina in 1945 and who was sentenced to death in France *in absentia*. For a while Ricord was involved with the French Connection; then, in 1970, he met some associates of Ng Sik-ho's in Japan and set up a distribution network for the supply of heroin to the USA through Rio de Janeiro to Asunción, where Ricord owned a hotel and a restaurant. Between 1967 and 1982 it is estimated that Ricord smuggled over five tons of heroin into the USA, making him the country's major importer of the drug. The downfall of Limpy Ho also rooted out Ricord, who was finally extradited from Paraguay in 1976 after the Americans threatened to cut off all financial aid.

With Ricord's arrest, the Triads and the Mafia changed tack. Panama, with its slack narcotics regulations, ineffectual policing, and its Canal conveying over twenty thousand vessels a year, offered ideal smuggling conditions and now became the focus for moving heroin into the USA. The importers also had the advantage of a compliant government. In 1971 the son of the Panamanian ambassador to Taiwan was arrested at Kennedy Airport in New York with seventy kilos of heroin in his baggage. His uncle, Guillermo Gonzalez, was also arrested. It was later estimated that between them they had smuggled in over half a ton of heroin.

Other routes into the USA include Hawaii, where there is a large oriental population, and the west coast ports of Canada, where many ex-Hong Kong police officers who fled the anti-corruption drives of the 1970s now live – mostly illegally. Many of these have maintained their Triad contacts in Hong Kong and some have established their own societies in Vancouver, Victoria, and over the US border in Seattle.

Until the crackdowns of the 1980s, the Canadian Chinese dealt through Mafia contacts. This collaboration began after the Mafia withdrew from associating directly with the Hong Kong Triads when two of Ng Sik-ho's men were arrested in the USA, but with the drastic reduction of Mafia power over recent years the balance has shifted decisively in favour of the Chinese groups in North America – though there are indications that the old-time mobsters are exploring ways of collaborating on an organized basis with the new Chinese criminals. In weakening the Mafia the authorities have, ironically, allowed the Triads to dominate the North American drugs market – not just in heroin and opium, but in other types of narcotics, such as Thai sticks (small bars of marijuana that have been immersed in hot opium). Both the FBI and the DEA are now having to respond rapidly to this new and even greater threat. Over the winter of 1987/88 the FBI transferred thirty of its agents from Mafia surveillance in New York's Little Italy to Triad-watching in Chinatown. During the same period, the DEA doubled its Chinese specialist force in New York to over twenty-five officers in an attempt to combat the Chinese dominance of New York's heroin market: in 1987 the Chinese share of this rose from 40 to 60 per cent. They are now believed to control the market completely.

Besides narcotics, the New York Triads also run the usual extortion and protection rackets against Chinese businesses in the city, and generally impose their rule on the ethnic community in the same ways as their counterparts in Hong Kong. (As in Hong Kong in the 1960s, Chinese gangsters in New York now have corrupt police officers on the payroll.) Gambling is another major area of their business, as are upmarket brothels, which are becoming increasingly popular with non-Chinese clientele. Many of the girls are immigrants and are kept virtually as slaves – to make sure they stay put, their passports are confiscated. The majority come from Taiwan (Taiwanese girls are said to be naturally subservient), though the Triads also employ Thai girls – less docile but usually having thinner waists and bigger breasts (a Western preference). The Taiwanese girls are enticed to America – known in Taipei, Taiwan's capital, as 'The Mountain of Gold' – as a means of escaping from poverty or menial jobs at home. They undertake to repay their fare from their earnings, and of course their employers contrive that they remain in debt to them for as long as they continue to attract punters. The girls may be sent to other Triad-owned brothels elsewhere in America and, as a number of the New York brothels are owned by Triad drug dealers, the girls are also used as couriers – for instance, they are sent across the USA-Mexico border with heroin in their baggage or on (or in) their person.

Within New York City's Precinct 5 (Chinatown) there are three tongs, as the secret societies are known colloquially, whose control of the Chinese business community in the city is total. According to the New York Police Department, one of these – the Hip Sing Tong, with its strong-arm unit of 49s known as the Flying Dragons – is fronted by the Hip Sing (NY) Federal Credit Union. Another, the On Lee Ong, also has a fighting unit, the Ghost Shadows. These two groups are in permanent contention over territorial rights, but the situation has worsened with the rise of another Triad, the Tung On, believed to be affiliated to the Sun Yee On in Hong Kong, who seem bent on gaining control of Chinatown and have already murdered a leader of the Flying Dragons.

Whether New York's Chinese criminals can be regarded as authentic Triads is debatable: it is not clear, for instance, how much emphasis is placed by them on the traditional initiation ceremonies and lodge rituals. Many undoubtedly make use of traditional secret signs and coded phrases, and their contacts with Far Eastern Triads, from whom they receive their heroin supplies, are good. These supplies include a new, cheaper heroin – known as China White, which has been responsible for increasing numbers of deaths amongst addicts and can be smoked, not injected.

The scale of Triad involvement in drugs in the USA is shown by several well-publicized recent incidents. In December 1987 three Chinese were arrested in the Queens

district of New York. Their car had been tailed from
Kennedy Airport, where they had arrived on a Flying Tigers
flight from Bangkok. The car was found to contain $1 million
and 165 pounds of heroin – at that time the fifth biggest haul
in America. In February 1988 a group of six Thais and Hong
Kong Chinese were arrested for smuggling heroin into the
USA worth $165 million. The drug was hidden in hollow
terracotta figures also shipped on a Flying Tigers flight from
Bangkok. The following month the DEA nailed their most
wanted drugs leader, a Chinese businessman called Kon Yu-
leung, also known as Johnny Kon. It is alleged that he has
smuggled heroin into the USA worth over $2 billion at street
value.

These successes, however, only highlight how much needs
to be done. Undercover work is essential; but so is public
awareness – always a powerful weapon against the Triads, as
the police in Hong Kong have demonstrated. The more the
Triad threat is publicized and discussed, the easier it will be
for law enforcement agencies to combat them effectively. In
any case, undercover work is still extremely difficult, even in
America. American agencies may have the apparent
advantage of ethnic officers, but in practice they face the same
difficulties as undercover agents elsewhere since American-
born Chinese often do not speak any Chinese dialect, and in
New York's Chinatown alone there are twelve different
dialects spoken.

Like the UK, Australia, and elsewhere, the impending
change of sovereignty in Hong Kong in 1997 is viewed with
disquiet by the American authorities, who recognize that
1997 will see an exodus of legal immigrants from the colony
that will provide both additional manpower and criminal
opportunities for the Triad groups who are already well
entrenched in the USA. And although the international trade
in cocaine is at present controlled by South American barons,
many people wonder, not if, but when the Triads will take
this over, too. The situation was summed up by a former head
of the FBI in New York, who observed in late 1987 that the
Chinese gangs in the city were at the same stage of develop-

ment as the Italian mobsters were in 1919 when the National Prohibition Act was enacted. Prohibition caused the Italian mobs to go corporate. The expectation is that the Chinese criminal societies will do the same.

When Mao Tse-tung's Communist forces finally defeated the Nationalist Kuomintang, one of their first moves was to make the growing of opium illegal – indeed a ban had already been imposed in those areas previously controlled by the Communists (in 1927 a commander in Mao's army, an ex-addict called Chu Teh, publicly incinerated ten thousand pounds of raw opium). The reason for the Communist prohibition was twofold. Firstly, they wished to reduce the appalling level of opium addiction amongst the people (in the mid-1920s there were an estimated fifteen million addicts in China). Secondly, the opium trade was controlled by the Triads, who were sympathetic to the Nationalist cause and who still, at this time, functioned partly as welfare organizations. The Communists clearly could not tolerate such a potentially dangerous political force to flourish at grass roots level, and Mao consequently set about cutting off a key source of income for the Triads and pursued a vigorous policy to eradicate them altogether.

Sun Yat-sen had also decided to make the growing of opium illegal in order to reduce China's addiction problem, though his revolution had failed before he could effect this. It is interesting to speculate how his Triad supporters would have reacted to this. Chiang Kai-shek similarly announced his intention to abolish the use of opium but quietly made no mention of poppy cultivation itself, since the ex-Triad office bearer derived useful income from opium interests.

There was, then, open hatred between the Communists and the Triads, an ideological gulf that simply could not be bridged. In 1927, the year Chiang Kai-shek came to power, a Communist-inspired workers' strike took place in Shanghai that was ruthlessly suppressed by Big-Eared Tu's men with arms obtained from the foreign concessions. Thousands of Chinese were massacred, including hundreds of innocent bystanders. Events like this made subsequent reconciliation impossible, and when the Communists came to power huge numbers of Triads and Kuomintang soldiers with Triad connections fled to Malaya, Laos, Burma, French Indo-China, Hong Kong, Macao, and Taiwan (Formosa) to escape inevitable retribution. But not all were able to escape, or indeed willing to leave their families or businesses, and went into hiding. The Communists were implacably thorough in their attempts to root out anyone associated with the Triads, who were also frequently denounced by those on whom they had previously preyed. When caught, rank and file Triads were usually sent for political re-education and rehabilitation; more senior members were either summarily shot or put through show trials before being executed.

But the source of the Triads' power remained: opium. In 1950 Chou En-lai ratified a government order that totally banned the cultivation of poppies and the smoking of opium, and rehabilitation schemes were set up for addicts. The youth of the new China were clearly informed about the evils of opium, whilst land on which opium poppies had been cultivated was seized from its owners and handed over to peasant farmers as part of the massive land reforms that took place in the early years of Communist rule. As an indication of the prevailing mood, in 1951 a festival was held in Canton to celebrate the centenary of the seizing of twenty thousand chests of Indian-grown opium in the city by the Prefect of Kwantung. Fifty thousand people attended the celebrations, including four thousand ex-addicts who were publicly lauded for breaking their drug habit.

If the victims of addiction were treated sympathetically by the Communist regime, drug dealers and traffickers received no mercy. Anyone convicted of growing or distributing opium was sentenced to death, and throughout the 1950s and 1960s many executions were carried out, mainly in the south and particularly involving members of the 14K. No mercy was shown to anyone involved in drugs: the authorities killed them when they caught them, expropriated their property, and destroyed the poppy fields. The result was that by the mid-1960s opium addiction was virtually stamped out in China. From the millions of wretched sufferers in the 1920s the number of addicts had been reduced to an estimated twenty-five thousand. The policies were severe, but effective, and they must be replicated if the world community wishes to put an end to the evils of drug dealing: the poverty that forces peasants to cultivate opium poppies must be eradicated; alternative crops must be forcibly introduced; traffickers and dealers must automatically expect to be treated with the utmost severity; and sequestration of all assets deriving from drug dealing must be standard.

But China still has a Triad problem, and it is increasing – particularly in the south. In the areas relatively close to Hong Kong, Triads formerly based in the colony are returning to China due to much relaxed cross-border restrictions on travel and are setting up familiar Triad operations – gambling, labour racketeering, prostitution, extortion, and pornography. The Chinese public security minister, Wang Fang, has publicly denounced the 'decadent bourgeois ideology' of Hong Kong that has allowed its criminal element to flourish and which is now spilling over its borders. The crime rate in southern China increased by 4 per cent in the year 1987–8, with serious crimes showing a massive 65 per cent jump. Like the West, China, too, is having to come to grips with what is literally a Triad invasion.

The Chinese authorities are also facing a re-emergence of the opium problem. For the first time since Chou En-lai's ban, opium poppies are once more being cultivated in China, under the sponsorship of Hong Kong based Triads and the drugs barons of the Golden Triangle. The poppies are being grown in isolated plantations in south-western China and the opium base is then transported through Burma to Thailand, where it is refined into heroin by Hong Kong trained chemists. Police raids in October and November 1988 uncovered the main laboratory for the operation containing Chinese-language textbooks and chemicals manufactured or purchased in Hong Kong.

Amongst the many factions involved in this network is one

run by a pro-Kuomintang ethnic Chinese called Laolee Sai-
lee, and this in turn is connected – perversely – with the
Burmese Communist Party (BCP), which deals in drugs to
finance its opposition to the Burmese government. The BCP
is no longer officially supported by the Chinese government
(though it does receive Chinese arms), but its contacts in
China are believed to help provide overland routing for
heroin from Thailand to Hong Kong. The most powerful of
the present Golden Triangle barons is the self-styled 'Opium
King', General Kuhn Sa (meaning 'The Prince of
Prosperity'), who presides over a 15,000-man force (the Shan
United Army). Political instability in Burma has allowed
Kuhn Sa's activities to flourish and he now controls something like half of all the opium grown in the Golden Triangle.
But Kuhn is only a part of an enormous criminal economy
based on the opium poppy. The 1988 harvest has been
estimated at some 2000 tons of raw opium at source. The
gigantic revenues that this harvest will eventually produce
will fuel Triad activities worldwide, resulting in untold
human misery and degradation. The whole Golden Triangle
system of cultivation, transportation, and refining is financed
by Triads; Triad-trained chemists oversee the refining operations and train local chemists; Triads handle the onward
distribution and further refine the Thai heroin into even more
powerful forms.

As far as the global community is concerned, the Triads are
Public Enemy Number One. Law enforcement agencies all
around the world have been slow to recognize the sheer scale
of the Triad threat. It is now time – if indeed it is not already
too late – for something to be done.

8

FIGHTING THE TRIADS

The first step in any attempt to eradicate the Triads must be to destroy their principal breeding ground in Hong Kong, which – although the Triads are not a single unified group – is to all intents and purposes the international 'headquarters' of Triad activity. Triad societies throughout the world look to Hong Kong as their spiritual home, and it is through Hong Kong that the Triads operate their international drug business and money-laundering operations. Hong Kong offers a perfect environment for the Triads to thrive: financially, politically, and geographically. It is not enough to strike at individual Triad members: the Triad menace will only be overcome by destroying the conditions that currently encourage their expansion and by creating in its place an environment that is intrinsically inimical to their activities.

The government of Hong Kong is acutely aware of the problems created by having the Triad heartland under its administrative control and is actively developing counter-measures for dealing with the Triads. For some time it has been running an effective advertising campaign against them, including street posters warning people about the full cost of Triad membership. The press is fully briefed on the nature and extent of Triad crimes, whilst television advertisements caution viewers – in particular teenagers – against associating with Triad groups. Teenage members are eagerly sought by the Triads, who require a continual supply of low-ranking troops who can be thoroughly inculcated with the Triad ethos from an early age. Countering Triad street recruitment is therefore seen as a crucial part of the government's counter-measures against the gangs.

The Immigration Department is also in the front line of the fight against the Triads since it has to deal directly with the Triads' illegal immigration rackets, their forging of travel documents and passports, and their control of illegal immigrants in Hong Kong – known colloquially as *Eye-Eyes*. For instance, in recent years Triad-dominated syndicates have been uncovered importing Thai, Malay, and Filipino girls into Hong Kong to work either in the brothels or as domestic servants. The Customs and Excise Department wages constant war against the Triads' narcotics operations and has to police the busiest harbour in the Far East (the second busiest in the world, with a greater container cargo traffic than Rotterdam and a busier sea-lane system than the English Channel). The CED also controls the busiest international airport in the Far East and is responsible for the fight against copyright infringements and the lucrative counterfeiting of consumer goods.

The third agency actively involved in fighting the Triads is the Independent Commission Against Corruption (the ICAC). It is an independent, non-government organization established in 1974 to combat the enormous amount of corruption – much of it Triad-related – that was then rife in government and particularly the police. The ICAC cannot prosecute offenders without the express sanction of the Attorney-General. It employs about 1000 officials in three categories: operations, prevention of corruption, and public relations. These officials, who have a wide range of powers, are overseen by a complex system of advisory committees and other safeguards to protect them from outside interference. Civil servants must, at the request of the ICAC, make a declaration regarding the property they own, expenditure, liabilities, and earnings from all sources; they also have to respond on behalf of their spouses, dependants, and relatives. Anyone suspected of corruption can be forced to relinquish their passports and the ICAC also has the power, with the approval of a magistrate, to freeze assets.

Since its inception the ICAC has eradicated virtually all syndicated corruption in the government of Hong Kong and has now turned its attention to non-governmental corruption – and here it comes up directly against the Triads. In this arena the powers of the ICAC pose a major threat to the Triad societies, in particular the ICAC's ability to probe corporate and financial corruption – stock market manipulation, insider dealing and other share frauds, and the whole range of white-collar crime: all areas in which Triad criminals are becoming increasingly involved.

But it is the Royal Hong Kong Police who are in the forefront of the battle against the Triad societies. The RHKP is divided into departments, formations, and units: police headquarters, which includes special units and the Criminal Investigation Department (CID); the Marine Police; and the three land regions: Hong Kong Island, Kowloon, and the hinterland of the New Territories. The regions are autonomous and are divided into districts in which all crime investigation and general policing comes under a district command. Each district has its own CID officers and each region has an overseeing CID unit which deals with more serious crimes, such as murder, armed robbery, and gang warfare. Each region and district has dedicated Triad and criminal intelligence units.

Within the police headquarters structure there are several specialist CID units, all of which regularly deal with Triad-related crime. The Commercial Crimes Bureau handles fraud, counterfeiting, and other white-collar crimes. The Narcotics Bureau concentrates on the drug trade. The Organized and Serious Crimes Group deals with the overall problem of syndicated crime – mainly of course Triad-related. The OSCG contains the Criminal Intelligence Bureau, which is itself subdivided into units specializing in gathering intelligence on Triad activities, as well as dealing with other organized crime groups.

The RHKP structure – the result of an in-depth report on the Triad societies and syndicated crime compiled in 1984 – has proved to be an effective weapon against Triad crime, backed up by stringent anti-Triad laws and attention to such matters as witness protection. Witnesses in Hong Kong are easily bought off: often witnesses do not turn up, or, if they do take the stand, conveniently lose their memories. And always there is the threat of assassination: a Triad hit-man can be hired for as little as eight hundred Hong Kong dollars (£75). Witnesses, and their families, therefore have to be protected, and relocated if necessary. Accomplices who elect to give evidence for the prosecution (in return for which their sentences are usually reduced by a third) also need protecting.

Methods used in other countries against organized crime are also under consideration: for example, the Grand Jury system, which has been used effectively in the USA against the Mafia and which can, among other things, offer witnesses immunity from prosecution. Another possibility is to introduce something like the American Racketeering Influenced and Corrupt Organizations Act, the so-called RICO Statute, which was passed in 1970 specifically to combat organized crime where one crime relates to another – for example, drug deals that finance gambling rackets, which in turn provide funds for legitimate real estate purchases. Under the RICO Statute courts can confiscate property and assets that have been accrued as a result of criminal actions, and victims are able to pursue claims against confiscated estates through the civil courts to the value of three times their loss. Clearly such measures would strengthen the Royal Hong Kong Police's armoury, but whether they will be adopted in Hong Kong, and elsewhere, remains to be seen.

Certainly many Triads are now quitting Hong Kong; but though this is due in part to more aggressive and effective policing the exodus is also the result of the desire of Triads to expand their activities in new markets and to protect their interests in advance of the Chinese takeover in 1997.

What the future holds for the Triads is a matter of conjecture and speculation. Indeed, for any enterprise – legal or otherwise – which has its roots in Hong Kong, the future is decidedly uncertain.

In 1997 Hong Kong reverts to the government of China. Originally, under a ninety-nine year leasehold treaty signed in 1898, only the New Territories (the mainland hinterland of

Kowloon) and some islands would be ceded back to China: the island of Hong Kong and the peninsula of Kowloon were given to the British Crown in perpetuity. The state of detente is such however that the British government has agreed to relinquish the sovereignty of the whole colony of Hong Kong on the due date.

What will happen after 1997 is still undecided. A 'basic law' is being drafted which will ensure that Hong Kong will not perceptibly change either its method of government or its way of life for fifty years. This includes the colony's legal framework. However, knowing the infamous mobility of Chinese politics, few Hong Kong residents believe that the fifty-year limbo will last more than a few years. It is in the interests of the Chinese government to change the laws of Hong Kong in order to combat the Triads. The fewer Triad societies there are in Hong Kong, the lower the crime rate generally. The Chinese government has already been made aware of the relationship between Triad societies in Hong Kong and the explosion of crime in areas of China adjacent to the colony.

Against the foreseen potential collapse of capitalism, free market enterprise, and the entrepôt status of Hong Kong, many Chinese residents are preparing for an uncertain future. Businesses are investing abroad, banking abroad and trans-ferring funds to 'offshore' havens in the Virgin Islands, the Channel Islands, and the like. The man in the street is also making his preparations: sons are being educated abroad in Canada or Australia, marrying abroad, and will, no doubt, in the not-so-distant future, fly out aged parents to be depen-dants in those foreign lands. Those Chinese who can are already emigrating in droves. Many are holders of British passports or British Commonwealth passports. Those who are not are going to be given, prior to the 1997 deadline, a worthless passport which maintains that they are British citizens abroad but have no rights of residence in Britain. The government in London is anxious not to have a vast influx of Hong Kong nationals into Britain as 1997 draws nigh: the lesson on that score was learnt at the time of the Amin *coup d'état* in Uganda when thousands of British-passport-holding Indians fled to Britain.

As in the past, when China fell to Mao Tse-tung's Communism, Chinese are fleeing ahead of the invader. And along with the emigrants go the Triad members. Wherever the Chinese are moving to now, Triad office-bearers are moving with them. Not only that: wherever money is being exported, investments transferred or businesses moved, then so is Triad money, investment and business shifting.

The home base of the Triad societies, Hong Kong, is under threat just as Canton and Shanghai were from the Communists, as Peking was from the Manchus and Mongols before them. History is repeating itself but there is a terrible difference. In the past, the Triads ran ahead of the enemy's advances but generally stayed within the boundaries of China or, at any rate, the Far East. Now, with a skilful invidiousness, they are spreading rapidly much further afield. This is, of course, not altogether new. Previous chapters have shown how Triads have travelled in the past. Yet now they are seeking not simply to move with Chinese communities and live parasitically off them but also to exist outside them, preying upon the world at large.

Within Hong Kong and expatriate Chinese communities, the Triad societies continue with their criminal activities at street level. They may become more sophisticated in their gambling operations, in their protection and extortion rackets, yet they are essentially unchanging. The kind of crimes they are involved in are their traditional activities. The only new development is the exportation from Hong Kong to other countries of the Chinese youth or street gangs. These are little more than accumulations of thugs, sometimes allied to Triads in that '49' soldiers are members of the gangs, and the gangs are used as recruiting grounds for the Triad societies proper, but they do not actually partake of the fruits of serious criminal activity.

These gangs are a poisonous nuisance rather than a real threat to law and order, and they usually operate only within the Chinese community, involved in petty crime and expending much of their energies on internecine warfare. This is not to say that their violence never spreads outside it. Chinese youth gang graffiti started to appear on London underground trains in the autumn of 1988, alongside the indigenous scrawls of vandals and football hooligans. At least one murder has occurred which had some of the marks of a Triad-style gang assassination, though it is not known for certain whether it was one. The victim, a Vietnamese youth, was garrotted from behind by a rope or thin strap, and his body dropped into the River Thames in the very heart of the city several hours after the murder in October 1988. When it was found, he was wearing a T-shirt bearing a spider-and-web design, though this was not what he had been wearing when he left home, and he was barefoot when discovered.

When these gangs' violence erupts from the Chinese communities, it is no different from that emanating from black street gangs in London or from Puerto Rican gangs in New York, or Hispanic gangs in Miami or Los Angeles. They are criminal in that they mug, steal from and occasionally rape people from outside their own racial groups but these are not ethnic crimes as such. The gangs are a manifestation of modern criminal activity.

While some of the Triad societies are not much higher up the criminal ladder than street gang operators there are others, on the international scene, way above this level of crime.

In recent years, the various United States law enforcement agencies have hit hard at syndicated crime in the USA, particularly at the Italian Mafia families whose power has been much reduced. Their grip has been loosened on the big-time criminal world of, particularly, narcotics. Actions against foreign governments and foreign political leaders (such as those of Panama and other South American Latin states) or moves to assist foreign governments (Turkey and Colombia) in the eradication of narcotics have further weakened the immensely lucrative narcotics trade. However, what the law enforcers have failed to do is stem the alternative system to the Mafia – the Triads. Today, where the Mafia have been hammered, the Triads are filling the void.

Despite a reduction in heroin addiction in some Western countries, the drug still poses a major threat not only to the health of addicts (and others, when one considers the interaction of addiction with AIDS) but also to international peace. The holy war in Afghanistan, fought against the Russians, was substantially financed by the extensive Pakistani heroin industry: Pakistan has a rapidly escalating level of addiction. The Lebanon civil war was for a long time financed by both heroin (or opiates) and marijuana; indeed, the latter is still a source of finance to the militia-men fighting in the rubble of Beirut.

An outspoken report by a convicted heroin courier, John Weston, has pointed a finger in another direction in the terrorist underworld. Weston claims that the IRA is running a drugs operation in Britain to finance its campaigns in Ulster. Weston, an Englishman who was pardoned after serving eight years of a thirty-three year gaol sentence for heroin smuggling in Thailand, claims that he met IRA representatives in Thailand while he was employed by a heroin dealer he calls Mr Asia. The contacts were made in Australia, in Melbourne, and Weston was employed to collect a consignment of heroin in Bangkok for delivery in London. Travelling on a false passport, he entered London through Heathrow Airport and booked in to the Intercontinental Hotel on Park Lane. Here he met two Irishmen and an Englishman who, after testing the heroin and weighing it, paid £300,000 for the delivery. From subsequent conversation, Weston understood that they intended to trade the heroin in mainland Britain for profits to support the IRA cause in Ulster. After returning to Melbourne, Weston claims, he discovered that expatriate Irish in Australia were funding the transactions in order to support their countrymen. Later, in gaol in Thailand, Weston learned from a convicted American drugs courier that the same actions were being carried out in the USA and that IRA funding from drug dealing was enormous. How much truth there is in these claims is debatable, but it would neither be out of keeping nor would it be surprising. And any heroin dealing that passes through Thailand also passes through the Triads. The potential Triad/IRA link is terrifying in its possibilities.

Wherever there is heroin there are massive profits to be made (and risks to be run); there is also much potential for political or social destabilization.

At present, the Triads operate the bulk of the heroin market (in the post-Mafia years) simply for their own profits. How long it will be before they assume a political significance, or are manipulated to do so, remains to be seen. Contacts between the Triads, organized Chinese criminals outside the Triad society system and international terrorist organizations are rumoured to exist but no knowledge has yet been made public: suffice it to say that, with the Triads' penchant for secrecy and administrative/organizational skills, the possibilities are not encouraging.

Links between the Mafia and the Triads have been mentioned. Association of Triads with other criminal fraternities also exist – with the Japanese Yakusa, with the Filipino criminal fraternity and, in recent years, with South American narcotics dealers. These may be tentative and they may lead to nothing, but the fact that they exist at all bodes ill for the future.

The Triads' links with the Japanese Yakusa organization, which also traces its roots back to an ancient historical past and uses ritual and symbol in the initiation of members, are interesting. Like the Triads, the Yakusa is a secret confederacy of criminal fraternities; but unlike the Triads, Yakusa activity extends beyond crime *per se* and includes some arms dealing and smuggling, terrorism, political corruption, and extreme nationalist politics, as well as vice and drugs. Up to the 1940s the Yakusa operated exclusively in Japan; now they are somewhat in evidence wherever there are expatriate Japanese communities. Inevitably the expansions of their activities have brought them into contact with the Triads, with whom they have occasionally formed alliances. Since the Japanese have long been regarded as China's natural enemies, once again the Triads are denigrating their historical past, as they did in Hong Kong during the Japanese occupation of the Second World War.

Just how closely the Triads and the Yakusa are collaborating is hard to establish at present. The Yakusa are known to have moved heroin into the USA by way of Hawaii and by packaging it in consumer electrical goods, and there are fears of a massive Yakusa/Triads narcotics operation directed at the USA using the routes developed by Limpy Ho for the Mafia.

In Japan itself there is comparatively little demand for heroin. There is a market for marijuana, however, and the Yakusa are now importing this from Thailand via routes jointly operated by the barons and the Triads. Cannabis is also obtained by the Yakusa through Triad groups with contacts in the Philippines, where cultivation is increasing.

In Hong Kong the authorities have long been aware of a Yakusa presence. Thirty per cent of tourists who come to Hong Kong are Japanese and the percentage is even higher for Bangkok, where the sex trade attracts large numbers of Japanese men (many of the clubs in Bangkok are Yakusa owned or co-owned). Inevitably, Yakusa members are amongst them. In 1978 the Japanese police arrested Yakusa members who were importing amphetamines from Hong Kong with the help of the 14K, and in 1985 the 14K were linked to a 'speed' and heroin shipment seized from Yakusa members in Honolulu and Hong Kong. Conversely, the Yakusa have supplied amphetamine production technology to Triad chemists in Hong Kong.

The relationship between the Yakusa and Taiwanese Triad societies – in particular the Four Seas and United Bamboo societies in Taiwan – is well established. Both groups are politically as well as criminally motivated and share vested anti-Communist interests. The Taiwanese Triads have been used since 1949 by the Nationalist Government of China in Taipei against opponents of Chiang Kai-shek and the Taiwan government. On more than one occasion they have been employed as hit men by the government. Even closer cooperation between the Yakusa and the Triads bodes ill for the future.

The lucrative narcotics trade apart, the Triads are now

embarking upon new criminal ventures which, potentially, can cause even greater harm. At the lower end of the spectrum, is the manufacture of fake 'designer' goods, particularly wrist-watches, designer handbags and ladies' accessories. The wrist-watches are manufactured to such a high quality that they are indistinguishable from the genuine article even at close scrutiny and, in some instances, utilize original parts such as faces and hands. Only the movements are other than the original and yet they are usually as reliable. Of course, gold casings are merely gold-coloured but not of a cheap manufacture. The gold does not necessarily wear off. The watches not only keep good time but the Rolex Oyster Perpetual imitation which looks exactly like the original is also guaranteed waterproof to thirty metres pressure: successfully claiming under such a 'guarantee' is unlikely. The makes mostly imitated are Hermès, Gucci, Rolex, Cartier, Dunhill and Audemars Pigeot. These watches sell in Hong Kong for about £30 ($HK 400) as opposed to anything upwards of £400 for the real article. Occasionally, trading standards or customs officers, under pressure from the franchisees of the genuine items, capture and destroy a batch of the fakes, but this hardly affects the market. Within Hong Kong, the fakes sell widely both to residents and tourists: low-quality imitations may be obtained on the street with the higher quality items available only through salesmen contacted through untraceable telephone pager numbers.

Ladies' handbags – Gucci is a favourite designer label copied in Hong Kong – are commonly found on sale at street stalls and in the markets. It is not uncommon for even Chinese clerks and shop-girls to be seen carrying a bag that would cost over £100 in London but for which they paid not more than £5. Once more, the fake article is indistinguishable from the genuine. Indeed, in 1987, a representative of one of the major European fashion houses was invited on to Hong Kong television to discuss the fakes trade and to be tested with the imitations: he stated one of the two bags he was handed was fake, the other genuine. When he had given his reasons it was disclosed that both were copies.

This is a small business alongside other Triad activities and it is not entirely Triad-controlled or -operated. Yet it is, if anything, indicative of the ingenuity of the Chinese criminal (or entrepreneur – the distinction can be a fine one at times) and it shows his uncanny skill for seeing a market niche and exploiting it to its fullest potential.

The fakes trade has another, more lucrative and potentially more dangerous side.

In Hong Kong, in Fuk Wah Street in Shamshuipo, an area of teeming pre-war tenements, thronged streets and cooked-food stalls, eel- and snake-sellers, dripping racks of overhead laundry and right beneath the Kai Tak international airport flight-path – the 747s pass over at five hundred feet – there exists the Golden Shopping Arcade. This area is firmly in the control, at street level, of Triad gangs: particularly the 14K and Sun Yee On groups.

The Golden Shopping Arcade is a mecca for computer buffs. Here one can purchase almost any hardware, often at manufacturers' basic prices or at cost. The micro-electronics industry in Hong Kong is massive and of the highest international standard. Many well-known brand-name computers are either made or assembled in Hong Kong, where labour is cheap and technical expertise very high indeed. Facilities for the mass-market micro-electronics industries are amongst the best in the world.

In this shopping arcade, which is raided from time to time, one can purchase not only hardware but also software. Every major software program is available here at a tiny fraction of its market price. Desk-top publishing programs, sophisticated stock market programs, word processing packages – everything from the biggest data base down to the latest arcade game or space invaders program is available. Where these carry no copy protection, they have been copied. Where protection exists, this has been skilfully and effectively removed or bypassed. The operator manuals are also reprints, perfect copies of the original most likely printed in Taiwan where, for many years, there has been an illegal thriving 'pirate' book, music and video industry operated by Triad or Triad-affiliated groups.

The amount of money the major international software houses are losing in Hong Kong is astronomical. Programs that cost thousands of pounds can be purchased for less than a hundred: they contain no computer viruses, no bugs, no faults whatsoever. The Golden Shopping Arcade's whizz-kid protection busters – usually young Chinese under the age of 25 who have been brought up in the computer age – are some of them potentially the next generation of super-criminals, Triad or otherwise.

In late 1988, however, the situation changed. Continual raiding of the Golden Shopping Arcade apparently eradicated the black market in copied computer software. In fact the software is still available, but no longer over the counter: it can be obtained, like fake watches, through telephone pager services. Once more, the Triads' readiness to adapt has beaten the system.

Already, the Triads are moving into the areas of white-collar crime, their soldiers no longer thugs on the street with meat choppers and iron bars as their weapons but highly educated young men with a considerable technological skill in computer hacking, accountancy, legal services, banking and the stock market. Once again, the criminal activities are widespread. The forgery of money is not as common as it was twenty years ago, though it does still exist on a small scale. What is a larger business is the counterfeiting of securities documents, bond certificates and stocks and shares certificates.

Within Hong Kong, the stock market is a potent force. Not only is it an intrinsic part of the financial success of Hong Kong and South East Asia but it is also popular with a great many Chinese, whose love of gambling is satisfied by the Stock Exchange as well as by the race-course. And just as horse-race betting has become Triad-organized off-course, so is the stock market becoming affected. Insider trading, manipulation of stock and the legitimate dealing in stocks, shares and commodities all now fall within organized criminal activity of which a part is Triad-related.

The Triads' other forte is the laundering of money. This is

of particular importance to them as their criminal income, especially from the international narcotics trade, is huge and has to be laundered. Hong Kong has no currency exchange controls, and it is one of the largest international finance centres. It is indubitably used by foreign criminal organizations as a safe haven or a laundry machine and, with their intricate communications with the banking systems of the rest of the world, the Hong Kong banks are used as a means of exporting illegal money in order to return it cleaned and untraceable.

Banking fraud is another area of operation into which the Triads are expanding. Accountants working for the Triads are expert money laundrymen, and they are also adept at income tax evasion and fraud. A Royal Hong Kong Police special task force was established in 1989 to be granted powers of access to income tax records in much the same way as that afforded to the ICAC. It is hoped that this will yield valuable information on Triad bank fraud and money laundering operations, as well as on their international narcotics dealings.

In recent years, financial fraud has come to include insurance swindles, often involving the deliberate arson of property for the claim. In Hong Kong, on occasion, not only has the property owner received insurance compensation, but he has also had the site of his burned-out building cleared of obstruction (either of concrete or planning permission) and ready for immediate redevelopment. At the lower end of the fraud market there is, as now in every major city the world over, a brisk trade in stolen or fraudulently-obtained credit cards.

Since the introduction of the anti-corruption commission in Hong Kong, Triad leaders realize that their money is no longer safe in Hong Kong banks where accounts can be scrutinized with a court order. As a result, they are exporting their earnings to the many offshore banks set up in recent years around the world. Furthermore, dirty money earned in Hong Kong is now being legitimately invested abroad, in real estate in North America and Australia. The alleged New

York real estate transactions carried out by the late Ferdinand Marcos of the Philippines show just how potentially easy it is for Far Eastern money to be transferred abroad to obtain a veneer of respectability.

What has saved Hong Kong from becoming the criminal bank of the world is the anti-corruption authority. Without this, the banks could – and most likely would – become riddled with corrupt officials all in the pay of their employers and the criminal bosses to whom they owed allegiance, whether through fear or an oath-taking ceremony. In this respect, history is not repeating itself: quite a number of the followers of Big-Eared Tu worked as lower management staff in the Hongkong and Shanghai Bank in Shanghai during his years as Triad controller of the city.

Of great worry is the recent realization of the infiltration of the Triad societies into the legal profession in Hong Kong, a subject which causes deep concern to some members of the Hong Kong Law Society. It has been discovered that a number of solicitors' practices have Triad office-bearers in their employ as legal clerks and executives. This came to light in the recent trial of 'Dragon Head' Heung, the leader of the Sun Yee On. He had been working for some years for a leading solicitors' firm. Recent police searches of solicitors' premises have discovered Triad documentation, membership lists and insignia, the possession of any of which constitutes an offence under Hong Kong law. This is now, it would seem, a direction in which the ICAC might act and this will be of grave concern to the Triad leaders who, at this level, are not the elders of groups of teenage hoodlums but the controllers of skilfully contrived organized crime syndicates.

The Triads have cause to worry about the future. When Hong Kong reverts to Chinese rule, the new authorities are going to come down hard upon them. Chinese justice can be as swift as it is merciless. That China is now entering a period of 'enterprise culture' may offer the Triads the hope of a social environment in which they might be able to operate, but the truth is that times will be much tougher after 1997. The deliberate intention of the Chinese government to seek to stamp out organized Triad crime is exemplified in their attitude towards Kowloon Walled City. The Hong Kong government has been given permission to enter the Walled City, to clear out its inhabitants and to demolish the whole place except the mandarin's *yamen* house in the centre and the temple nearby. The whole of the city block is to become a public park. The *yamen* is destined to be a museum.

Every week, visas or immigration passes are approved by the governments of the USA, Australia, and Canada in particular. Australia alone receives 160,000 immigrant visa applications from Hong Kong each year. These countries cannot prevent this influx from Hong Kong for most of those applying for permission to enter are legally entitled to it. The vast majority of immigrants are law-abiding citizens; yet, in their midst, there will be Triad office-bearers. Some will enter quite legally, others will arrive as illegal immigrants and disappear into their new countries with false papers – papers probably as indistinguishable from the real thing as a fake Gucci handbag is from the genuine one. Where Australia is concerned, this has been going on, at a much lower level, for over a quarter of a century: in the early 1950s Morgan noted in his traditional history of the Triad societies that Australia in particular was named as a country to which office-bearers were moving.

Already, the shift of criminal activity is beginning to show. Australia is a country where the situation is indicative of what is going to happen elsewhere. Furthermore, Australia is ripe for the picking: it is near to Hong Kong, it has the open policy and ability to absorb immigrants, and it has an increasingly affluent society in which drug dealing (and taking) can be expanded. In short, it is what America was a hundred years ago, a young land hardly out of its pioneer phase. The pioneers, however, are not just the gold prospectors and the opal miners or the businessmen with an eye to an opening market.

In Sydney, the local Chinatown district is expanding quickly and Triad-related crimes are increasing at an alarming rate. The Australian authorities admit publicly that they are being swamped and can see no way to halt, let alone wipe out, the danger. Heroin addiction in Australia is soaring and 90 per cent of the heroin reaching the streets is of Thai origin – in other words Triad-society exported from the Golden Triangle.

In September 1988 Sydney police and customs officers seized their biggest-ever haul of heroin: £22,000,000-worth was discovered in a suitcase in the house of a 27-year-old Australian Chinese called Sunny Wong. He was originally from Hong Kong. In Hong Kong thirty other suspects were apprehended in a joint Hong Kong-Australian police exchange of information and co-operation.

Within weeks of this event, Australian police seized an even greater haul of narcotics on board the *Zoë*, a yacht en route from Hong Kong to Sydney. The seizure was of forty-three and a half kilos of No. 4 heroin.

For the Australian authorities, this is but part of a wider growing problem. In the last few years, prostitution in Australia has increased dramatically where Oriental girls are concerned. Over two hundred young girls, mostly of Thai or Malay origin, have been arrested on illegal immigration charges and a Chinese woman working for the Australian consulate visa section in Hong Kong has also been arrested and charged with issuing visas for narcotics couriers. In addition, six men have been arrested in Sydney and arraigned on drugs charges. It is claimed that they are members of the 14K and have extensive business interests in Sydney and Melbourne. Hong Kong and Australian police have uncovered cases of Chinese criminals entering Australia legally with business migrant visas. The prostitutes face deportation but the businessmen are less easily dealt with.

Quite how the Triad problem is to be handled internationally has yet to be seen. The predicament it raises is still in its infancy.

In Hong Kong, the police reckon that most Triad members are merely street criminals on the take, despite the international contacts such societies now possess either through the fraternity of drug dealers or the emigration of members.

There measures are being taken to contend with the Triad society presence: efficient policing, public education programmes (even teaching packs for schools) and the anti-corruption authority, not to mention a specific legal system tailored for the job (and under continual reassessment and improvement). Certainly, the Triad societies still have some glamour attached to them from both traditional stories and modern Triads-and-cops films, but the public, by and large, sees through this surface gloss.

Outside Hong Kong, massive and immediate provision must be made to prepare for Triad criminal activity. Already, drugs dealers are being more harshly dealt with through the various laws that exist for the confiscation of wealth, the extension of prison sentencing and the harshness of penalties for even the small-time narcotics criminal. Yet even destroying the narcotics trade – were it possible – would not eradicate the Triad societies. They adapt very quickly and one cannot but wonder what criminality they are dreaming up for the future. Computer blackmail with computer viruses? International stock market manipulation? The development of new narcotics? What will succeed China White? How long will it be before 'crack' and cocaine are overtaken by yet another super-drug of Triad invention?

In America, the RICO Statute is of tremendous value in dealing with Triad crimes; elsewhere, there is little provision being made. In Britain, the laws are inadequate to handle the kind of racketeering that Triad societies bring with them and which Britain has never really known. What is being seen now is the beginning of a potentially huge international crime wave. Wherever the Triad societies exist, they are expanding very quickly, very proficiently. And they are not all toughs waving meat cleavers.

It is almost too late. In another few years, unless the tide is turned, the war will be lost. A fast, international, co-ordinated response is essential – yet it seems not to be under way.

It is certain, of course, that the police and drugs enforcement agencies around the world are becoming aware of the impending – if not developing – situation. What is less certain is whether they will be able to contain and crush this immigration of criminal elements, better organized than the Mafia ever were, merciless, bound together not only by the remnants of a centuries-old tradition but also the honour of the oath, harder to infiltrate, better educated and infinitely better equipped than most previous organized crime syndicates, and sufficiently well-connected to conduct a supremely well-orchestrated international crime network if they wish. And it seems clear that they have every intention of doing so.

THE RED TURBANS REVISITED
An Afterword

While this book was being edited, the abortive democratic uprising against the Communist government of China occurred, possibly heralding a new phase in Triad history and demanding comment.

Those events in China of the late spring and summer of 1989 surprised and then shocked the world. Suddenly, from the grass roots of the universities and colleges sprang, almost spontaneously, a pro-democracy movement spearheaded by thousands of students and intellectuals and, for a brief period, wooed by the masses. Encouraged by a slight relaxation of the strict rules of Marxist Communism, with luxury goods appearing in the shops and free enterprise being sanctioned, many considered China was on the verge of, if not Western-style democracy, then at least something nearer to it than Far Eastern, mainstream Communism.

This was an instance of history repeating itself: the only seminal difference from the uprisings of the past was that the educated protesters were not failed Imperial civil service examination candidates. Yet they were disaffected thinkers, erudite people questioning the status quo. Furthermore, they were airing grievances not only on their own behalf but on that of the masses, of the Chinese people. They were also reacting against Peking, the capital manned by predominantly Northern Chinese which could be equated in some of their minds with Manchu rulers. The 'old men of Beijing' were regarded no more nor less than as emperors without crowns and heavenly thrones: they had the same elite privileges and power base as the extinct Imperial court.

When the People's Liberation Army turned its guns on its

own countrymen in Tiananmen Square, another example of history coming full circle, more than students and democracy were affected; so was the modern history of China and the Triad societies, particularly in Hong Kong but also internationally, since they face an uncertain future.

In Europe, the emergence of a new continental Triad grouping, the Tai Hung Chai, colloquially known as the Big Circle, with affiliations in North America and China, and founded by ex-People's Liberation Army officers who were disgraced in the Cultural Revolution of the 1960s, is threatening inter-faction warfare between itself and the 14K over the control of heroin. Additionally, the 14K are seeking to re-assert the sale of their own heroin product which has lost some of the market share due to lower-priced but high quality imports from Pakistan and Iran – the latter had been using the narcotics trade as a source of foreign currency during the protracted war with Iraq. Indeed, the invention of China White smoking heroin, which is cheaper to produce and therefore to sell on the streets of cities, particularly in the USA, indicates how the Triads are bending to market forces and producing what they hope will be a loss leader. Pakistan, of course, continues to be a source of heroin.

To complicate matters on the European drug front, the Triads are soon likely to confront fierce competition from the Colombian drug barons who are establishing themselves in Spain and Amsterdam in readiness for the opening of European Community borders in 1992. The possibility of Triad–Colombian gang warfare is not a welcome thought.

Inter-society fighting continues to erupt in Britain: the Wo Shing Wo, the 14K, the Wo On Lok and the Shui Fong societies continue to struggle to maintain dominance within the Chinese communities, especially of London and Manchester. On occasion, the police hear of attacks and arrests are made, deportation orders or prison sentences passed. Yet this does little to curb the violence: the accused are frequently acquitted from lack of evidence (and an inevitable dearth of eye-witnesses), those given bail jump it and are spirited out of Britain by their brothers and those deported return under cover when it suits them, often arriving via Eire and Ulster. The authorities are essentially powerless to prevent these evasions. The Metropolitan Police in London have a special Chinese monitoring unit to gather intelligence on the Chinese criminal fraternity but this is hardly an effective weapon against them.

The Canadian authorities are becoming necessarily more organised. Toronto police, who have in their jurisdiction a Chinese–Vietnamese population of over 175,000 and two major Triad societies (the 14K and the locally inspired Kung Lok), have their own Oriental Crime Unit partly staffed by ex-Hong Kong Chinese police officers. In Vancouver, the Oriental population is similarly huge and increasing in size as thousands emigrate from Hong Kong every month, the exodus accelerated by the approach of the 1997 hand-over of Hong Kong to Chinese sovereignty and the memory of the Tiananmen Square massacre. The Triad societies in Canada, of which the authorities declare there are ten, a number likely to be somewhat conservative, are spreading out from the centres of Chinese population to other cities with insignificant Oriental communities, like Winnipeg and Calgary.

Business is as usual: the shakedown of local Chinese businessmen with a few new developments. One of these is 'invasion robbery'. The Triads break into the home of their intended victim and hold his entire family (even their servants) hostage until their demands are met. The 'soldiers' who carry out this thuggery are often Vietnamese, hired by the Triad society involved. The Vietnamese element is worrying. In with the flood of genuine boat-people travel the flotsam of criminals with secret society backgrounds, fleeing arrest in Communist Vietnam: these are now establishing their own expatriate societies in Canada. Furthermore, although Canada's gun laws are strict, the USA is only a car ride away and firearms more readily obtained. Canadian Triads and their 'soldiers' are subsequently very well armed.

The American authorities are now bent on destroying the narcotics problem in the USA, spurred on by President Bush's dedicated determination. The indictment of General

Noriega of Panama has heralded the beginning of the big battle against the cocaine barons. As far as the Triads are concerned, a similar dilemma is facing them, for the Burmese authorities are now collaborating with the US Drug Enforcement Administration to spearhead an attack against Kuhn Sa in the Golden Triangle. The Chinese-backed Burmese Communist Party is in disarray, with the leaders in exile in China and the forces collapsing. This gives the Burmese army access to the Shan states where the opium is grown and affords a chance to move militarily against the Golden Triangle opium lords. However, a secret deal is purported to have been struck between Kuhn Sa and the Thai and Burmese governments, allowing valuable teak to travel through his domain in exchange for unhindered drug mule-runs. Despite this, the Burmese authorities are now publicly burning huge stocks of confiscated opium, morphine and heroin. The situation is rather unclear but it bodes ill for the Triads, giving the Americans and western governments entry into the Golden Triangle, threatening to disrupt if not destroy the cultivation of opium poppies.

Furthermore, the Triad narcotics dealers in America are coming up against a new threat to their trade. Although China White, manufactured in South East Asia, is cheap at US$10 per 0.05 gm packet and popular (being smoked, it avoids the risk of shared hypodermic needles and therefore the peril of contracting AIDS) and is being used by crack and cocaine addicts as an antidote to the notorious bouts of depression which follow a cocaine-induced high, it is beginning to be undermined by opium poppy cultivation in Mexico and Guatemala. Here, impoverished Latin American farmers are turning to poppy growing with Mexican refining chemists producing the resultant heroin. An upsurge in China White imports into the USA as a result of high-yielding poppy harvests in the Golden Triangle and the appearance of Mexican heroin, coinciding with the antici-pated reduction of cocaine imports as a result of the war against the Colombian drug cartels, promises a massive explosion in heroin addiction and therefore greater Triad profits, but only in the short term. In the long term, they may have to react to increasing competition from 'home-grown' heroin and more vigilant authorities.

The problems are much the same in Australia as they are in Canada, but there has surfaced something unseen for decades – a legal, non-criminally orientated Triad society. Behind the Exford Hotel in Melbourne is Waratah Lane where, at No. 7, is the headquarters of Mun Ji Dong – or People's Governing Society – Triad society which constructed the building thirty-five years ago. It has a brother lodge in Sydney known as the Ji Gung Tong or Public Society. The Mun Ji Dong was founded as the Yee Hing (or Brotherhood) Society in the Victoria goldfields in the middle of the last century in order to bring together and look after the welfare of the coolies. It has been registered as a 'masonic charity' for over eighty years.

As a result of the increasing Triad criminal activity in Australia, and the extensive publicity this has gained, the senior officers of the Mun Ji Dong have publicized their presence. They are a legitimate society of local businessmen, staunchly proud of being Triads, which fact they do not deny, honoured to trace their line back to the Hung League and contemptuous of the criminals. They have opened their lodge to press scrutiny and claim they have no contacts with criminality and have never had, save for one episode in the 1900s when they collected 'fees' from illegal Chinese gambling houses. The Mun Ji Dong even has a non-Chinese member, a Caucasian Australian.

The leaders of the society, who have gone so far as to allow their photographs to appear in the Australian press, claim there are no criminal Triad societies in Australia, only former Triad-related crime sydicates working on the fringes of Australia's Chinese communities, existing as contacts for narcotics and prostitution. The Mun Ji Dong stress they are a society with secrets, not a secret society and that their main aim is the retention and maintenance of Chinese culture and patriotism.

It is tempting to wonder if the Mun Ji Dong is the forerunner of a new breed of Triad societies, a link between what might come to pass and the true historical roots of the Hung League.

After the Tiananmen Square massacre in June, 1989, large numbers of pro-democracy leaders – most of them students and intellectuals, members of an educated and dedicated elite – went underground just as had their historical revolutionary forebears. Many sought to escape from China, but this is more easily said than done for China does not have an accessible land boundary with any stable non-Communist country save Hong Kong and the neighbouring minuscule Portuguese colony of Macao. These border crossing points are easily kept under surveillance. Some who succeeded in escaping did so with Triad assistance.

For many years, the Triad societies have had drug smuggling routes through China. These were now employed to smuggle people. The itineraries were various but some involved the pro-democracy 'counter-revolutionaries' travelling through China to the far south-west then crossing by sea to the island of Hainan. From here, they were taken on coastal junks or cargo boats to Hong Kong. Others succeeded in reaching Hong Kong by sea from Canton. Every day, hundreds of vessels ranging from motorized sampans to steamers make this journey, for Hong Kong imports huge quantities of food from China; additionally, it has a large ocean-going and inshore fishing fleet, long used as a cover for importing narcotics. In doing all this, the Triads reverted to their original *raison d'être*, the undermining of the Chinese government based far away in the north.

It was interesting to notice how old traditions still die hard in China, even under a totalitarian regime: albeit ignorant of the historical significance of their action, protesting students in Tiananmen Square wore headbands of white or red cloth in exactly the same way as had been worn by the Red Turban rebels of 600 years ago and are still worn by officers in traditional Triad ceremonies.

The future for the Chinese pro-democracy movement is in a manner of speaking to imitate the Triad and secret societies of old, to go underground to plot, manoeuvre, destabilize and infiltrate, to go into exile and raise support from overseas Chinese communities and foreign governments – the course followed by Sun Yat-sen and Chiang Kai-shek. One wonders if the Tai Hung Chai society in Europe might become a patriotic/criminal fraternity? This is a possibility which cannot be ruled out and it would give the society much influence and potential for growth: somewhere in the wings, perhaps, there lingers a modern Tu Yueh-sheng, waiting for the big chance. Whether or not the monies gathered in the name of China will be accrued by 'squeeze' or an appeal to patriotic sentiment or both, remains to be seen. It would be neither impossible nor original for the democratization of China to be financed in part by the sale of China White in America or No.4 heroin in Europe.

What seems certain is that the established Triad societies will not be prepared to forego their criminal incomes to assist the patriots: they may consider that they have little to gain from the democratization of China. On the other hand, they might feel they have much to gain from its destabilization. That country in turmoil would present a well-tilled ground for graft, corruption, drug dealing and smuggling, and exploitation as in the old days of Imperial and Republican rule. Perhaps there will be a two-tier Triad structure, the criminal and the patriotic, as there once was, the one aiding the other: equally, there might now be a resurgence of Triad groupings actively gaining international support, a percentage of which it must be expected will filter into criminal activity.

It is impossible to predict the way ahead either for China or the Triad societies wherever they may be. The situation is in a state of flux and all that can be done is to understand it, counteract it where it has a criminal intent and, ironically, succour it where it might be patriotic. It remains to be seen which way the winds of change will blow the incense smoke through the City of Willows.

APPENDIX 1:

'OVERTHROW THE CH'ING AND RESTORE THE MING'

The apparent meaning of this motto is deeper than might appear. On the surface, it means what it says: get rid of the Manchus (Ch'ings) and put a Chinese (Ming) back on the throne. Yet there is more to it. The Ming Dynasty translates into 'The Dynasty of Light', for the Chinese calligraphic character for *ming* means 'light'. The character for *ch'ing* (sometimes spelt *ts'ing*) means 'dark', 'darkness' or 'black' – at least, it *almost* does. A tiny alteration to the character referring to darkness, the addition of a short bar and two dots to the front of the character, is all that is required to turn the character for Manchu/Ch'ing into abominated darkness. The political motivation is, therefore, easily transmuted into a religious one and vice versa.

Yet, typically, there are other levels of meaning and calligraphy. *Ch'ing* also refers to the vital forces in mankind, to the passions (as in the meaning of the famous philosophical book, the *I Ching*), and it means 'clear' or 'void': mystically, it means the 'light of the spirit encased in a material wrapping'. It was therefore to the advantage of anti-Manchu factions to tamper with the calligraphy to alter this to the opposite.

The different interpretations, be they linguistic, literary or magical, give the whole matter added arabesques and, therefore, more significance to the Chinese. (Even the name T'in Tei Hui, the Hung Society under its alias of 'The Society of Heaven and Earth' has an alternative: depending on the construction of a sentence, *t'in* can mean 'man' and *tei* 'wife' – the implications of unity, of morality and of stability are evident.)

APPENDIX 2:

FROM *THE HUNG SOCIETY*
(J. S. M. Ward and W. G. Stirling, 1925)

The traditional history as recorded by Ward and Stirling is as follows:

The foundation of our Order dates back to the time of the Emperor K'ang Hsi. In those days in the State of Silu there lived a great General named Phang Lung Tien, who was instructed by the Prince of that state to invade China at the head of a large army.

The General obeyed the command and advanced, spreading destruction far and wide. No one was able to resist him and the news of his successes struck terror into the heart of the Emperor K'ang Hsi, who summoned his ministers before him and ordered them go out against the enemy. So great, however, was the terror inspired by Phang Lung Tien, that none of the Imperial ministers ventured to undertake the task.

In this predicament it was suggested to the Emperor that he should issue an appeal, which should be posted up throughout the whole Empire, calling for volunteers, and offering a huge reward and high honours to anyone who could raise an army and defeat the invaders.

These notices were posted up all over the country, and it chanced that a certain monk, who came from the Siu Lam monastery situated in the Prefecture of Foochow, saw the appeal, and, taking it down, carried it back with him to the monastery and showed it to the abbot.

On reading it, the abbot cried out, 'In all the Empire are there not to be found any officers brave enough or sufficiently capable to lead an army against these invaders? If this be so, it is our duty to see what can be done to save our country in its hour of peril, for we constitute a well-trained body of men, since we have always been well-versed in athletics.'

This suggestion was heartily approved by all the monks, and after some discussion they unanimously decided to set out for the Court of the Emperor and offer to form the nucleus of an army to fight the enemy.

Accordingly, next day, they armed themselves and the whole of the monks, to the number of one hundred and twenty-eight, set forth, in due course reaching the Court of the Emperor in Peking. Here they presented a written petition praying that they might be allowed to go forth against the invaders. On reading this petition, the Emperor summoned the abbot and monks into his presence, and was greatly impressed by their manly appearance. He accepted their offer, and the monks prostrated themselves and thanked him for thus giving them, although not soldiers, an opportunity of showing their skill in the art of war and their loyalty and patriotism.

The abbot and his monks thereupon withdrew and proceeded to the city against which the invaders were rapidly advancing, and which was destined to be besieged within a few days. In command of this city were two Generals who, thinking that it was a relief force, opened the gates with joy, but were astonished and disappointed to find that the party consisted of 'nothing but a band of bald-headed monks', for so they called them.

With true politeness, however, they refrained from making any comments and invited them to take tea, at which the abbot informed the Generals that they had come to defeat the Eleuths.

'We are highly honoured at your gracious condescension in leaving your monastery and hastening to our assistance, but was there not any experienced military commander deemed worthy of the task?' enquired one of the Generals.

The abbot replied, 'His Imperial Majesty, out of the kindness of his heart, enquired of the civil and military officers which of them would like to undertake the task of repulsing the Eleuths. Strange to say, however, none of them was willing to undertake the responsibility and, after ripe consideration, suggested to His Majesty that he should issue an edict, which should be posted up throughout the Empire, calling for volunteers and offering to appoint as commander of the army anyone who seemed to possess the requisite abilities. In this proclamation, His Majesty departed from the usual practice in such matters, called on everyone of whatever rank or position, whether soldiers or officers, merchants, priests or sorcerers, to offer their services. When my attention was drawn to this proclamation, I took down a copy and, accompanied by my monks, proceeded to the capital and presented myself before His Imperial Majesty. With truly royal condescension His Majesty was graciously pleased to accede to my humble petition, and I have therefore come hither to fulfil my promise and save the Empire.'

After this explanation the Generals and the abbot proceeded to talk on general subjects until a substantial feast had been spread, of which all partook, which being finished the abbot began to ask various questions concerning the positions the enemy had taken up, and to discuss plans for defeating them. As the conversation proceeded the Generals were astonished at the military knowledge evinced by the abbot, and greatly impressed and encouraged by his obvious familiarity with military tactics.

Having ascertained the exact character of the country, the position of the roads and passes, and where the rivers were situated, the abbot announced his intention of making an attack upon the enemy next morning. At dawn, after having invoked the spirits, he marched out of the city and skilfully laid an ambush at a point which the invaders would be obliged to pass on their way to the city.

Having carefully selected his men and posted them in strategic positions, he gave them precise instructions as to how they should act. This done, he drew his sword, made sundry magic passes, and uttered a series of powerful spells. He invoked Heaven and the spirits Luh-ting and Luh-kah, summoning them to his aid. Then the battle was opened, and at its height the spirits, obeying his behest, suddenly poured down a rain of stones and sand. This was accompanied by a mighty wind, so that the dust obscured the sky, and the Eleuths, unable to distinguish friend from foe, turned their weapons upon each other.

Gradually the great host was thrown into complete disorder, panic seized the soldiery and they turned in flight. They soon reached a ravine, named Hu-hu-chu, where the bulk of the monks were lying in ambush. Bombs and fiery darts came whistling from every side, while mines were exploding underfoot. The dense smoke, mingling with the sand-storm, entirely obscured the pass. Phang Lung Tien and all his officers were slain and the whole host of the enemy annihilated.

Having thus utterly routed the invaders, the abbot and his monks returned in triumph to the city, and after two days rest bade farewell to the Generals and proceeded to Peking.

On their arrival they were immediately admitted in to the presence of the Emperor, to whom they related all that had transpired.

The joy of the Emperor knew no bounds and he commanded that for three successive days they should be led in triumph through the city, and that the people should do them every honour. For many days he feasted them in the Imperial Palace, and wished to shower rank and rewards on them. He offered the abbot an important position at the Court, and tried to persuade him and his monks to enter his service. The abbot, however, on behalf of himself and his monks respectfully declined, thanked the Emperor for his gracious favour, and begged that they might be allowed to return to their life of peaceful meditation now that the crisis was over. The Emperor fully appreciated the motive which led them to decline the honours offered, and esteemed them the more, but insisted on bestowing various presents on the monastery, and in particular presented to it an Imperial seal, a jade ring, and a sword of honour.

This seal gave the monastery extensive powers over the district, for any edict issued by the abbot and chopped [stamped] with this seal had the force of one emanating from the Emperor himself. It was triangular in form and is the origin of the first seal used by the Hung Society. It contained four characters, but at a later date was replaced by our present seal, which has only one character – 'Hung'.

Thus laden with presents for their monastery, bestowed on them as a mark of recognition for the splendid service they had rendered, the monks returned to their abbey rejoicing.

Sometime later the Emperor K'ang Hsi died, in the 61st year of his reign, and was succeeded by his son Yung Cheng. Eleven years after that date a new Prefect was appointed to the Judgeship in the Foochow district. This man was as avaricious as he was dishonest, and greatly coveted the Imperial gifts, especially the Imperial seal, which he saw in the Siu Lam monastery when visiting it one day.

He was fully aware of its history, and of how it came into the possession of the monks, also of the real powers which it placed in their hands. He therefore began to scheme and plot how he could obtain it, and at first tried to persuade the monks to give it to him on various special pretences, and in return for a substantial bribe.

The abbot, however, replied that it had been entrusted to them by the Emperor as a special mark of his favour, in recognition of the service which the monastery had rendered to the State, and he therefore could not hand it over to anyone else. He added that its possession was not only a high honour but a solemn responsibility, for it bestowed on its holder almost unlimited power, including that of condemning a man to death. Such a seal he could not entrust to a stranger, lest it should ultimately pass into unworthy hands and become the instrument of injustice and oppression.

The refusal infuriated the Prefect, the more so as he perceived that the abbot was under no delusions as to his true character. He therefore decided to obtain it by any means within his power.

In pursuance of his wicked design he wrote to the new Emperor at Peking, Yung Cheng, saying that the monks of the Siu Lam monastery were a menace to the peace and security of the realm, for by means of the Imperial seal which they possessed they were able to oppress the whole countryside, defy the authorities and, worse still, were now plotting to overthrow the Emperor. He further pointed out that from their previous military exploits and the strength of the mountain fastness in which the monastery was situated, if they did revolt the situation would be most serious.

In conclusion he prayed for instructions as to how he should act.

The Emperor was horrified when he received this letter from the Prefect, whom he completely trusted, but he could hardly believe the information and wrote to him to that effect, adding that he thought that he had been misinformed and instructing him to make further and more searching enquiries.

Herein the Emperor acted wrongly and as does not befit a monarch, for clearly if the Prefect's report was not to be trusted he should have sent an independent investigator. As it was, the treacherous Prefect merely replied that the situation was as he had previously stated, and added further falsehoods, all tending to prove that the monks were on the very point of breaking out into open rebellion.

On receiving this second answer the Emperor was very wroth that the men whom his father had honoured for their fidelity and loyalty should thus abuse the privileges bestowed upon them, and conspire to bring about the downfall of their benefactor's son. At the same time he was seriously perturbed, and hesitated to take open action lest this should precipitate the supposed revolt.

He therefore asked the wicked Prefect for his advice, which, of course, suited the treacherous Tang Shing excellently, and he thereupon suggested the following abominable plan, which was approved by the Emperor Yung Cheng.

He advised that the monks should be slaughtered and the monastery razed to the ground. In order that the troops might fall upon the monks before they had time to arm themselves, or to man the passes which led to the monastery, he advised that resort should be made to treachery, adding,

'Let the Emperor send a New Year's gift to the monastery, consisting of poisoned wine, as a mark of his continued favour, but let it be accompanied by a large body of troops, ostensibly as a further mark of honour and to protect the gift from the possible depredations of brigands.'

He also suggested that he himself should take charge of the embassy, and see that the Emperor's commands were carried out to the letter.

Accordingly the expedition set out, and as it approached the monastery fell in with a man named Ma I-fuh, who was the seventh man in physical prowess in the monastery, and for that reason was known as 'A'Tsat'.

But though his physical powers were great his character was vile, and in consequence of his lewd and lawless conduct he had been expelled from the monastery by the abbot, after having been well beaten.

In consequence he hated the holy abbot and the monks, and was always meditating how he could be revenged upon them. He knew that the Prefect also hated them, and so he made common cause with him and told him that unaided he would never be able to slay all the monks, as there were many ways of escape from the building, and secret paths through the mountains by which many could make their way to safety. He therefore offered to show the Prefect these spots, and to conceal soldiers all round the monastery so that none could escape alive. While this was being done by A'Tsat, the Prefect advanced openly to the monastery with the remainder of his retinue and the Imperial gifts. He presented the wine to the abbot, declaring that the young Emperor sent them this present as a proof that he, like his father, continued to hold them in the highest esteem.

The abbot, suspecting no evil, was highly gratified, and invited the Prefect and his soldiers to join them at a feast, whereat the wine was solemnly opened. But as soon as he smelt it, his suspicions were aroused. He immediately sent for his magic cup, made from the horn of a rhinoceros, and as soon as the wine was poured therein it began to smoke and give off noisome fumes.

Seeing that his treachery was detected, the Prefect threw off all disguise, and ordered his soldiers to attack the monks and fire the monastery. The monks were unarmed and most of them were cut down on the spot, but the abbot, followed by a handful, rushed into the temple and, throwing themselves before the statue of the Buddha, called on him for aid.

It was indeed a great iniquity that so many of the monks of the Siu Lam monastery should thus perish miserably. They were sincere and disinterested men, who by their fidelity had saved the State in the hour of peril, and being men of a virtuous life their injured ghosts were unappeased, and the wrong done to them reached the Heavens. Their cries mingling with the prayers of the abbot moved the Holy Dharma-Buddha, who cried, 'The destruction of the Siu Lam monastery was predestined by Fate, but these few who have not perished shall yet set their hands to a mighty task, and I ought therefore to save them and show them a way of escape.'

He thereupon changed a yellow and black cloud into a long causeway. The temple filled with smoke, great clouds billowed about the statue, and the monks, one of whom was carrying the seal, seeing this causeway, made their escape thereby.

On finding themselves outside the burning monastery they saw the traitor monk, A'Tsat, helping the soldiers. This roused them to fury and, regardless of the fact that it meant almost certain death, for they were unarmed, they determined to slay the traitor. They therefore hurled themselves among the soldiery, tearing the weapons from their hands, and never resting until they had meted out to the traitor the death he so richly deserved. Nevertheless, it was at a terrible price, for only five succeeded in making good their escape along the causeway. This led them to a bay near Shih-san-li, at Ufan, where the cloud roadway joined the Heavens. Here they were hidden by two boatmen named Sieh and Wu.

Next morning the soldiery, having found that a few of the monks had escaped, made their way towards the sea, saw the five monks and followed in pursuit. After fleeing ten miles their further progress was barred by the ocean and all chance of escape seemed to be lost, for their pursuers were closing in upon them fast. In their dire extremity they threw themselves upon their knees and raised their voices in prayer to Heaven, saying, 'O Lord Buddha, we, the monks of the Siu Lam monastery, have rendered meritorious service to the gods of the land. We served the late prince with absolute fidelity, and now see how we are stricken by a traitor. A hundred and twenty-three of our number have perished in the flames of our monastery and only we five remain. Having fled to this place we find all hope of escape cut off. Before us is the ocean, and behind us our enemies close in upon every side. To Thee we call; have mercy and save us!'

As they ceased praying the two genii, Chu-kwang, and Chu-kai, appeared before them, seated on the end of a cloud, and, pointing with their fingers, cried, 'Hasten!'

The monks then saw a yellow and black cloud which changed before their eyes into a bridge of two planks, one of iron and the other of brass. When the soldiers came to the spot they saw nothing, neither was there any bridge, only the open ocean. They therefore returned to the wicked Prefect.

These monks are the Five Ancestors, the Founders of our Order. By good fortune it chanced that one of them had upon his person this precious triangular seal at the time of the burning of the monastery and thus brought it with him into safety.

In due course they reached the temple of Kao Chai, near which was a stream, and desiring to quench their thirst they stooped down to drink, when they beheld a white porcelain censer floating in the stream. On lifting it out they saw that it had two handles, or ears, and on it were the characters 'Overthrow Ch'ing and restore Ming'.

'This is the will of God,' they cried, and hid the censer in their clothing. Henceforth it became one of their most precious possessions, and today no Triad Lodge is without a copy.

Again continuing their flight they came to the spot where Cheng Kiun Tah was buried. This man had been one of their companions during the war with the Eleuths and it was his wife and sister-in-law that Ma I-fuh had tried to outrage. Ma I-fuh was the same man as A'Tsat, and it was this particular offence which led to his expulsion from the monastery.

When the Emperor ordered the massacre of the monks of the Siu Lam monastery he at the same time sent messengers to Cheng Kiun Tah ordering him to commit suicide, falsely accusing him of treachery, but he was as innocent of the charge as were his friends, the monks. On arriving at this grave they found Kuo Sin Ying, the dead man's wife, and Cheng Yu Lan, her sister, praying there, and joined their prayers with those of the widow and the sister-in-law, and also the two sons of the dead man.

At this moment their pursuers appeared in sight and the fugitives were in despair, but just as they had given up all hope the ground opened and a magic sword of justice made of peach wood shot forth. On one side of the handle were engraved certain characters, which meant 'Two dragons disputing over a pearl', and on the other 'Overturn Ch'ing and restore Ming'.

Kuo Sin Ying seized the sword and on striking at a soldier was amazed to see his head fall off, although she had not even touched him. She thereupon rushed at the rest of the Imperial troops, several of whom were similarly slain, while the remainder took refuge in flight.

Soon after the monks left the women and proceeded on their journey, but it was not long before the officer in command of the Imperial troops, hearing of what had happened, descended upon the house of Kuo Sin Ying. Hearing that they were coming, she gave the sword to her two sons, who fled and joined the five monks, and it is in this way that the magic peach sword came into the possession of the Hung Brotherhood.

When the soldiery reached the house of these illustrious women they endeavoured in revenge to outrage them, and the two fled, pursued by the ravishers towards the river. The ferryman was about to take them on board when their pursuers called out that the women were traitors whom they were about to arrest, and thus misled as to the true facts the boatman left them to their fate.

Seeing all hope of escape thus cruelly cut off, and valuing their honour more than their lives, these brave and loyal-hearted women threw themselves into the San Ho river and were drowned. Their bodies floated to Kang Wei, where they were recognized and honourably buried.

When the news of this latest outrage reached the monks they determined to avenge it at all costs, and to this end hid themselves in a wood near Cheng Kiun Tah's house. As soon as the leader appeared at the head of his troops they hurled themselves on him and cut him in half, and then escaped from the enraged soldiers owing to the assistance given them by the five horse-dealers, who are now known to the Society as the Five Tiger Generals.

These men had been unjustly oppressed and compelled to become outlaws, although upright and honourable in character, and it was because they had learnt of the gross injustice which had been meted out to the monks that they wished to join them.

Soon after the band met an outlaw, Chan Kan Nam. The reason for his outlawry was that he had killed a man who had molested his wife and child. Owing to his high moral character, great personal strength and undoubted magical powers, the others chose him as their leader, and he subsequently became Master of the first Lodge. It is for this reason that the Master of a Hung Lodge is always called Chan Kan Nam.

The whole band then journeyed until they came to the Red Flower Pavilion where they rested the night, and while there a red flame suddenly burst from the censer which they had brought with them. They considered that this was a sign from Heaven that they should devote their lives to avenging the treacherous conduct of the Emperor Yung Cheng.

They therefore swore a solemn oath of brotherhood, and first of all, having no incense sticks, took three pieces of grass, and for candles lighted two pieces of wood.

Herein they followed the excellent example of our illustrious predecessors Lui Pei, Kwan Yu and Chang Fei.

As they had no divining blocks they used two tea-cups and asked if they should avenge the wrongs of the Siu Lam monastery and strive to overturn Ch'ing and restore Ming. The cups were thrown, and in falling did not break, which they accepted as a sign of approval.

They then pricked their fingers and, mixing the blood with wine, drank it and swore an oath of brotherhood, pledging themselves to undertake this task, raise soldiers, buy horses and collect all the braves of the Empire under their standard.

While they were doing this a young boy appeared and asked leave to join them. His whole appearance was uncommon and he was clearly of noble descent, but the brotherhood at first refused to admit him when they learned that he was only fourteen years old. Thereupon he said that he was the great grandson of the Emperor Tsung Ching Wang of the Ming dynasty, born of a concubine. He added that his name was Chu, and his surname Hung Chieh, for his ancestor was the great Emperor Hung Wu, founder of the Ming dynasty.

The young man then said, 'If I do not attempt to recover my Empire, how can I face my ancestors in the next world? Let me join you, and if you recover my throne I will rebuild the Siu Lam monastery.'

They demanded of him a proof and he thereupon produced a perfume bag of Imperial make, on seeing which the band prostrated themselves, crying, 'Heaven has sent us the Prince Imperial. This is according to the will of God. Let us obey Heaven and act righteously.' They thereupon agreed to support his claims.

They therefore lifted him up and placed him upon a high seat, and prostrated themselves before him, but the young Prince raised the brethren from the ground, saying, 'I am not yet worthy of so high an honour, neither would I venture to accept it.'

They made their way into the province of Canton where on a certain day they arrived at a monastery which was situated in the Camp of Universal Peace. From this there came out an abbot, who was named Wan Yun Lung, and asked them who they were who came with so large a force behind them, for by this time they had gathered a large number of troops. As he spoke he made signs to them with his hand, and thus encouraged they told him the whole story of the destruction of the Siu Lam monastery, whereupon he exclaimed in a loud voice, 'O finish, finish.'

Encouraged by his compassionate tones, the brethren asked him to be their Elder Brother (Grand Master), to which he consented.

Now Wan Yun Lung was a man of enormous strength and size, being twelve feet high and eight feet in circumference, with red hair, a head as large as a bushel and arms like the branches of trees. He made up the number of leaders to fifteen. These events took place on the 25th day of the 7th moon, which date is still kept by us as a solemn festival.

They then appointed officers as follows: Wan Yun Lung was made Commander-in-Chief. Chan Kan Nam was appointed Incense Master, and Hwang-ching-yin was made leader of the Vanguard, his name being changed to Thian-yu-hung, which is the name always borne by the Vanguard in the Lodge. The rest of the brethren adopted the surname of Hung and took as their watchword, Patriotism.

On the 20th day of the 8th moon, having by then raised a considerable army, they came in sight of the Manchu troops. They thereupon sacrificed to their standards and commenced the attack. Day after day the conflict raged and lasted till the 9th day of the 9th moon. Suddenly Wan Yun Lung lowered his hand, ceased fighting, and fell dead on a sharp paving stone.

The Five Founders who were watching the course of the battle from the ramparts led forward the reserves, routed the enemy, and recovered his body. The victorious brotherhood took up the corpse and the head of their dead leader and marched north-eastwards, and as they were doing so there appeared in the north-east a cloud of five colours. The Five Founders thereupon declared that, though Wan Yun Lung had fallen, Heaven had sent this as a sign to show that though dead he was still Grand Master. They buried him with full honours on the left side of Five Phoenix Hill, near Lake Chu. The grave lies at the south-east and faces the north-west, while its geomantic position is Yin-Shin-fan-kin.

Their Master Chan Kan Nam raised over the hero a mound, 30 feet broad and 218 feet 3 inches long, which he named the Octagonal Camp, and on it erected an obelisk of triangular form, 9 feet high and 3 feet 6 inches broad. On the front were written sixteen characters, to each of which was added the character for 'three drops of water', and before the grave a nine-storeyed pagoda was erected.

After the funeral rites were ended the Master Chan Kan Nam consulted the Fates and declared that the destiny of the Ch'ing dynasty was not yet fulfilled, and instead of continuing a hopeless struggle they should disperse over the face of China and organize themselves, so as to be able to continue the struggle at a more auspicious date.

The band decided that this was the wisest policy, and before separating solemnly constituted the Tien Ti Hui or Hung Society, dividing it into five Provincial Grand Lodges, each under one of the five monks, allotted to each an appropriate banner and appointed signs and passwords by which brethren might at all times recognize each other.

The five horse-dealers were placed in charge of five lesser Lodges, but it is the five monks of the Siu Lam monastery whom we venerate as the Five Ancestors of our Order.

On parting, the five Ancestors made a verse:

> Ng yan fan hoi yat shau shi
> Shan seong Hung Ying mo yan chi
> Chi sz chuen Tak chung Heng Tai
> Hau Ioi seong hui tuen yuen sze

[The gist of this is as follows: On dividing, the Five Ancestors composed a poem which Hung warriors carry secretly; but if brothers see it they understand and immediately all quarrels are healed.]

The Five Original Provinces of our Order were: Fukkien, Kwangtung, Yunnan, Hukwang, Chekiang, and their respective banners are: black, red, yellow and carnation, white, green.

This, O Recruits, is the history of the foundation of our Order, and may Heaven protect Hung and righteousness spread throughout the Empire.

APPENDIX 3:

FROM *TRIAD SOCIETIES IN HONG KONG*

(W. P. Morgan, 1960)

PLAN OF THE LODGE

The Lodge is representative of the Triad city of Muk Yeung, 'City of Willows'. It is square shaped and surrounded by a large wall. Gates are set in the wall at the four cardinal points and each is guarded by a legendary General. These four guards are known as the 'Four Great Faithful Ones', their names being:

(*a*) North Gate: Lee Cheung Kwok
(*b*) West Gate: Hon Fuk
(*c*) South Gate: Cheng Tin
(*d*) East Gate: Hon Pang

Even in large ceremonies it is customary to have a representation of the East gate only. The North and South gates do not figure in the performance and the West gate is generally a simple exit from the Lodge.

Inside the city walls, near the East gate, are flown the banner of the Leader of the celebrant society and the 'Recruiting' banner. On the ground close to these banners are placed three paper effigies representing the Triad traitors, Ma Ning Yee the renegade monk, Chan Man Yiu the Magistrate of Po Ting district, and Hong Hei the Ch'ing Emperor.

The banner of the Leader of the society is square shaped and red coloured. It is the flag of the Leader of the celebrant society only and is quite distinct from the banner of the main Lodge to which the society belongs. In the centre of the banner is the surname of the Leader. Down the side of the banner is inscribed the name of the celebrant society. In our example the name is given as 'Chung Kwok, Hung Mun, Chung Yee Wui, Mo Tin Shan, Chung Yee Tong China, Hung Mun, Loyalty & Righteousness Association, Mo Tin Mountain, Loyalty Righteousness Hall'. The words 'Mo Tin Shan' indicate the actual society performing the ceremony, the other words are common to all societies of the 2nd Lodge of Kwangtung and Kwangsi. We have used fictitious names for the Leader of the society and for the society itself.

PLAN OF THE TRIAD LODGE

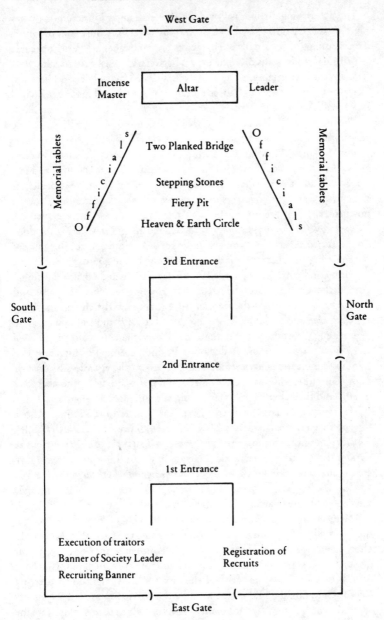

The 'Recruiting' banner is flown whenever an initiation ceremony takes place. It is not displayed when a promotion ceremony only is in progress. The meanings of certain of the characters on this banner are rather obscure.

Within the city walls on a line drawn between the East gate and the West gate are three entrances, or arches, each guarded by two Triad Generals. Recruits must pass through these entrances prior to reaching the main hall in which the altar is located.

The first entrance is guarded by Man To Lung and Man To Fong. Above the entrance are the characters *chi yin kwong chai* indicating that multitudes of virtuous men are assembled within the gate of mercy. These characters are said to have been derived from an inscription above the fifth and last doorway leading to the main altar hall of Siu Lam monastery. At the left of the entrance are the characters *to chi tei mo yee mok loi* meaning 'Proceed no further if you are not virtuous'. At the right of the entrance are the characters *yap ki mun fei chung mat wong* meaning 'On entering the door do not proceed further if you are not loyal'. On either side of the gate are flags bearing the character '*man*', the surname of the guards.

The second entrance is guarded by Cheng Ki Yau and Chan Ting Shing. Above the entrance are the characters *chung yee tong*, 'Loyalty and Righteousness Hall'. At the right of the entrance are the characters *chung yee tong chin mo tai sai* , 'Before the gate of loyalty and righteousness all men are equal'. At the left of the entrance are the characters *hung fa ting noi yau chuen pei*, 'Inside the Red Flower Pavilion are men of high and low standing', indicating that membership is open to all regardless of class or rank. On either side of the entrance are flags, one having the character '*cheng*' and the other '*chan*', these being surnames of the guards.

The third entrance is guarded by Ng Kam Loi and Ng Wun Yi. Above the entrance are the characters *kin kwan huen*, 'Heaven and Earth Circle'. At the right of the entrance are the characters *sha tsz pei chung chong lit shi*, 'Under the Yellow Covering the Martyrs Hid'. At the left of the entrance are the characters *kin kwan huen noi chut hung ying*, 'Through the Heaven and Earth Circle are Born the Hung Heroes'. On either side of the entrance are flags with the character '*ng*', the surname of the guards.

The location of these three entrances is baffling. Although placed within the city walls the recruits are said to have reached the City of Willows only after they have passed through them. It is possible that they represent passes or check-points leading to the city and for ceremonial purposes have been brought within the walls of the city for convenience and secrecy. Recruits entering the first entrance under the crossed swords of the guards are said to be 'Passing the Mountain of Knives', which seems to indicate the passage through a guarded check-point in the open air. Alternatively, it may be wrong to interpret the word 'city' too literally. The ancient Chinese palaces often covered an immense acreage and were comprised of a number of pavilions for the accommodation of favoured courtiers and concubines or for purposes of relaxation and pleasure. Such pavilions not only contained dwellings for the occupants and their staff but were set in their own grounds, distinctively landscaped, and containing the smaller garden type 'Pavilion' with which we more commonly associate the word nowadays. Each of the main pavilions was given a specific name and in the old Imperial Palace at Peking one such pavilion was called the 'City of Willows'. It is quite possible that if the society was, in fact, organized at any one place, the headquarters was in a large estate, surrounded by a wall with reception halls and main and subsidiary pavilions. The three entrances in this case would be within the main wall of the estate and might lead to reception halls beyond which would be the pavilion of the 'City of Willows'.

After passing through the three entrances, the recruit comes to the main hall in which is located the Triad altar. At the rear of the altar and on the walls of the hall are hung memorial tablets to the society founders and to various incidents in the adventures of the First Five Ancestors. Other tablets commemorating society heroes and incidents may be displayed according to the whims of the celebrant society.

The Hung Fa Ting, 'Red Flower Pavilion', is not shown on the plan. While an integral part of the 'City of Willows', it is not used until the 'face washing' ceremony which takes place three days after the main initiation and the whole Lodge is altered to represent it. The time lapse is dictated by practical rather than symbolic reasons for the old authentic initiations often spread over three days and nights. At the end of the ceremony a large scale feast and celebration was scheduled for the recruits and society officials and, while rest periods were taken during the ceremony itself, it was felt that justice could only be done to the meal if all concerned were completely fresh. For that reason the ceremony was terminated prior to the 'face washing' episode and the recruits returned after three days to undergo this small section of the ceremony and then immediately take part in the general celebrations. The rest period might well have been one, two, or any other number of days but it is natural that the society should have used their sacred number 'three' to determine the actual time prescribed. A possibility that cannot be ignored is that this three day period may be linked with the traditional account of the resurrection of So Hung Kwong into the Vanguard Tin Yau Hung and it may signify that the recruit must undergo a symbolic death stage before being re-born as a Hung hero. It will be noticed that in some other accounts of the society the 'face washing' precedes the main initiation and is said to be for the purpose of removing the dirt of the Ch'ing from the recruits. Our informants state that the main object of the initiation ritual is to symbolize the re-birth of the recruit into the Hung family. For this reason the 'face washing' should be placed at the end of the ceremony in accordance with normal practice whereby the child (recruit) is cleansed after it has been born (initiated). The 'Red Flower

Pavilion' wherein this ritual takes place is also entirely feminine in nature, and therefore symbolic of birth, as is shown by the fact that all memorial tablets displayed therein are to the female deities of the society. The tablets read:

Central tablet: The spirit seats of the foundresses of the Hung Mun. Lady Kam To; Lady Kam; Lady Fuk Sau; Lady Shui Mo.

Right hand tablet: Night rain may perch on the flowers for half a morning.

Left hand tablet: The pavilion never keeps the lucky clouds apart overnight.

Should the hall in which the ceremony takes place be of sufficient size, the recruit, after passing through the third entrance, would proceed in a straight line towards the altar encountering along the way the various episodes in the ritual such as the 'Fiery Furnace', 'Two Planked Bridge', etc. Seldom are such large premises available and the normal practice is for each episode to be enacted separately with the recruits returning to their original positions at the end of each episode.

It is most unlikely that any elaborate representation of the Triad city will be found nowadays. At an initiation the walls of the room where the ceremony is held will represent the city walls and the entrances, etc., will be represented by pieces of red paper bearing characters to indicate their meaning.

MEMORIAL TABLETS ABOVE THE MAIN ALTAR

[There is] a main tablet inscribed with the characters *cham tai wang fa* (Extensive Conversion; Blending with Heaven), written horizontally. Below it are four vertically inscribed tablets bearing the matched couplets:

(a) Faithful ones may join the society
(b) Disloyal ones must not offer incense here
(c) The heroes are supreme
(d) The brave ones have no equal

A main tablet written in white characters on black paper and placed immediately below the Tsam Tai Wang Fa tablet. The translation of this tablet is as follows:

The
Spirit-seats
of the
Hung Family
Founders, Foundresses
&
The early Martyrs.
Emperor Kai Shing and his wife, the Lady Pei.

Emperor of the Ming.
Prince Chu Hung Ying and his wife, the Lady Kam.
Man Wan Lung. Chan Kan Nam. Tse Pong Hang. Ng Ting Kwai.
Hon Pang. Hon Fuk. Cheng Tin. Cheung Kwok.
Tsoi Tak Chung. Fong Tai Hung. Ma Chiu Hing. Wu Tak Tai. Lee Shik Hoi.
Ng Tin Shing. Hung Tai Shui. To Pit Tat. Lee Shik Tai. Lam Wing Chiu.

A main tablet with the characters for Hung Ka Temple written horizontally. Below it, two tablets with the characters written vertically as follows:

(a) The lone efficacious tortoise from the wide ocean shows promise of success. Nine numbers by Yin and nine numbers by Yang. Nine times nine make eighty one numbers. Every number goes back to the three big doctrines (i.e. Taoism, Buddhism, Confucianism). Morality comes from the Primal Celestial Excellency. Complete single-heartedness is inductive.

(b) The two gay phoenixes on the lofty mountain signify prosperity. Six calls from the hen and six calls from the cock. Six times six make thirty-six calls. Each call penetrates the nine divisions of Heaven. Heaven produced the holy Emperor of the Great Ming. May he live forever.

A main tablet to Man Wan Lung written in white characters on black paper bearing the phrases:

(a) Tablet of Ancestor Man
(b) Pagoda (of) Priest Tat Chung Kung
(c) Received office at Siu Lam Monastery
(d) Opened Mountain (society) number one branch
(e) Heaven produced Heaven. (The) Nourished Heaven bestowed blessings
(f) Myriads (of) children. Myriads (of) grand-children. Myriads (of) years length (of time)

Tablet to the deceased brethren of the society. Placed on the right hand side of the altar just above floor level. Written in black characters on yellow paper in the form of a couplet:

(a) When will be the end of enmity?
(b) Regrets will remain for ever

and headed: The Spirit seats of deceased brothers.

MEMORIAL TABLETS DISPLAYED ON THE WALLS OF THE LODGE

Tablet to the Two Planked Bridge

Top horizontal characters – Two Plank Bridge.
    Right hand two sets of vertical characters form the couplet:

(a) Brethren pass the head of the two plank bridge
(b) The confluence of the three rivers flow for myriads of years

Central two sets of vertical characters form the couplet:

(a) The Yellow River will one day become clear. (Implies that the Ch'ing will be exterminated)
(b) How can it be that the Hung brethren will not obtain the opportunity to achieve their desires

Left hand two sets of vertical characters form the couplet:

(a) Having a beginning and an end (in view) marks a true gentleman
(b) To be persistent from start to finish is a virtuous thing

Tablet to the Long River and Huge Sea

Written in black characters on green paper.

Tablet to the Ko Kai Temple

Written in black characters on red paper. Headed with the three horizontal characters 'Ko Kai Temple'.
    Right hand vertical characters indicating: 'Place guarding Ko Kai. A range of mountains and rivers which will be for ever glorious'.
    Left hand vertical characters indicating: 'Entrance facing the big sea. The confluence of the three rivers will flow for myriads of years'.

Tablet to Cheung Sha Bay

Written in black characters on red paper. Headed Cheung Sha Bay.
    Right hand vertical characters indicating: 'Heaven and Earth. The mixed atmosphere of Heaven and Earth . . .' (remaining characters are of ancient form and present meaning is unknown).
    Left hand vertical characters indicating: 'Drizzling rain. Continuous rain. Frost. Snow. Mist. Fine and sleet-like rain'.

Tablet to the Fiery Pit

Written in black characters on red paper. Headed 'Fiery Pit'.
    Right hand vertical characters indicating: 'Changeable winds (i.e. evil persons) are not to be admitted into the Quarters of the guards'.
    Left hand vertical characters indicating: 'Fiery pits are only for traitors to enter'.

Tablet to the 'Yee Hop' Shop

Written in black characters on red paper. Headed 'Righteousness United Shop'.

Right hand vertical characters indicating: 'Help faithfully and loyally the kingdom of Han'.

Left hand vertical characters indicating: 'Destroy the Ch'ing with all your heart and might'.

Tablets to the 'Black Dragon' river and to Cheng Kwan Tat, his wife and sister

Both written in black on red paper. The large arch type tablet is headed 'Black Dragon River'. The right hand vertical characters indicate: 'Black, red, vermilion, white, and green combine together to prosper the Han'. The vertical left hand characters indicate: 'Dragon, Tiger, Tortoise, Snake, Assembled together to exterminate the Ch'ing'.

The smaller, square tablet, is inscribed with the characters for: The spirit seats of Marshal Cheng Kwan Tat and the two sisters-in-law Cheng Yuk Lin and Kwok Sau Ying.

Tablet to the Fuk Tak Temple

Written in black characters on red paper. This is considered a most important tablet and is placed on the wall of the main hall close to the third entrance door. Its primary purpose is to protect the Lodge from any harm. The name 'Fuk Tak' is given to many temples and there is a famous one in Hong Kong where the birthday celebrations of the To Tei (God of Earth) are performed. The central tablet bears characters to indicate: 'Fuk Tak Temple. Spirit seats of Buddha Ka Lam; the God of Earth; the God Wong Cheong, the Goddess Chung'. The smaller tablet on the right side bears characters indicating: 'If there is dust in a happy place, the wind itself will bear it away'. The tablet on the left side bears characters indicating: 'A virtuous house is without trouble, and its door is open every day'.

Tablets to the presiding officials

There are actually two tablets: the one on the left hand side is displayed whenever an initiation or promotion ceremony is held and the one on the right hand side is only displayed when a promotion ceremony is scheduled. The right hand side one lists the names of those scheduled for promotion, the left hand side one lists the names of the presiding officials. The characters shown indicate:

(a) Left hand tablet

Chung Yee Tong, Mo Tin Shan (of the) Hung Mun Chung Yee Wui (of) China (this being the name of the celebrant society).
    Tung Chu (Society Leader) ....

(*Note:* Tung Chu is a rather more common expression for the ceremonially correct title of San Chu).

Heung Chu (Incense Master)   ....
Sin Fung   (Vanguard)   ....
Pa Kwat   (Guards)   ....

Dated this ...... day, ... month, ... year of Hung Mun.

(b) Right hand tablet
Chung Yee Tong, Mo Tin Shan (of the) Hung Mun Chung Yee Wui (of) China.

Names of nominees on the Golden Placard.

Office.	Name.	Protector.
426	....	....
415	....	....
432	....	....

Hung (members) extend to ten thousand cities.

Dated this ...... day, ... month, ... year of Hung Wan.

Tablet to the Red Flower Pavilion
Consisting of three tablets hung above and on either side of the entrance to the pavilion. Written in black characters on red paper. Above the entrance are the characters for 'Red Flower Pavilion'. To the right of the entrance are the characters for 'Flowers bloom for ever. It is the will of Heaven that Ming be restored. Then we will sing praises in honour of the prosperous age'. To the left of the entrance are the characters for 'Before the pavilion we swear the oaths. Fate decrees that Ch'ing is to be annihilated. Then we will see the omen of a plentiful year'.

Also displayed on the walls should be:

(a) a small tablet bearing the characters for 'Tai Ping Market'
(b) a small tablet bearing characters for 'Chung Sum (Centre) Street'
(c) An arch type tablet headed 'Ka Fong', this being the guard house at the pass guarding the entrance to the Triad city. The right hand side of this arch should have the characters for 'Find out (by weighing) the loyal ones and make them our brethren'. The left hand side of the arch should have the characters for 'Seize the treacherous and treat them as the chicken'

Above the West gate of the city should be inscribed the characters for 'To Prosper The Nation'. On the right hand side of the gate should be the characters for 'To promote the national spirit in order to prevent the people of a noble country from falling into the hands of foreign enemies'. On the left hand side of the gate should be the characters for 'Combine our strength to lead the heroes from all over the country for the purpose of taking back our rivers and mountains'.

Above the East gate of the city should be inscribed the characters for 'Loyalty; Filial Piety; Moral Integrity; Righteousness'. On the right hand side of the gate should be the characters for 'To be of the same mind, the same conduct, and the same liver and gall'. On the left hand side of the gate should be the characters for 'Let us unite ourselves in benevolence, righteousness, and sworn brotherhood'.

No tablets are posted above either the North or South gates since these are not used during the ceremonies.

THE MAIN ALTAR
At the commencement of the ceremony the following articles will be found on the altar in the Ko Kai Tau type of ceremony:

(*a*) The Tau and contents. These will be described in detail later

(*b*) A sheet of red paper bearing the characters *Hung fat man chun* 'Hung family Expand Ten Thousand cities', indicating the hope that the society will flourish throughout the country. The Tau is placed on top of this piece of paper

(*c*) Two brass, single stem, lamps known as the Ku Shu 'Ancient Trees'. These represent the tree branches used instead of candles by the First Five Ancestors when worshipping the Precious Censer

(*d*) A brass lamp with seven stems often referred to as the Seven Stars Lamp. Believed to be symbolic of the seven planets, Sun; Moon; Saturn; Venus; Mars; Jupiter; Mercury; which were regarded as the seven rulers of the heavens. It is also said to represent the seven mows of land which legend has it were encompassed within the walls of the Triad city

(*e*) A pot of wine and five wine bowls. The five wine bowls are said to represent the five wells said to have been in the Triad city

(*f*) A pot of tea and three tea bowls. The three bowls are said to represent three ponds in the Triad city

(*g*) An incense pot for holding joss sticks

(*h*) A portable incense pot used for worshipping the memorial tablets at various points around the hall. This pot has a red paper cover bearing the character *cheng* 'Well'. It is surrounded by five circles and decorated with the characters *yu* and *kwai* which are frequently used by the society for such purpose. The character *yu* is taken from the top of the Ling Wong Temple seal and the character *kwai* from the bottom

(*i*) A dish of fresh fruit. There should be one each of five different kinds of fruit representing the five orchards in the Triad city but it is quite common to use five of the same kind

(*j*) A dish of groundnuts. Any other kind of nut would serve the same purpose except the Ma Tai 'Horse's Hoof' type of water chestnut since its name is too reminiscent of the traitor monk Ma Ning Yee. Groundnuts are favoured since their name is *fa sang* and *fa* means 'Flower' while *sang* means 'Grow' or 'Birth' and can thus signify, in a rather oblique manner, that many heroes will be born into the Hung family

(*k*) A dish of fresh flowers. A normal adornment of altars during religious performances

(*l*) A dish of red dates. Used for sacrificial purposes and also given to the recruits to eat. That the word for date is pronounced exactly the same as the word for early is also taken to signify the desire for an early overthrow of the Ch'ing dynasty

(*m*) A dish containing vegetables, three pieces of bean curd and two pieces of fungi. The significance of this dish is unknown

(*n*) A dish of Chinese tobacco and betel nuts. These are signs of hospitality to honoured guests

(*o*) A bowl containing water and pomelo leaves. The leaves are believed to possess the power of driving away devils. Water from this bowl is sprinkled over the altar to purify it

(*p*) A bowl containing a mixture of wine, sugar, and cinnabar. Recruits drink this mixture after blood from their own fingers, blood from the slaughtered cock, and ashes from the 36 oaths have been added

(*q*) The hand-book of the society. Such books are practically non-existent and a folded piece of brown paper is used to represent it

(*r*) A sheet of paper bearing the name, date of birth and place of birth of each of the recruits. In theory these particulars should be recorded from the recruits by an official as they enter the East gate of the city. The list should then be handed to the Incense Master who places it on the altar

(*s*) Five small flags each bearing one of the elemental character – *muk* 'wood'; *fo* 'fire'; *kam* 'metal'; *to* 'earth'; and *shui* 'water'. These flags are used in conjunction with the portable censer by the Vanguard official when he sacrifices to the five cardinal points prior to 'executing' the three Triad traitors

(*t*) A needle threaded with red thread. Used by the Incense Master to prick the fingers of the new recruits

(*u*) A supply of joss sticks to be used for purposes of worship

THE TAU

This is a large wooden tub painted red and filled with rice, each grain of which is said to represent a society member. The Tau is capable of holding a 'peck' which is a common measure for dry commodities such as beans, rice, etc. The 'peck' measure also denotes abundance and the ability of the Tau to hold a 'peck' of rice symbolizes the countless thousands of loyal brothers in the Hung family. It is of interest to note that a similar type of tub is often used during the religious ceremonies in Taoist temples.

Around the outer circumference of the Tau, at what might be called the cardinal points, are the four characters *chung* 'pine', and *pak* 'cedar', both of which signify 'longevity', and *to* 'peach', and *li* 'plum', which signify 'loyalty'.

On the front are the three characters *muk yeung shing* 'City of Willows' and surrounding them are four other characters built up from contemporary and ancient Chinese numerical characters. These characters are:

(a) *Muk*
Consisting of the character *sap* 'ten', and *pat* 'eight'. Together they signify the 18 monks who escaped from Siu Lam monastery

(b) *Lap*
Consisting of the character *luk* 'six', and *yat* 'one'. Said to commemorate the alleged date of the burning of the monastery, the 1st day of the sixth moon

(c) *Tau*
Consisting of the old style characters *chat* 'seven', and *sap* 'ten'. Signifying the 70 days spent by the First Five Ancestors in fleeing from the Ch'ing pursuers

(d) *Sai*
Consisting of the old style characters *sam sap* 'thirty', and *yat* 'one'. Said to commemorate the 31 battles fought by the First Five Ancestors against their enemies. This is the first intimation we have had that the monks fought such a number of engagements and it is very doubtful if this is, in fact, the correct interpretation of the character

The Tau contains all the 'Precious Objects' of the society as well as the Lodge flags, Warrant flags, etc. We shall deal with each of these objects separately starting with the different flags. To clarify matters it should be noted that each Lodge is allotted one of the First Five Ancestors and one of the Second Five Ancestors as its patrons. Each of these patrons has his own surname flag and a complementary Lodge flag both of which are in the Lodge colours. It should also be noted that when a flag is mentioned as having a border, the border is serrated and consists of nine serrations along the hypotenuse and twelve along the base. These serrations are said to be in memory of the jagged hole in the wall of Siu Lam monastery through which the First Five Ancestors escaped.

(a) *1st Lodge. Fukien and Kansu area*
Flag of First Five Ancestor, Tsoi Tak Chung
Black with red border. Bearing surname character '*Tsoi*'.
Complementary Lodge Flag

Black with red border. Bearing character *lung* 'dragon'.
Flag of Second Five Ancestor, Ng Tin Shing
Black with red border. Bearing surname character '*Ng*'.
Complementary Lodge Flag
Black with red border. Bearing character *piu* 'glorious'.

(b) *2nd Lodge. Kwangtung and Kwangsi area*
Flag of First Five Ancestor, Fong Tai Hung
Red with black border. Bearing surname character '*Fong*'.
Complementary Lodge Flag
Red with black border. Bearing character *fu* 'tiger'.
Flag of Second Five Ancestor, Hung Tai Shui
Red with black border. Bearing surname character '*Hung*'.
Complementary Lodge Flag
Red with black border. Bearing character *sau* 'ages'.

(c) *3rd Lodge. Yunnan and Szechuan area*
Flag of First Five Ancestor, Ma Chiu Hing
Vermilion with green border. Bearing surname character '*Ma*'.
Complementary Lodge Flag
Vermilion with green border. Bearing character *kwai* 'tortoise'.
Flag of Second Five Ancestor, To Pit Tat
Vermilion with green border. Bearing surname character '*To*'.
Complementary Lodge Flag
Vermilion with green border. Bearing character *hop* 'united'.

(d) *4th Lodge. Hunnan and Hupeh area*
Flag of First Five Ancestor, Wu Tak Tai
White with vermilion border. Bearing surname character '*Wu*'.
Complementary Lodge Flag
White with vermilion border. Bearing character *sh'e* 'snake'.
Flag of Second Five Ancestor, Lee Shik Tai
White with vermilion border. Bearing surname character '*Lee*'.
Complementary Lodge Flag
White with vermilion border. Bearing character *wo* 'harmonious'.

(e) *5th Lodge. Chekiang; Kiangsi; Honan area*
Flag of First Five Ancestor, Lee Shik Hoi
Green with white border. Bearing surname character '*Lee*'.
Complementary Lodge Flag
Green with white border. Bearing character *wui* 'assembled'.
Flag of Second Five Ancestor, Lam Wing Chiu
Green with white border. Bearing surname character '*Lam*'.
Complementary Lodge Flag
Green with white border. Bearing character *tung* 'together'.

The expression formed by the combined characters on the complementary flags of the First Five Ancestors – 'Dragon, Tiger, Tortoise,

Snake, Assembled' – is frequently used in the Triad ritual, as is the expression 'Glorious Ages Harmoniously United Together' formed by the combined characters on the complementary flags of the Second Five Ancestors.

Flags of the Five Tiger Generals

It is uncertain whether or not five historical characters known as the Five Tiger Generals ever existed, but in Chinese fiction at least they are frequently mentioned. In the Triad, the title is used to indicate the commanders of the regiments raised by the five Lodges. These Generals are said to have been:

(a)	Eastern area	–	Ng Tin Yau
(b)	Southern area	–	Cheung King Chiu
(c)	Western area	–	Fong Man Shing
(d)	Central area	–	Yeung Man Cho
(e)	Northern area	–	Lam Tai Kong

These Generals are not delegated to individual Lodges but command armies at the five cardinal points signifying unity and strength of the brotherhood throughout the land. This sense of universal support is also evident in the fact that the flags of the Generals bear the characters for the five elements, believed in ancient days to be the basic elements from which the earth was formed.

The flags of the Generals are all black coloured with red borders. The elemental characters delegated to them are:

(a)	Eastern General	–	*muk*	'wood'
(b)	Southern General	–	*fo*	'fire'
(c)	Western General	–	*kam*	'metal'
(d)	Central General	–	*to*	'earth'
(e)	Northern General	–	*shui*	'water'

Flags of the Four Great Faithful Ones

These are the flags of the guards of the main gates in the walls of Muk Yeung City. They are all red coloured with black borders. The distinguishing characters are:

(a)	North Gate. Flag of Lee Cheong Kwok.	Character *fa*
(b)	West Gate. Flag of Hon Fuk.	Character *wang*
(c)	South Gate. Flag of Cheng Tin.	Character *tai*
(d)	East Gate. Flag of Hon Pang.	Character *cham*

These four characters, taken in the sequence *cham tai wang fa*, form another common Triad expression. It is difficult to interpret them literally but a possible translation could be 'Extensive Conversion; Great

Blending'. The intended significance is that the divine purpose of the brotherhood will grow and spread throughout the land.

Warrant Flag of the Society Leader

This is a yellow coloured flag with a red border. The name of the celebrant society is written down the side of the flag and in this instance we have used the fictitious name of Mo Tin Shan Chung Yee Tong. In the centre of the flag is the main character *ling* 'warrant'. This flag is the authorization from the Leader of the society for the Incense Master to perform one of the three main types of initiation ceremony as under:

 (*a*) Muk Yeung (Main)
 (*b*) Muk Yeung (Secondary)
 (*c*) Ko Kai

These are elaborate ceremonies which can only be performed by accredited Incense Masters of the main societies. Less elaborate ceremonies performed by branch societies can be one of three types:

 (*a*) Chung Sum
 (*b*) Hung Shuen
 (*c*) Kam Toi

and do not require the special warrant flag from the Society Leader.

Warrant Flags of the Incense Master

These flags are red coloured, no borders, bearing the main character *ling* 'warrant'. The number of such flags in the Tau depends upon the number of officials participating in the ceremony. Each official must be handed one of these warrant flags by the Incense Master before he can assume his duties.

Warrant Flag of the Army Commander

This flag is in the shape of an upright oblong. It is black coloured with a red surround and bears the characters *sam kwan sze ming* 'Order of the Commander of the Three Armies'. The origin or meaning, if any, of this phrase is obscure. One of our informants connects it with the ritual verse:

 '*THREE* sages made their true compact in the peach garden.
 The *ARMY* Adviser Chu-Kot was an excellent statesman of the Han,
 The *COMMANDER* roamed over the five lakes and four seas,
 ORDERING us in future to adhere to the Ming ruler'

The three sages were Kwan Yu, Lau Pei and Cheung Fei whose oath of loyalty sworn in the peach garden is held as a model for the brothers of the society. Chu-Kot is Chu-Kot Leung, the strategist behind the adventures of the three sages. The word 'Han' is sometimes used to indicate the Chinese people generally and is not restricted solely to the dynasty of that name. The Commander is unknown but may refer to Tin Yau Hung who, prior to resurrection as a Triad General in the body of So Hung Kwong, had roamed the earth in spirit form seeking to avenge the death of the Ming Emperor Sung Ching. The expression 'Five lakes and four seas' is an ancient expression used to indicate the whole earth. The foregoing is, of course, conjecture, and it is possible that the phrase is not purely Triad in origin. It is a fact that this phrase, or the very similar 'Commander of the Three Armies', frequently appears both in Chinese fiction and in certain Taoist and Buddhist funeral rites which would indicate that a spiritual rather than temporal interpretation should be placed upon it. Some sources state that the flag represents the actual charter of the Society and this may well be the case, for while many of the other flags are frequently omitted in these ceremonies, this flag is always present.

All the above mentioned flags, with the exception of the warrant flags of the Incense Master and the Army Commander, have two red pennons attached to the top bearing the characters *shun tin hang to*; *fan ch'ing*; *fuk ming* 'Act according to the will of Heaven; overthrow Ch'ing; restore Ming'.

The other articles in the Tau are:

The Red Club

This is the symbol of punishment and is said to represent one of a pair of such clubs kept at Siu Lam monastery for that purpose. It can be of any measurement involving the figures 3 and 6, i.e., three feet six inches, since it is the numerals and not the scale of measurement that is the important feature. These numerals signify the 36 oaths of the society for breach of which various degrees of punishment are laid down.

On the top and bottom surfaces of the club are the characters *fan ch'ing*; *fuk ming* 'Overthrow Ch'ing, Restore Ming'. On the front surface of the club are four vertical characters *ping ching*; *chui kan* 'Act justly; exterminate traitors'. Above these are four horizontal characters *yee lung tsang chu* 'Two dragons fighting for a pearl', signifying the two Emperors of Ch'ing and Ming struggling for the throne of China. Below the vertical characters are four more horizontal characters *sheung fung chiu yeung* 'Two phoenix facing the sun', signifying the resurgence of the Ming dynasty. The phoenix is a mythical bird said to be re-born from the ashes of its own funeral pyre. Here one bird is dying in representation of the earlier phase of the Ming rule and its resurrected self represents the phase to come. On the rear surface of the club are the characters *tan sum yat pin* 'Together with one heart'.

The Sword of Loyalty and Righteousness

Representing the sword of Kwan Kung the God of War, and the god worshipped by the Triad as the embodiment of loyalty to sworn brothers. It is used for the symbolic execution of the three Triad traitors.

The Peach & Plum Wood Sword
Representing the magic sword that sprang from the graves of the wife and sister of Cheng Kwan Tat. Also known as the Seven Stars Sword. The Seven Stars are believed to refer to the mythical rulers of heaven who dwelt in the planets Sun, Moon, Jupiter, Mars, Mercury, Saturn, Venus. Its connection with the grave is also shown by the fact that it was a common custom for Chinese coffins to have seven holes drilled in the bottom plank and that particular plank was called the Seven Stars Plank.

Grass Sandal
Made from closely woven dried grass or rice straw with securing loops and thongs of hemp. It represents one of a magic pair of sandals belonging to Tat Mo the deity of Siu Lam monastery. Tat Mo is actually the Chinese name for Bodhidharma who went to China in about AD 526 as a Buddhist missionary. After his death he was worshipped as Buddha. He is said to have visited and stayed at Siu Lam monastery in the course of his journeying. His sandals were saved from the burning monastery by the First Five Ancestors. Besides being able to turn into boats they were said to enable the wearer to cover huge distances in the manner of the 'Seven League Boots' of European fables and for this reason the official messengers of the society are known as the Cho Hai 'Grass Sandal' officials. Both sandals were lost during a battle with Ch'ing troops at the Wu Lung river but one was subsequently recovered by Ng Ting Kwai who has since been recognized as the first Cho Hai official. In some sources it is stated that the missing sandal was replaced by a metal one known as the Tit Pan 'Iron Sole' but our informants do not support this and state that Tit Pan is merely a Triad slang term for shoes.

Yellow Umbrella
This is simply a representation of the Imperial Umbrella of the Ming Emperors. There are no characters or secret marks inscribed on it. An ordinary umbrella is frequently employed.

White Paper Fan
Constructed of bamboo and white paper, it has two thick outer ribs and thirteen thin inner ribs. These represent the administrative division of the country under the first Ming Emperor, the two thick ribs being the capitals of Peking and Nanking and the inner ribs being the thirteen provinces. On both sides of the fan are verses said to be allegorical poems relating to the future of the Ming dynasty. The hidden meaning or interpretation of these poems is not now known. On the outer surface of the two main ribs are the characters *chung ching wing sai kai* 'restore a flourishing world', and *choi cho kam kin kwan* 'reconstruct a beautiful world'. It would appear that the phrases on these two ribs vary considerably in the different societies and

Lodges. Those quoted above are said to have been created by Dr Sun Yat Sen in comparatively recent times and are much favoured by societies in the Kwangtung area as a mark of respect to him. It is common also to have a drawing of a white peony on the front surface of the fan and a red peony on the reverse side. The white peony represents the Ch'ing dynasty and the red peony the Ming dynasty. Turning the fan illustrates the favourite Triad expression of 'Overthrow Ch'ing; Restore Ming'.

Abacus
The Chinese calculating instrument. On this the sins and debts of the Ch'ing will be totalled in order that the people may exact just recompense when the dynasty is overthrown. Alternatively it symbolizes a means of calculating the time most favourable to start a successful rebellion against the Ch'ing.

Foot Rule
A normal foot rule said to be for the purpose of measuring the area of land lost to the Ch'ing and to ensure that every inch is recovered from them. Alternatively it represents the magic rule of Lo Pan, the patron saint of carpenters and can be used to measure the dominions of the Hung family extending over heaven and earth.

Scales
The symbol of justice, denoting that when the Ming is restored all people, regardless of wealth or rank, will be treated as equal. Alternatively used to weigh the virtue of the Ming against the Ch'ing, the Ch'ing of course always being found wanting. There is also a suggestion that it can be used to weigh the hearts of members to detect those who are not faithful.

Writing Brush and Ink Stick
Normal implements used for writing Chinese characters. It is said that with these will be written the proclamation calling on the people to rise and overthrow the Ch'ing. They are also closely bound up with the precious 'Pat Kwa' (Eight diagrams) of the society since together these represent the method and means by which man was enabled to record his words and thoughts.

Three Hung Cash
This red paper cut-out represents the three cash coins that should be given to each recruit on completion of the initiation ceremony. Formerly, each recruit brought 600 cash to the Lodge wrapped in a piece of red paper bearing the characters *luk pak man* 'six hundred cash'. Of this sum, 597 was paid over to the society at various stages in the ceremony. The remaining three cash were for retention by the recruit but special Hung cash were substituted for them. The Hung cash were of specific weights, being:

(a) 3.3 mace
(b) 3.6 mace
(c) 3.9 mace

making a total of 10.8 which commemorates the 108 heroes of Triad history. Additional characters were also inscribed on these coins as follows:

		Front		Reverse
(1)	*Hung ying.*	'Hung Hero'	*Kei tak.*	'Remember'.
(2)	*Hung lung.*	'Hung Dragon'	*Shik tak.*	'Recognize'.
(3)	*Hung mo.*	'The Ming Emperor'	*Sau tak.*	'Obey'.

Such coins are not given to the recruits nowadays but the three paper cash can be torn from a single sheet of paper and the method of doing so is shown to the recruits and can be used as a form of identification between members.

Purse
This is simply a red paper packet in which the recruits carry their initiation fee. It is marked *luk pak man* 'six hundred cash'.

Scissors
Ordinary scissors symbolizing that the dark clouds of the Ch'ing rule will be ripped away to reveal the red sky of the Ming.

Mirror
Usually a small hand mirror. Said to represent its magical counterpart which was originally in the possession of the society founders. It is the Mirror of Truth in which man's innermost soul is revealed so enabling the false to be detected from the loyal. It is supposed to have been donated to the society by Nui Wo, one of the Heavenly Empresses of Chinese mythology.

Five Coloured Silks
Five small bundles of black, red, vermilion, white and green silk. Said to represent the five main Lodges of the society. It is mentioned in the ritual that such silks could be purchased in the market of Universal Peace and it is possible that there was a deeper significance to these items than is now recognized, especially since they are the colours of the five elements.

The Hung Candles
Two red candles placed in brass candlesticks and used for purposes of worship. They are said to symbolize the brightness of the Ming dynasty.

The Hung Lamp
The ancient bowl and wick type of oil lamp. Said to have burned with a red

flame at the original initiation ceremony in Muk Yeung city. By its light it was said [to be] possible to distinguish the true from the false.

The Precious Censer
A representation of the precious censer found by the First Five Ancestors during their flight from Siu Lam monastery. It should stand on three legs and have a handle on each side. The original is said to have weighed 52 catties and 13 taels which would have made it a most bulky object. It is believed, however, that this weight was chosen purely for the significance of the numbers, i.e.:

52 catties	=	5 main Triad Lodges
		2 capitals of the Ming administration
13 taels	=	13 provinces of the Ming administration

On the bottom of the censer are written the abbreviated characters for *fan ch'ing; fuk ming* 'Overthrow Ch'ing; Restore Ming'. On the front are the abbreviated characters for *shun tin hang to* 'Act according to the will of Heaven'. Inside is a sheet of red paper bearing an allegorical poem relating to the future fortunes of the Ch'ing and Ming dynasties. The top of the censer is sealed by another sheet of red paper bearing a number of characters. This seal is said to have been placed there by Chan Kan Nam, one of the first officials of the society.

Wooden Clappers
In memory of the monks of Siu Lam. Similar clappers were used by monks to mark the rhythm during the recitation of prayers.

Bloodstained White Robe
In memory of the monks who died in Siu Lam monastery.

Rosary
Also in memory of the monks of Siu Lam

Allegorical poem found in the Precious Censer

Three three year year, two years three.
Bloodstains form a river and bones cover the hills.
White flower open, red flower blooming.
But not known in which year this will take place.
Three three make nine, eighteen years.
Bright moon raises troops to uphold the righteous flag.
Black ape and black pig fight together.
Naturally there will be a time of peace.
Three slaughters at the same time, another three slaughters occur.
Two eight beautify woman, two eight high.
Although no vehicles or horses for communication on land.
For communication on water are wooden boats.

Time comes when it is neither Ch'ing nor Ming.
The two capitals on this day will be very clean.
Master and servant stop shedding tears.
Brightness is again restored after both eyes are wiped dry.
There is always a mountain higher than another.
Myriads of waters will eventually meet in one.
Viewing from a distance you can only see vast plains of grass.
You can see only a pair of phoenixes in Kwangtung.
Fifty years ago the whole affair started.
One war after the other annihilated the Ch'ing dragon.

Cover on the 'Precious Censer'

(a) *Ka*   These four characters were said to have been engraved on a sword
(b) *Hau*   presented to the monks of Siu Lam by the Emperor Hong Hei
(c) *Yat*   after their defeat of the Eleuths.
(d) *Shan*
(e) The Triad insignia of a triangle containing the character *hung*.
(f) Combined character *kit man wai kee* 'myriads united'.
(g) Combined character *kung tung wo hop* 'peacefully united'.
(h) Combined character *tan sum yat pin* 'together with one heart'.
(i) Combined character *chung sum yee hei* 'loyal and righteous'.
(j) Character *piu* 'ornamental' (or beautiful, glorious, etc.).
(k) Character *sau* 'ages'.
(l) Abbreviation for *hung shun tong* 'Hung obedience hall'.
(m) Abbreviation for *kam lan kwan* 'golden orchid district'.
     Note: (l) and (m) form the Triad designation for the 2nd Lodge. If the celebrant
     society belonged to one of the other Lodges the designation of that Lodge
     would appear at (l) and (m).
(n) The character *kin* 'observe'. Frequently used together with (o) which is the top
     part of the seal of Ling Wong Temple, to form a decorative framework around
     certain characters or on official seals. The bottom of the character *kin* is
     extended to close the frame. The curls in the extensions, four on the left and five
     on the right, signify the ancient Chinese expression for the world – 'four seas
     and five lakes'. Other characters, apart from *kin* are used in this method of
     decoration.

(p)	Numerical code of the First Five Ancestors		Numerals	33.
(q)	,,	,, ,, Head of society		489.
(r)	,,	,, ,, Senior officials		438.
(s)	,,	,, ,, Hung Kwan official		426.
(t)	,,	,, ,, Pak Tsz Sin official		415.
(u)	,,	,, ,, Cho Hai official		432.
(v)	,,	,, ,, Ordinary member		49.

Coconut Bowl

Representing a begging bowl used by the monks. Any type of bowl, not
necessarily a coconut shell, will serve the same purpose.

The Gall of the Tau

A peculiar object which is intricately folded from a single sheet of paper and
once unfolded it is almost impossible for the uninitiated to reconstruct it.

The secret of folding the 'gall' is kept by the Incense Master of the main societies and seems to serve almost as his badge of office. Each main society should have only one Incense Master and he, on retiring, hands the 'gall' to his successor at a special ceremony and instructs him in the secret of its construction. It must always be placed near the front of the Tau where all can see it and the Incense Master cannot perform the ceremony unless he so produces it and places it in the Tau. On the inside of the paper, not visible when folded, is the character *tau* surrounded by an ornamental framework formed by the characters *ling* and *kwai*. The character *kwai* is extended in the same way as the character *kin* on the censer seal to symbolize the four seas and five lakes. Referring to the characters on the illustration above, we have:

(*a*) Hung
(*b*) Abbreviated characters for *shun tin hang to* 'Act according to the will of Heaven'
(*c*) Abbreviated characters for *hung shun tong* 'Hung obedience hall' (Official title of the 2nd Lodge)
(*d*) Abbreviated characters for *shun tin chuen ming* 'Obey Heaven and restore Ming', or, more precisely, 'Turn the present dynasty back to Ming according to the will of Heaven'
(*e*) *Hung*, (*f*) *fat*, (*g*) *man*, (*h*) *chun*. 'Hung family extend ten thousand cities'. Expressing the hope that the society will flourish throughout the land
(*i*) Abbreviated characters for *kit man wai kee* 'myriads united'
(*j*) Abbreviated characters for *kung tung wo hop* 'peacefully united'
(*k*) Abbreviated characters for *chung sum yee hei* 'loyal and righteous'
(*l*) Abbreviated characters for *tan sum yat pin* 'Together with one heart'
(*m*) *Cham*, (*n*) *tai*, (*o*) *wang*, (*p*) *fa* 'Extensive conversion, blending with Heaven'. The same characters that are found on the flags of the Four Great Faithful Ones who guard the gates of the Triad city.

The above completes the list of articles that should be contained in the Tau during the Ko Kai type of ceremony.

On the front of the main altar is pinned, or otherwise attached, a large sheet of yellow paper known as the:

Sha Tsz Pei (Yellow Gauze Quilt)

This is a representation of the yellow curtain that fell over the eighteen surviving monks during the burning of Siu Lam monastery. It is difficult to give an exact translation of the characters 'Sha Tsz' but they indicate a type of paper or cloth made from strong, loosely woven threads. On the reverse side of the Sha Tsz Pei are inscribed the 36 oaths of the society and a translation of these will be found on page 193.

On the front of the paper are the four characters *fan ch'ing; fuk ming* 'Overthrow Ch'ing; Restore Ming', at the four outer corners. Part of the corner and character *ch'ing* should be burned away to indicate that the curtain was slightly burned when guarding the monks from the flames. In the centre are the four large characters *ping ching: chui kan* 'Act justly: exterminate traitors'. At the top are the five characters *hung mau tan ham yui* 'red peony budding', and at the bottom are the five characters *pak mau tan hoi fong* 'white peony blooming'. These two phrases signify that the Ch'ing dynasty (white peony) is presently flourishing but that the Ming dynasty (red peony) is soon due to burst forth in all its glory. On the left hand side are the characters *sheung fung chiu yeung* 'Two Phoenix Facing the Sun', and on the right the characters *yee lung tsang chu* 'two dragons fighting for a pearl' indicating the struggle of the Ch'ing and Ming Emperors for the throne of China. Below the central characters, *ping ching; chui kan*, are inscribed the names, dates of birth, and places of birth of the recruits attending the initiation ceremony. After the oaths have been read out and the recruits have passed under the 'protection' of the Sha Tsz Pei, the paper is burned and the ashes mixed with the wine, blood, etc., which the recruits will later drink.

Also within the Lodge, ready for use during the initiation are:

THE STEPPING STONES
These are three pieces of paper each bearing one of the characters *ting hoi fau* 'floating on the calm water'. They represent the stepping stones used by the First Five Ancestors to cross the river under the 'Two Planked Bridge'. They are laid out on the floor in triangular form and at the commencement of this episode the recruit stands at the base of the triangle.

THE TWO PLANK BRIDGE
Representing the bridge under which the Ancestors crossed the river by means of the stepping stones mentioned above. It is very simply represented by means of two long tapes, one white and one red. It is guarded by three legendary heroes, Lee Shun and Man Ko Wong at either end, and a female, Lee Sin Fa in the centre. This is the only occasion on which a female takes any part in the initiation ritual and, since women were not allowed to hold official rank under the old Triad system, the wife of one of the society's officials temporarily adopted her husband's rank in order that she might play this part.

THE HEAVEN AND EARTH CIRCLE
This is a large bamboo hoop with sprigs of pine and cedar, the Chinese symbols of longevity, on the sides. At the top and bottom of the hoop are pasted strips of red paper cut with a number of serrations, nine at the top and twelve at the bottom. These serrations represent the jagged edges of the

hole through which the monks escaped from Siu Lam monastery. During the initiation, the hoop is held upright and rests on a sword placed on the floor. The recruit passes through the hoop by kneeling on his right knee and putting his left leg through the hoop first. This has a double significance in the ritual. First it commemorates the escape of the monks from the monastery and secondly it has the even more important significance of symbolizing the re-birth of the recruit from his former life into the Hung family. The very name given to the hoop, The Heaven and Earth Circle, is symbolic of birth since the Triad religion, if it can be so described, is based on the belief that the three principal forces of nature are Heaven, Earth, and Man; and that it was from the union of the first two forces that Man was born. A more material indication of this sense of re-birth can be found in the common Triad identification phrase 'My mother's vagina has teeth', referring to the serrations at the top and bottom of the hoop.

THE FIERY PIT

This simply consists of a quantity of joss paper which is placed on the floor and set alight. The recruit steps over the flames to commemorate the passage of the Ancestors over the flames of the burning monastery and hillside.

This concludes the list of objects found in the Lodge with the exception of the clothing worn by participating officials.

It will be noted that no mention is made of a portrait to the god Kwan Kung, nor is mention even made of a memorial tablet to him. When the Lodge is decorated to represent Muk Yeung City only memorial tablets to those who actually helped form the society, or the deities who extend their protection to the members, are displayed. Kwan Kung, while revered as the symbol of true brotherhood, did not take part, in flesh or spirit, in the founding of the society but was later adopted to signify loyalty. His portrait, which is almost always displayed in the society meeting hall on normal occasions, is therefore covered when an initiation or promotion ceremony takes place.

THE THIRTY SIX OATHS OF THE SOCIETY

1. After having entered the Hung gates I must treat the parents and relatives of my sworn brothers as my own kin. I shall suffer death by five thunderbolts if I do not keep this oath.
2. I shall assist my sworn brothers to bury their parents and brothers by offering financial or physical assistance. I shall be killed by five thunderbolts if I pretend to have no knowledge of their troubles.
3. When Hung brothers visit my house, I shall provide them with board and lodging. I shall be killed by myriads of knives if I treat them as strangers.

4. I will always acknowledge my Hung brothers when they identify themselves. If I ignore them I will be killed by myriads of swords.

5. I shall not disclose the secrets of the Hung family, not even to my parents, brothers, or wife. I shall never disclose the secrets for money. I will be killed by myriads of swords if I do so.

6. I shall never betray my sworn brothers. If, through a misunderstanding, I have caused the arrest of one of my brothers I must release him immediately. If I break this oath I will be killed by five thunderbolts.

7. I will offer financial assistance to sworn brothers who are in trouble in order that they may pay their passage fee, etc. If I break this oath I will be killed by five thunderbolts.

8. I must never cause harm or bring trouble to my sworn brothers or Incense Master. If I do so I will be killed by myriads of swords.

9. I must never commit any indecent assaults on the wives, sisters, or daughters, of my sworn brothers. I shall be killed by five thunderbolts if I break this oath.

10. I shall never embezzle cash or property from my sworn brothers. If I break this oath I will be killed by myriads of swords.

11. I will take good care of the wives or children of sworn brothers entrusted to my keeping. If I do not do so I will be killed by five thunderbolts.

12. If I have supplied false particulars about myself for the purpose of joining the Hung family I shall be killed by five thunderbolts.

13. If I should change my mind and deny my membership of the Hung family I will be killed by myriads of swords.

14. If I rob a sworn brother or assist an outsider to do so I will be killed by five thunderbolts.

15. If I should take advantage of a sworn brother or force unfair business deals upon him I will be killed by myriads of swords.

16. If I knowingly convert my sworn brothers' cash or property to my own use I shall be killed by five thunderbolts.

17. If I have wrongly taken a sworn brother's cash or property during a robbery I must return them to him. If I do not I will be killed by five thunderbolts.

18. If I am arrested after committing an offence I must accept my punishment and not try to place the blame on my sworn brothers. If I do so I will be killed by five thunderbolts.

19. If any of my sworn brothers are killed, or arrested, or have departed to some other place, I will assist their wives and children who may be in need. If I pretend to have no knowledge of their difficulties I will be killed by five thunderbolts.

20. When any of my sworn brothers have been assaulted or blamed by others, I must come forward and help him if he is in the right or advise him to desist if he is wrong. If he has been repeatedly insulted by others

I shall inform our other brothers and arrange to help him physically or financially. If I do not keep this oath I will be killed by five thunderbolts.

21. If it comes to my knowledge that the Government is seeking any of my sworn brothers who has come from other provinces or from overseas, I shall immediately inform him in order that he may make his escape. If I break this oath I will be killed by five thunderbolts.

22. I must not conspire with outsiders to cheat my sworn brothers at gambling. If I do so I will be killed by myriads of swords.

23. I shall not cause discord amongst my sworn brothers by spreading false reports about any of them. If I do so I will be killed by myriads of swords.

24. I shall not appoint myself as Incense Master without authority. After entering the Hung gates for three years the loyal and faithful ones may be promoted by the Incense Master with the support of his sworn brothers. I shall be killed by five thunderbolts if I make any unauthorized promotions myself.

25. If my natural brothers are involved in a dispute or law suit with my sworn brothers I must not help either party against the other but must attempt to have the matter settled amicably. If I break this oath I will be killed by five thunderbolts.

26. After entering the Hung gates I must forget any previous grudges I may have borne against my sworn brothers. If I do not do so I will be killed by five thunderbolts.

27. I must not trespass upon the territory occupied by my sworn brothers. I shall be killed by five thunderbolts if I pretend to have no knowledge of my brothers' rights in such matters.

28. I must not covet or seek to share any property or cash obtained by my sworn brothers. If I have such ideas I will be killed.

29. I must not disclose any address where my sworn brothers keep their wealth nor must I conspire to make wrong use of such knowledge. If I do so I will be killed by myriads of swords.

30. I must not give support to outsiders if so doing is against the interests of any of my sworn brothers. If I do not keep this oath I will be killed by myriads of swords.

31. I must not take advantage of the Hung brotherhood in order to oppress or take violent or unreasonable advantage of others. I must be content and honest. If I break this oath I will be killed by five thunderbolts.

32. I shall be killed by five thunderbolts if I behave indecently towards the small children of my sworn brothers' families.

33. If any of my sworn brothers has committed a big offence I must not inform upon them to the Government for the purposes of obtaining a reward. I shall be killed by five thunderbolts if I break this oath.

34. I must not take to myself the wives and concubines of my sworn

brothers nor commit adultery with them. If I do so I will be killed by myriads of swords.

35. I must never reveal Hung secrets or signs when speaking to outsiders. If I do so I will be killed by myriads of swords.

36. After entering the Hung gates I shall be loyal and faithful and shall endeavour to overthrow Ch'ing and restore Ming by co-ordinating my efforts with those of my sworn brethren even though my brethren and I may not be in the same professions. Our common aim is to avenge our Five Ancestors.

APPENDIX 4:

COMMISSIONERS' REPORT ON PENANG RIOTS, 1868

Report of the Commissioners Appointed under Act XXI of 1867 to enquire into the Penang Riots together with Proceedings of the Committee, Minutes of Evidence and Appendix, Penang, 1868.

The Commissioners appointed under Act XXI of 1867, to enquire into the origin and causes of the recent riots at Penang, have considered the matter referred to them, and have agreed to the following Report.

Subjects of Enquiry

1. The subjects of enquiry as stated in Article 1 of the Act are:
   1st. The origin and causes of the recent riots;
   2ndly. How far the Secret Societies existing in Penang, have been concerned in instigating, or fostering such riots.
2. As the second subject treats of matters explanatory of the first, the Commissioners consider it better to report upon that subject in the first instance.

Societies concerned in the Riots

3. It is evident to the Commissioners, that there were four of the Secret Societies of Penang which were solely concerned in the late riots. Two of these Societies are composed of Chinese, and two of Malay and Kling (natives of India) members.
4. The names of these four Societies are the Ghee Hin, the Toh Peh Kong, (otherwise called Kien Teck), the White Flag and Red Flag.

Ghee Hin Society

5. The Ghee Hin Society or Hoey, was formed in China, some centuries ago, for the purpose of overthrowing the Tarter rule, and replacing the Ming dynasty upon the throne of the country. This original object has been practically lost sight of by the branch at Penang, whose only real object has been, to carry on amongst its members a government of its own, as far as possible, independent of the Government of the Settlement.

6. The rules of this *Imperium in Imperio*, are given by two of the evidences before the Commission. One (No. 36) describing his initiation into the society says:

'A fowl's head was cut off and I was told, that whenever I was called by the Society, I was to come immediately; when called on to subscribe, I was to do so; when there was a funeral, I was to attend, if called; if called to a marriage, I was to go; if called on at any time assistance was required, or to go and fight, I must go at once, and that if I did not obey these Rules, I would meet with the fate of the decapitated fowl then before me.'

The other evidence (No. 53) gives these additional regulations:

'One member assaulted by another member, must bring his complaint before the headmen, and not before the Police; if he complained to the Police he would be punished. Should a member commit robbery, arson, or murder, the chiefs are bound to assist him in escaping from justice, and a chief would be punished, if he refused assistance. A criminal, assisted by the Society to escape, has his passage paid, and a sum of money given him to make a new start in life.'

7. The members of this Society are bound by an oath, which is rendered more binding, in their estimation, by the ceremony of drinking one another's blood. The blood is extracted from their forefingers, and mixed with spirits and water, in a bowl, from which all the new members drink.

8. There are three principal Headmen, and a *Sing Seng* or Secretary, the latter of whom manages all matters of business.

9. There are also Councillors, whose number is not restricted, twenty of whom reside in George Town.

10. The number of members is stated, in evidence (No. 55) to be from 25,000 to 26,000, 14,000 to 15,000 of whom live in Province Wellesley: The total population of this Settlement being about 125,000. The members belonging to this Society, consisting entirely of adult males, it must be evident, may, at any time, become highly dangerous to the peace of the Settlement.

11. The punishments awarded by the chiefs of the Society against its offending members, are excommunication, flogging, cutting off the ears, and beheading; but the witness who gave the evidence (No. 8) regarding this adds: 'But this is never done in this country.' Another witness (No. 13) was present, not many months ago, when a member who was sentenced to 108 blows, the greatest number allowed, received 36 blows on the buttocks, with a stick 3 feet long and one inch in diameter. The punishment was for paying his addresses to another member's wife. This witness also states: 'We don't inflict these extreme punishments (cutting off the ears and death) here.' Another instance of flogging is given by witness (No.

36), for refusal to call members together when ordered to do so. Although there is no direct evidence, that the severer punishments have been carried out in this country, the Commissioners cannot but believe, that they have sometimes been enforced. Considering that the witnesses before the Commission have all struggled to conceal the worst features of their societies, it is not surprising, that there has been no direct evidence on this point. It is enough, however, in support of the Commissioners' opinion, to state that they have succeeded in obtaining sufficient evidence to prove how unscrupulously evil these societies are, and that the rules framed for the government of these Societies in this very place, permit the infliction of these extreme and barbarous punishments.

12. The Ghee Hins of Penang consist chiefly of the labouring and artisan class, and are principally men from Canton.

13. The *Sing Seng* or Secretary of the Ghee Hins, appears to have been the leading and most influential person amongst them – the Chief being a very quiet person, and not disposed to be the cause of any disturbance. The Secretary (i.e., Boey Yoo Kong) has been deported from the Colony by order of the Government, in consequence of the prominent part he took in the bringing about of the late riots.

Toh Peh Kong Society

14. The Toh Peh Kong Society or Hoey, was instituted in Penang about twenty-four years ago, under one Khoo Ten Pang.

15. The Society was founded by men from the Ho Kien Province of China, who have always been antagonistic to the Cantonese, who form the greater part of the Ghee Hin Society.

16. Khoo Ten Pang was succeeded about fifteen years ago, by Khoo Thean Tek, who at the time of the riots was the headman of the Society, and who is now a convict undergoing a sentence of seven years' transportation, being a commutation of his original sentence of death, passed upon him for aiding and abetting in certain cases of murder during the riots.

17. The Rules for admitting members, and the objects and regulations of this Society, are similar to those of the Ghee Hin.

18. The Rules for pensions and gratuities, to those who may be the sufferers, during their fights with other societies, would lead to the supposition, that the headmen, and better-to-do class of members, never intended to risk their own lives and persons on such occasions – the amounts of compensation being so small.

19. The Toh Peh Kongs number amongst their members most of the wealthy merchants and shopkeepers of Beach Street, and include, also, the manufacturers and sellers of fire-arms and ammunition.

These proprietors of fire-arms are bound, in times of disturbance, to supply the members of their Society with muskets, and it was in this manner, that so many of the Toh Peh Kongs were armed during the late riots.

20. The number of Toh Peh Kongs in the Settlement, is about 5,000 to 6,000, the greater part of whom are in Prince of Wales' Island, very few residing in Province Wellesley.

21. The most influential person, next to Khoo Thean Tek, during the riots was Khoo Poh, a man described by one of the witnesses (No. 35) as clever and bold, and who gave advice to the headmen on all subjects. This man has been deported from the Colony by order of the Government.

White Flag Society

22. The White Flag was established as a Society about ten or twelve years ago.

23. The object of the Society at the time of its establishment, was a religious one, viz., to attend and assist at the religious ceremonies of its members, such as marriages, funerals, circumcisions, etc., and its rules contained nothing bad or injurious to the Public. Of late years the religious matters have been neglected, and as described by a witness (No. 37): 'All manner of evil is done, mischief plotted, and combinations made, to help members out of trouble, instead of having recourse to the authorities.'

24. The White Flag Society is in alliance with the Ghee Hins, and the Head of it, Tuan Chee, and about thirty others, entered the Ghee Hin Society about two years ago.

25. This Society is composed of Malays and Klings, and during the late riots took part with the Ghee Hins. The town members of these two Societies inhabit the same quarter of the town.

Red Flag Society

26. The Red Flag is another Society of Malays and Klings, and was established about eight years ago for religious purposes, but like the White Flag, it has lost its religious character, and adopted the same bad practices.

27. The Head of the Society at the time of the riots, was Che Long, a Malay, who is described by one of the witnesses before the Commission, as a desperate character. Che Long is now a convict under sentence of 21 years' transportation for the crime of arson, committed during the late riots. He appears to have taken an active part in the riots, and to have issued muskets, which were supplied to

him on the order of Thean Tek, the Head of the Toh Peh Kongs, to
the members of the Society.

28. In the year 1863, a fight took place between Che Long's (The Red
    Flag), and the Toh Peh Kong Societies, after which, these two
    Societies became friendly, and entered into an alliance for offensive
    and defensive purposes.

29. The members of both Societies occupy the same quarter of the town.

Erroneous opinion regarding Hoeys

30. There is an opinion generally entertained, that the Chinese Hoeys
    are necessary and beneficial to the Chinese community, as Benefit
    Societies. The Commissioners are, therefore, anxious before leaving
    the subject of the Societies, to record that this opinion is erroneous.

31. Every Chinese tribe has its own Benefit Society, which is entirely
    free and independent of any Hoey. It is only a member of a Tribe
    who can be the head of it, and he is appointed the Head, in virtue of
    his social position in the Tribe. The head of a Hoey, on the contrary,
    may be a member of any Tribe, and members of the same tribe are
    frequently to be found in different Hoeys.

Explanation of terms

32. The word Hoey means 'Brotherhood', 'Society' or 'Association',
    and the word Congsee or Kongsee, so frequently used in the
    evidence, means 'Company'. A Hoey is a Secret Society. A Congsee
    is any Company, but the word is frequently made use of to denote a
    Hoey. The Congsee House is the meeting house or club of the
    Hoey.

Origin and causes of the Riots

33. In order to ascertain the origin and causes of the recent riots, it is
    necessary to go back some years into the history of the Societies
    concerned in them. It has already been mentioned, that the Toh Peh
    Kong, was, from the day of its foundation antagonistic to the Ghee
    Hin Society. It has latterly desired to gain the ascendance over its
    rival, and its late Chief, Thean Tek, appears to have been determined
    to carry out this object.

34. It has also been mentioned that the Red Flag, and the White Flag
    Societies, very soon dropped their religious character, and took to
    quarrelling and fighting, and that, lately, they had joined in alliance,
    the one with the Toh Peh Kongs, and the other with the Ghee Hins,
    for offensive and defensive purposes.

35. The first cause which appears to have brought about the particular riots, which are the subject of the present enquiry, was a quarrel about some trifle, between the Red Flag and White Flag Malays, during the last Mohurrum festival. This quarrel continued, and led to constant assaults, by individuals of the one party on those of the other, which resulted in the murder of a diamond merchant, a Malay, in the Toh Peh Kong quarter, by one of the Red Flag party.

36. This led to the Malay quarrel being taken up by the Chinese.

37. Thus things went on until about the 1st or 2nd July (1st of the 6th moon), when the peace was disturbed in the following manner – (*vide* Evidence No. 4).

38. A Toh Peh Kong Chinaman was looking through the palings, bounding the premises of a White Flag Malay in Pitt Street. The Malay threw a rambutan skin at the Chinaman, and called him a thief. The Chinaman went away, but returned with ten or twelve Toh Peh Kong friends. The Malay's friends then turned out, and a fight with stones and clubs ensued. The Malays drove back the Toh Peh Kongs, as far as their Congsee House, and then the stones thrown by the former, struck the Toh Peh Kong signboard, upon which the Toh Peh Kongs turned out in great numbers, and fire-arms are said to have been used. The Police interfered, and succeeded in putting a stop to the disturbance for the time.

39. About the 8th of the month (July), a meeting took place of the chiefs of the Toh Peh Kong, Ghee Hin, White Flag and Red Flag Societies, who, assisted by arbitrators, patched up a settlement of grievances.

40. This settlement was, however, of no effect, for the following day the Toh Peh Kongs and the Red Flag Malays, attacked and entered some of the houses of the White Flag Malays, and injured and destroyed their property.

41. After this, frequent assaults and murders were committed by both parties, and so matters continued until the 1st August, when a false charge was made by Thean Tek, the Head of the Toh Peh Kong party, that some White Flag Malays and Ghee Hins, had stolen from the Toh Peh Kong cloth dyers, some cloth that had been put out in the street to dry, after having been dyed.

42. A meeting took place on the following day (at the house of Cheow Sew, one of the arbitrators, and a non-Congsee man) of the Headmen of the two Chinese Societies and their arbitrators to try and settle the case of the stolen cloth; but in consequence of a quarrel between Thean Tek and the *Sing Seng* or Secretary of the Ghee Hins, no settlement of differences was come to, and both these men left the meeting determined to fight.

43. There is no doubt, from the evidence, that Thean Tek was prepared and determined to do this beforehand, and that the false charge

about the stolen cloth, was only made to bring about a *casus belli*.

44. Accordingly, on the morning of the 3rd of August, the Toh Peh Kongs attacked the Ghee Hins, and thus commenced the riots, into the origin of which the Commissioners under Act XXI of 1867 were appointed to enquire.

Conclusion

45. The conclusion, arrived at by the Commissioners, is, that the late riots had their origin in a trifling quarrel between two rival Muhammadan Societies during the late Mohurrum Festival, and that they were fostered by two other rival Societies of Chinese, with one of which, each of the former had joined in alliance. That all these Societies joined in the riots by the direction, and under the instigation of their respective Headmen or Office-bearers, who directed their principal movements, and who, from the funds of their Societies, supplied them with provisions and arms, with rewards for the heads of their enemies, and with gratuities and pensions for the wounded and for the relations of those who were killed when fighting. That the organization and discipline of the Societies appear to be as complete as that of any disciplined force of the Government. That it is therefore evident, that these Secret Societies are extremely dangerous to the peace and welfare of the community. A notable circumstance, and one which has rendered these Societies more harmful of late, is, the combination of the Mussulmans and Hindoos with the Chinese, with whose customs their religious prejudices are so much at variance.

Suggestions

46. Although not required to do so by the Act, the Commissioners consider, that it is not altogether beyond their province, to make a few suggestions, concerning the means of preventing future injury to the Public, arising from Secret Societies in this Settlement. They would, therefore, recommend the entire suppression of these Societies, which, it has been before stated, have no claim to be considered Benefit Societies, in the same manner as it has been done by legislation in Hongkong. Should it, however, be found impossible to suppress the Societies by legal enactment, the Committee would suggest:

1st. That all Societies, of whatever nature, should be registered (under penalty) at the Office of the Commissioner of Police. The registration should furnish the names of the Head, and other Chiefs of the Society, its object, number of members, etc. The registration should be annual, and a fee should be charged for registering, except in the case of Benefit Societies, and there should be a penalty for making a false registration.

2nd. All oaths, of every description, should be prohibited, and any person guilty of administering an unlawful oath, should be liable to a penalty.

3rd. The Head of the Society or any of the Chiefs, if the Head is not forthcoming, should be liable, in case of any riot, in which his Society should be concerned, to be prosecuted by any Police Officer, and to be fined in a penalty not less than $(—), and not exceeding $(—), without prejudice to the amount of any damage or injury committed, and in default of payment of the fine, the Congsee or Meeting House of the Society, with all the premises attached thereto, and all other property, belonging to, or standing in the name of the Society, should be forfeited to the Crown.

4th. The Head of the Society, as well as every other member of it, should also be held liable in an action for any damage, or injury to property, committed by the Congsee to which he belongs.

5th. That a heavy penalty should be imposed upon any person found guilty of preventing by force or intimidation, any individual from making his complaint to the Police, or to any Magistrate, or other judicial authority, or from prosecuting any individual before any of the Courts of Law.

6th. That a member of a Society, forcing on any individual, a rule of his Society, which is contrary to law, should be liable to a heavy penalty.

7th. That all opportunities of collision between rival Societies or Religious Sects, should, as far as possible, be prevented by not authorizing processions of the members of such Societies or Sects, in the public streets, or high roads of the Settlement, and by confining such ceremonies to the grounds or compounds of such Societies or religious communities.

A. E. H. Anson,
Lt.-Governor and President.
Lawrence Nairne.
Walter Scott.
James Lamb.
Bernhard Rodyk.
Foo Tye Sin.
Nina Merican Noordin.
Ong Attye.
Lee Phee Chuan.
(Signed in Chinese characters).

Prince of Wales'
Island, (Penang)
14th July, 1868.

SELECT BIBLIOGRAPHY

Bard, Emile. *The Chinese at Home* (Newnes, 1901 [?]).

Blythe, Wilfrid. *The Impact of Chinese Secret Societies in Malaya* (OUP, 1969).

Chesneaux, Jean, and others. *China from the Opium Wars to the 1911 Revolution* (Random House, 1976).

Chesneaux, Jean. *Secret Societies in China in the Nineteenth and Twentieth Centuries* (Heinemann, 1971).

L. F. Comber. *Chinese Secret Societies in Malaya* (Augustin, 1959).

Fairbank/Reischauer/Craig. *East Asia: Tradition & Transformation* (Houghton Mifflin, 1973).

Fleming, Peter. *The Siege at Peking* (Hart Davis, 1959).

Goldsmith, Margaret. *The Trail of Opium* (Hale, 1939).

Lethbridge, H. J. *Hard Graft in Hong Kong* (OUP, 1985).

Li Chien-nung. *The Political History of China* (Van Nostrand, 1956).

Lubbock, Basil. *The China Clippers* (Brown Son & Ferguson, 1914).

McCoy, Alfred W. *The Politics of Heroin in Southeast Asia* (Harper and Row, 1972).

Morgan, W. P. *Triad Societies in Hong Kong* (The Government Printer, Hong Kong, 1960).

O'Callaghan, Sean. *The Triads* (Star, 1978).

Pickering, W. A. *Chinese Secret Societies and their Origins*.

Robertson, Frank. *Triangle of Death* (RKP, 1977).

Seagrave, Sterling. *The Soong Dynasty* (Harper and Row, 1986).

Shi Nai'in and Luo Guanzhong. *Outlaws of the Marsh* (Allen & Unwin, 1986).

Soothill, W. E. *The Three Religions of China* (OUP, 1929).

Tan, Chester C., *The Boxer Catastrophe* (Octagon Books, 1983).

Tu, Elsie, *Elsie Tu – An Autobiography* (Longman, 1988).

Tyson, Godfrey. *A Hundred Years of Banking in Asia and Africa* (National and Grindleys Bank, 1963).

Ward, J. S. M., and Stirling, W. G. *The Hung Society* (The Baskerville Press, 3 vols. 1925).

PHOTO ACKNOWLEDGEMENTS

Hong Kong Government Press:
Kot Siu Wong
A street poster

Royal Hong Kong Police:
A legal Triad Society march
Chang Si Fu with the deputy
    commander of his Shan United Army
The altar in a lodge
A Triad Society altar in a lodge
Triad Society members in a meeting
Hand signs at an altar
Hand signs during a Triad ceremony
A police officer dressed in the uniform
    of an Incense Master
The Incense Master at the altar
Heroin in a tin of lychees
Forty-two condoms containing heroin

A packet of opium
A ship's fire extinguisher containing
    drugs
A stuffed toy turtle containing drugs

Granada Television
Spectators at the opening of a
    Manchester Restaurant

News Limited, Sydney
Edmund Louey, Cheung Yin-ng and
    Mr Poon

Associated Press:
Protesting Students in Tiananmen
    Square
A pro-democracy protester in Peking,
    1989

INDEX

Afghanistan, 140

Amin, Idi, 137

Amitabha Buddha, 7

Amoy, 11–12

Amsterdam, 112–14; *see also* Holland

Anson, Colonel *(later* Major-General Sir) Archibald E. H., 65, 204

Asia Minor, 123

Auden, W. H., 79

Australia, xii, 148–9, 156

Beirut, 124, 140

Big Circle Boys, 97

Big Knives (Ta Tao Hui), 12

Blue Gang, 74

Boey Yo Kong, 199

Bomb Associations, 44, 53

Booth, Chief Inspector Roger, 94

Boxer Uprising (1900), 12, 14

Boxers (I Ho Chuan; the Righteous Harmony Fists), 12–14

Bristol, 116

Britain: Triads in, xii, 115–23; and heroin distribution, 116–17, 121; laws, 150

Britannicus, 46

Buddhism, 4–8, 11, 19, 175

Burma, 132, 155; *see also* Golden Triangle

Burning the Yellow Paper (ritual), 37

Butterfield and Swire *(now* Swire Group), 47

Canada, xi, 125–6, 154

Carr, Julian S., 76

Central Intelligence Agency (CIA), xii, 109

Cha So (treasurer), 34

Chan Tai Tong of the Lin Cheung Kwan (Twenty-nine Tai), 29

Chan Chak, Admiral, 45

Chan Kan Nam, 20, 25–7, 167–9

Chan Man Yiu, 22–3, 25

Chan Sau Hong, 26

Chan Siu Kun, 26

Chan Tai-ling, Inspector Harry, 94

Chan Yeun *(formerly* Tsoi Tak Chun; also known as Fat Sam and Ching Fong), 23–4, 28–9

Chang Ching-chang (Curio Chang), 78

Chang Chueh, 5

Chang Fei, 5, 167

Chang Hsiao-lin, 74

Chang Keng Wee (society), 66

Che Long, 200–1

Ch'en Ch'i-mei, 77

Ch'en Chieh-ju, 78

Chen Hsen (Mrs Chung Mon), 114

Cheng Ch'eng-Kung (Koxinga), 10

Cheng Hak Song, 20

Cheng Kiun Tah, 166–7

Cheng Kwan Tat, 21–2, 25

Cheng Shing Kung, 20–1

Cheng Yat So, 29

Cheng Yu Lan, 166

Cheng Yuk Lin, 21, 25–6

Cheng Yuet-ying, 82, 84, 86

Cheow Sew, 202

Cheung Chau Bun Festival (Hong Kong), 100

Cheung Kin Chau, 22–3

Cheung Oi Wan, 31

Cheung Poi Chai, 29

Chi Kung Tong group, 15

Chi Sang, 121

Chi Yuen, Abbot of Siu Lam, 21

Chiang Kai-shek: and Kuomintang, 45; suppresses opium, 49, 129; and Tu, 57, 72, 77–80; marriages, 78; and American Chinese, 123; and Taiwan Triads, 142

Ch'in dynasty, 2

Ch'in Ah Yam (society), 66

Chin Keong Yong, 119–21

Chin Kin, 28

China: imperial history, 2–12; development of private associations in, 4–5; Europeans in, 12; republican movement in, 14–16, 31, 42; opium in, 47–9, 129–31; surviving Triads in, 131, 137; growth of crime in, 137; anti-Triad measures, 147–8

Ch'ing dynasty (Manchus), 8–11, 14–15; rebellion against, 16, 19–31, 159, 166–9

Ching Lin Tong of the Fung Wong Kwan, 28

Ching Mun see Green Party

Ching Nin Kwok Ki Sh'e (society), 43

Chiu Chau Triad, 100, 113, 124

Chiu Kwong (group), 54

Chiu Yuk, 31, 60

Cho Hai (official), 35

Chou En-lai, 130–1

Christianity, 62–3

Chu Chi (leader), 34

Chu Hung Ying (formerly Chu Hung Chuk), 26–7

Chu Teh, General, 129

Chu Yuan-chang see Hung Wu, Emperor

Chuen (society), 42–3

Chui Shun-kwok, 97

Chung Man Kwan, 25

Chung Mon ('Unicorn'; 'The Fearless One'), 113–15, 118

Chung Wo Tong Society, 15, 42, 53, 71

Chung Yee (group), 54

Chung Yee Wui Society, 58

cocaine, 48–9, 83, 128; see also heroin

Communists and Communism: Triad antagonism to, 57–8, 60, 91, 129–30; in Malaya, 67; Tu and, 75–6, 129; in Shanghai, 80; ban on Chinese opium growing, 129; power in China, 129–30

computer trade: in Hong Kong, 144–5

Confucianism, 4, 18, 175

Confucius, 2

Congsees, 201

Copper Horses (group), 5

Corsica, 124

counterfeiting, 145; see also fakes and copies

Dai Bei-tang (Big-nose Tang), 96

Darul Ma'amur Football Club (Penang), 70

Dent and Company, 47

Deposit Taking Companies (DTCs), 102

'Dragon Head' Heung, see Heung Wah-yim

Drug Enforcement Administration (USA), 85, 116, 126

Drug Squad (UK), 117

Dunman (of Malaya), 63

Dylan, Bob, 87

Eastern (Later) Han Dynasty, 3

Eastern Chin, 6

Eight Diagrams (Celestial Principles) Sect, 6, 12

Eighteen Sages of Rozan, 7

Eleuths (tribe), 9, 161

Elliott, Elsie (Madame Tu), 89–90, 92
Eon (Hwui-yin), 7

fakes and copies, 104, 143–4
Fang Kuo-chen, 6
Federal Bureau of Investigation (FBI),
    xii, 116, 126
Federal Drugs Administration (FDA),
    xii
festivals, 100–1
film industry, 103–4
First Five Ancestors, 24, 28, 166–9
fishball stalls, 102–3
Five Continents Overseas Chinese
    Hung League, 57–8
Flag Societies, 70
Flying Dragons, 127
Fong Pan Leung, 20
Fong Tai Hung (Fat Mo; Ching
    Cho), 24–5, 29
Four Seas (society), 142
14K Society, xii, 53, 56–60, 81, 91,
    98, 100, 105; overseas, 114–17, 122,
    149, 153–4; and Communist
    suppression, 130; see also Ngai
    Triad faction
426 Fighters, 15
Fraser's Magazine, 67
French Connection, 124–5
Fu Ching Yuen, 19
Fu Chu Chi (deputy leader), 34
Fu Shan Chu (deputy lodge leader),
    33, 35
Fuk Yee Hing (society), 42–3

gambling, 101–2
Ghee Hin (society), 9, 65–6, 70, 115,
    197–9, 200–3
Ghost Shadows (society), 103, 127
Godber, Chief Superintendent Peter,
    89, 91
Golden Shopping Arcade, Hong
    Kong, 144–5
Golden Triangle, 83, 109–10, 119,
    123, 131–2, 149, 155

Gonzales, Guillermo, 125
Green Gang, 72, 74, 77–9
Green Pang Society, 31, 52
Green Party (Ching Mun), 28, 32
Guat San Sih, 119–20

Hai San Society, 66, 70
Hak Chai, 97–8
Ham Fung, Emperor, 30
Han Shan-tung, 7
Hanging the Blue Lantern
    (ceremony), 100
Hannibal (Carthaginian General), 46
Hawaii, 125, 142
Heaven and Earth Society, 6
heroin, 48, 52, 83–4, 104; production,
    processing and distribution, 108–
    13, 115–16, 121, 125, 132, 141,
    153, 157–8; in USA, 127–8; and
    financing of international unrest,
    140–1; in Australia, 149
Heung Chu (Incense Master), 33–5, 37
Heung Wah-yim ('Dragon Head'),
    54, 98, 147
Hing Ah Kee Kwan (organisation), 45
Hing Chung Wui (society), 31
Hip Sing tong, 127
Ho Seng (society), 68
Hoeys, 201
Hok Beng Society, 69
Holland, 85, 112; see also Amsterdam
Hong Hei, Emperor, 20–2
Hong Kong: as Triad city, 40–4, 88–
    9, 100–5, 107, 133; Japanese in,
    45; opium in, 49, 108; northern
    Triads in, 52; taxis in, 89–90; street
    traders, 90; riots in, 91; festivals,
    100; crime gangs, 105; population,
    105; anti-corruption drive, 117,
    134–5, 146–7; 1997 sovereignty
    change, 128, 136–7, 147; and
    mainland Triads, 131; counter-
    Triad measures, 133–4, 150; Triad
    exodus from, 137–8, 148; computer
    manufacture and trade, 144;
    financial dealings and fraud, 145–7

Hong Kong Customs and Excise
    Department, 134
Hong Kong Immigration
    Department, 134
Hong Kong Police *see* Royal Hong
    Kong Police
Hong Kong Precious Stone
    Company, 84
Hong Tai Shui, 29
Hung Cheong Wui (Red Spear, or
    Cannon, Society), 30
Huang Chih-jung (Pock-marked
    Huang), 74–5, 77
Hung Chieh Chu, 161
Hung Chun Min, 30
Hung Fat Shan Chung Yee Wui, 58–
    9; *see also* 14K Society
Hung Hsiu-ch'uan, 10–12
Hung Kai Shing, 19
Hung Kwan (Red Pole; official), 34–5
Hung League, 6
Hung Mun Society, 15
Hung Sau Chuen, 30
Hung Shun Tong of the Kam Lan
    Kwan (Twelve Tai), 29
Hung Society (Tien Ti Hui), 8–10,
    18, 39, 159; founding and history,
    19–31, 160–9; lodge described,
    170–96
Hung Tai Shui, 25
Hung Wu, Emperor (Chu Yuan-
    chang), 6–7, 168
Hunt, Superintendent Ernest
    ('Taffy'), 91–2
Hutchison and Company, 47

Incense Burning Society, 8
Independent Commission Against
    Corruption, Hong Kong (ICAC),
    93, 134–5, 146–7
Irish Republican Army (IRA), 140
Iron Shins (group), 5
Isherwood, Christopher, 79

Japan, 44–5, 141–2

Jardine, Matheson and Company, 47
Ka Hau Tong of the Fuk Po Kwan
    (Nine Tai), 29
Ka Hing, Emperor, 30
Kam Shun, 19–20, 28
Kam Toi Po Luk (*Kam Toi* Precious
    Records), 20, 26
Kam Wong, 118
K'ang Hsi, Emperor, 8–9, 160, 162–3
Kao Chai temple, 166
Khoo Poh, 200
Khoo Ten Pang, 199
Khoo Thean Tek, 199–202
Kin Lung, Emperor, 30
Ko Lo Wui (*formerly* Ko Tai Wui;
    Elder [and Younger] Brothers
    Society), 29
Kon Yu-leung (Johnny Kon), 128
Kot Siu Wong, Lieutenant-General,
    57–9, 91, 109
Kowloon Walled City, 55–6, 148
Ku Ting Lam, 19
Kuang Hsu, Emperor, 12
Kublai Khan, 6
Kuhn Sa, General, 132, 155
Kung Hsiang-hsi, 77
Kung Lok (society), 154
Kuo Sin Ying, 159
Kuomintang (KMT), 45, 60, 72, 78,
    123
Kuomintang New Society Affairs
    Establishment Federation, 60
Kwan Ti (deity), 9, 100
Kwan Yu (Kwan Ti), 5, 167
Kwok Li, 118
Kwok Man Tong (National People's
    Party), 31
Kwok On Wui Society, 15, 31
Kwok Sau Ying, 21, 25–6
Kwok Shui Li, 118
Kwok Yuen, Abbot of Po Tak, 25
Kwong Hon, 29

labour, market: managed by Triads,
    50–1, 101
Lam Song Man, 30

Lam Wing Chiu, 25, 30
Lam Wing-kei, 97
Laolee Sai-lee, 132
Lao-tzu, 4
Larut Wars (Malaya, 1872–4), 66
Lau, Superintendent Douglas, 118
Lee Shik Hoi (Chi Yau; Ching
  Kwan), 24, 30
Lee Shik Tai, 25, 29
Leung Fat-hei, 85
Leung Hung, 97
Li Chi Shing (Li Chong), 19, 26
Li Choi Fat, 52
Li Jarfar Mah, 119–21
Li Lap Ting, 30
Li Mi, General, 109–10
Li Ping-heng, 13
Li Wen-huan, General, 110
Limpy Ho see Ng Sik-ho
Liu Pei, 5
Liverpool, 115–16
Lloyd, Captain, 68
Lo Cho, 28
Lo Hsing-han, General, 110
Lo Shing, 82
loan sharking, 102
Loh Siah, 63
London: Triad activity in, 107–8,
  115–16, 153–4; police infiltration
  of Triads, 119; Chinese youth
  gangs, 139
'Lot Drawer', 73
Low, Hugh, 68
Luen (society), 43
Lui Pei, 167
Luo Dao-gang, 10

Ma Chi-man, Constable ('Rodney'),
  94–5, 97–8
Ma Chiu Hing (Yan Wai; Ching Kit),
  24, 29
Ma I-fuh ('A'Tsat'), 164–6
Ma Man-chuen, 97
Ma Ning Yee, 25–6
Ma Yee Fuk (Ma Ning Yee), 22–3

Macao, 102
Mafia: broken in USA, xii, 126, 136,
  139; organization, 1–2; Ng Sik-ho
  negotiates with, 84–5; and drug
  control, 108, 113, 123–5;
  association with Triads, 141–2
Mak Mei-kiu, 97
Malacca, 69
Malaya (Malaysia), 61–71, 119; see
  also Penang
Man Chi Tong (Overseas Chinese
  Democratic Party), 60–1
Man On Society, 42
Man Shing Tong, 42
Man Wan Lung (formerly Wu Tai
  Hei), 20
Manchus, 8, 15, 19, 41; see also
  Ch'ing dynasty
Mao Tse-tung, 91, 129, 138
Marcos, Ferdinand, 147
May Wong (Mrs Shing Moori Wong),
  119–21
Ming dynasty, 7–10, 19–20, 26, 159,
  166
Ming Wang (Big and Little; i.e. two
  prophets), 7
Ming Yee Toi Fong Luk (Records of
  the Enemies of Ming), 19
Ming Yeu Tong, Kam Toi Shan, 27
Mo Yat, 24
Mongols, 6–7, 9
Morgan, W. P.: Triad Societies in
  Hong Kong, 18, 36, 148; extract,
  170–96
Muk Yeung (City of Willows), 39
Mun Ji Dong (society), 156

Nanking, Treaty of (1842), 40
National Bank of India, 47
National Prohibition Act, 1919
  (USA), 129
Nationalist China, 57–60, 91, 129
New York, 126–8
Ng Chun-kwan, 83, 86
Ng Ping, 86
Ng Sam Kwai, General, 19

Ng Sik-ho (Limpy Ho): background and career, 81–8; convicted, 86; and Chung Mon, 113–15; overseas interests, 116, 142; and Ricord, 125
Ng Tin Shing, 28
Ng Ting Kwai, 25
Ng Wah-hei ('Tai Lo'), 97
Ngai Triad faction (of 14k Society), 94–8, 102
Nine Mansions Society, 6
numerology, 8, 35

On Lee Ong, 127
opium: qualities, 46; in China, 46–9, 131; growing made illegal, 49, 129–30; derivatives, 48; Triad control of, 108–10; see also heroin
Origin of Chaos Society, 8
Origin of the Dragon Society, 8

Pak Tsz Sin (White Paper Fan; official), 35
Pakistan, 140
Panama, 125
Penang, 64–5, 70–1; 1868 riots, 197–204
Perak, 68–71
Phang Lung Tien, General, 160, 162
Phao Sriyanonda, General, 110
Pickering, W. A., 67–8
Po Ko Wui (Robe of the Elder Brother Society), 29
prostitution: managed by Triads, 50, 102–3; in Singapore, 64; in USA, 126–7; in Australia, 149
protection rackets, 51–2, 61
public services, 101
Pullinger, Jackie, 56
Pun Ching, 28

Racketeering Influenced and Corrupt Organisations Act, 1970 (USA; RICO Statute), xii, 136, 150
Read (Singapore magistrate), 64
'Red Eyebrows' (society), 3, 9–10
Red Fists Society, 12

Red Flag Society, 65, 70, 197, 200–2
Red Gang, 73–5
Red Pang Society, 52, 54
Red Turban Rebels (14th century), 7
Red Turbans (19th century), 12
Ricord, Auguste, 125
Roman Catholic Church, 62
Royal Hong Kong Police: penetrated by Triads, 42, 90, 92–3; traffic division, 89–90; Triad Bureau, 91–2; corruption in, 91–3, 117; success against Triads, 93–9, 119; counter-Triad measures, 135–6; organization and departments, 135

Sam Hop Wui (Three United Association), 29
Schultz, Captain, 68–9
Second Five Ancestors, 25
Selangor (Malaya), 69
sex, 102–3; see also prostitution
Shan Chu (lodge leader), 33, 35
Shan United Army, 132
Shanghai, 73–5, 129
Shao Lin monastery see Siu Lam monastery
Sheppard, Assistant Commissioner John, 98
Sheung Fa (officer), 35
Shing (society), 43
Shing Heung Shan, 28–9
Shu Kingdom, 5
Shui Fong (society), xii, 122, 153
Shun Chi, Emperor, 19
Shun Society, 59
Sin Fung (Vanguard; officer), 33–5, 38
Singapore: Triad activities in, 61–4, 67, 71; death penalty in, 119
Sino-American Press, 76
Sitiawan (Malaya), 70
Siu Lam monastery, Foochow (Shao Lin; Shiu Lam), 9–10, 20–3, 38–9, 153, 163–7, 169
Sixteen Kingdoms, 6

Small Knife Society, Shanghai, 12
So Hung Kwong, 27
Society of God Worshippers, 10
Soong, Ai-ling, 76–7
Soong, Charlie (Han Chao-shun), 76–7
Soong, May-ling (Mrs Chiang Kai-shek), 78, 80
Sopsaisana, Prince, 111
South America, 125, 139
South China Morning Post, 98
Speedy, Captain, 66
Su Hung-u, 8
Sui dynasty, 6
Sun Yat-sen, 14–16, 30–1, 58, 71, 76–8, 123, 129
Sun Yee On (San Yee On; society), xii, 53–6, 98, 105
Sunday Morning Post (Hong Kong), 93, 98
Sung dynasty, 6
Sung Ching, Emperor, 19, 26
Sung Heung-lau, 97
Sze Ho Fat, 19, 27
Sze Kam Ming, 27
Sze Kau (49s), 35

Tai Chi-kwong, 97
Tai Hung Chai, 153, 158
Tai Lik Shan (society), 30
Tai Ping Shan Sports Association, 54
Taiping Rebellion, 10–12, 14, 41, 62–3
Taiwan, 142
Tak Wan, 21
Tamar, HMS (Hong Kong dockyard), 43
Tah Ah Choon, 63
Tan Wee Kow, 64
T'ang dynasty, 6–7
Tang Shing, 164
Taoism, 4–5, 8, 11, 18, 175
Thailand, 83, 109–10, 113, 119, 125, 132, 140–1, 149
Thean Tek *see* Khoo Thean Tek
Thian-ti-hui (Malayan groups), 61

Thian-yu-hung (Hwang-ching-yin), 168
Third Force, 60–1
Three Harmonies Triad, 74
Three Kingdoms, 5–6
Three United Society (Hung Society), 8, 29
Tien Ti Hui (Hung Society), 169
Tientsin, 48
T'in Tei Hui (Hung Society), 9, 159
Tin Hau Festival (Hong Kong), 100
Tin Yau Hung, General, 26–7
To Kwong, Emperor, 30
To Pit Tat, 25, 29
To Shui Boxing Club, 54
To Yeun, 28
Toh Peh Kong (Kien Teck; society), 65, 197, 199–203
trade unions, 43
Triad Society: formed, 6, 8
Triads: origins and background, 1–9; and number three, 8–9; oppose Ch'ing dynasty, 10–11; and opium trade, 11–12, 46–9; and Boxer rebellion, 14; overseas activities, 15, 107–8, 137–8, 148–50; and establishment of Chinese Republic, 15–16; tradition and legend, 17–32; organization, 33–7, 105–6; initiation, ceremonies and rituals, 37–9, 58, 99–100, 170–96, 198; as benevolent societies, 43–4, 201; and Japanese, 44–5; and patriotic movements, 57; street operations, 88–9; political inclination, 90–1; infiltrated by police, 94; business operations and rackets, 101–4, 122–3, 126, 143–6; counter-measures against, 133–4, 150–1; emigration from Hong Kong, 137–8, 148; replica manufactures, 143; lodge described, 170–8; punishments, 198–9
Tse King Chin, 26

Tse Pong Hang, 25–6
Tsui Ping-wing, 97
Tu Wei-ping, 79
Tu Yueh-sheng (Big Eared Tu):
  supports Chiang, 57, 72, 77–9;
  character, 71; background and
  career, 72–5, 77, 80–1, 86–7, 88;
  appearance, 73; hostility to
  Communism, 75–6, 129; in Hong
  Kong, 78–9, 147; decline and
  death, 80
Tuan Chee, 200
Tuan Shih-wen, General, 110
T'ung (society), 42
T'ung Meng Hui (society), 71
Tung (society), 42–3
Turkey, 124, 139
Tzu Hsi, Dowager Empress, 12–14

Uganda, 138
United Bamboo (society), 142
United States of America: and
  suppression of Mafia, xii, 126, 136,
  139; and Triad groups, 60; heroin
  addiction in, 112–13; Triad
  activities in, 123–8; Grand Jury
  system, 136; see also New York
United States Customs and
  Coastguard, xii

Vickers, Superintendent Steve, 94
Vietnam, 124–5, 154

Wai Chow Triad, 100
Wan Li, Emperor, 9
Wan Yun Lung, 168–9
Wang Fa Tong of the Lung Sai Kwan
  (Forty-seven Tai), 30
Wang Fang, 131
Wang Mang, Emperor, 3
Ward, J. S. M. and Stirling, W. G.:
  The Hung Society, 18; extract:
  160–9
watches: copies and fakes, 104, 143
Wei Kingdom, 6
Wenchow, 47

Western Chin empire, 6
Western (Early) Han dynasty, 2
Weston, John, 140
White Flag Society, 65, 70, 197,
  200–2
White Lily Society, 6, 8–9
White Lotus Society, 6–9, 12
willow pattern story, 39
Wo (society), 42–3
Wo Hop To (society), 53–4, 98
Wo On Lok (society), xii, 54, 153
Wo Shing Tong, 54
Wo Shing Wo (society), xii, 53–4, 56,
  59, 81, 101, 105; in Britain, 116–17, 153
Wo Yung Yee (society), 53
Wo Shing Yee (society), 54
Wong, May see May Wong
Wong Cheong, 25
Wong Chun Mei, 21
Wong Hei Chung, 19
Wong Po Chau, 19
Wong Shing Yan, 26–7
Wong Shuen Shan, 19–20
Wong Sui, 74
Wong, Sunny, 149
Wong Wan So, 31
Wu Kingdom, 6
Wu Ping Yiu, 30
Wu Tak Tai (Lun Hau; Ching Shing),
  24, 29
Wuchang Rising (1911), 71

Yakusa (Japanese organization),
  141–2
Yat Chi, Abbot of Ling Yan, 28
Yee Lung Shan Tong (Two Dragon
  Hill Society), 29
Yee On (society), 43
Yellow Turbans, 5
Yeow, Molly, 140–1
Yeung Sau Ching, 30
Ying Fat Sports Association (Hong
  Kong), 94
Yu Hsien, 13
Yu Kam-cheung, Constable ('Sandy'),
  94, 97

Yu Shi-cheung, Inspector Michael, 94
Yuan dynasty, 6–7
Yuan Shih-k'ai, 13, 16
Yuet Tung Society, 59
Yung Ch'eng, Emperor, 9

Yung Cheng, Emperor, 163–4,
    166–7
Yung Ngan, 28

Zoë (yacht), 149